# The Waldemar Cookbook

MEMORABLE SAVORINGS
FROM THE WALDEMAR
KITCHEN

LAURA PIPKIN KRAMER

FIRST EDITION

Copyright © 2001
By Waldemar, Inc.

Published in the United States of America
By Eakin Press
A Division of Sunbelt Media, Inc.
P.O. Drawer 90159 ☜ Austin, Texas 78709-0159
email: eakinpub@sig.net
💻 website: www.eakinpress.com 💻

1   2   3   4   5   6   7   8   9

ISBN 1-57168-439-5

**Library of Congress Cataloging-in-Publication Data**

Kramer, Laura Pipkin
    The Waldemar cookbook: memorable savorings from the Waldemar
kitchen / Laura Pipkin Kramer.—1st ed.
        p.    cm.
    Includes index.
    ISBN 1-57168-439-5
    1. Cookery, American.  I. Camp Waldemar (Tex.) II. Title.

TX715 .K8924   2000
641.5973— dc21

                                                      00-059279

# CONTENTS

*I feel a recipe is only a theme, which an intelligent cook
can play each time with a variation.*
— Madame Benoit

*Waldemar, Sea of Woods. Located on the cypress-lined banks of the
Guadalupe River in the western region of the Texas Hill Country.
It is a tradition seventy-five years strong among thousands of young girls
spanning the state and beyond. It is a place that offers opportunities
to learn skills, establish lifelong relationships,
and to foster an appreciation for the
spiritual qualities of a
loving, living place.*

# Special Thanks

SPECIAL THANKS TO the Elmore clan: Teak and George Anne, Meg and Clayton Clark, Josh and Allison, and Marsha and Dale, for the opportunity to write this book, and for all of their "tasting" wisdom. And I want to mention that George Anne has ably assisted in many of the details in getting this project to completion. Also, many thanks to my sisters, Liz Pipkin Pohl and Catherine Pipkin, and our "adopted" sister, Rachel Meriwether, my favorite samplers and supporters. Their tireless encouragement and positive response kept me on my toes and moving forward! To Connie Reeves, for her endless support and inspiration. May we all live with as much life as she does. To Julie Menges, for her patience and conversation. To Susan Gordy, for her laughter and encouragement and her baker's perspective. To Lori Appleton, for her balance, energy, and positive outlook. To Kirsten Parker, for her exemplary typing ability.

Waldemar has always been a community of support. This project has been no exception. A special thank you of course to my son, John, who always tells me I am the "best cook in the world" and who accepted "life on hold" for the duration of this project; to my parents, Linda and John Pipkin, for their kind encouragement and enduring acceptance; and to Aunt Lois—Lois Shrout—whose professional advice and encouragement have been a blessing. And last but certainly not least to Angela Buckley, my very patient, thorough, and encouraging editor, who has helped me immensely in bringing this project to fruition. Ultimately, without Angela, this book would still be sitting in my computer. Thank you, Thank you, Thank you.

# Dedication

ORA JOHNSON, an educator with a vision to create an environment for young women to learn and experience life to its greatest potential, founded Camp Waldemar for Girls in 1926. After her untimely death in 1931, her beloved niece took over the running of Waldemar and carried the vision in her heart for the next fifty years. Without any children of her own, Doris sold the camp to the next best thing: A woman who loved the camp just as much as she did. Marsha English Elmore came to Waldemar as a camper. She returned as a counselor, both before and after she had children. Marsha fit Doris' profile to carry the torch lit by Ora so many years ago. And over the past twenty years she has supported the vision created with so much love. Her daughter Meg, a camper and counselor as well, has now taken over the running of the summer camp. In addition to the summer camp, Meg and her brothers Teak and Josh have run an off-season conference resort since 1980. Doris had also done this by letting several families enjoy Waldemar's grounds as a dude ranch.

One important constant that has persisted through all these years is an absolute dedication to delicious food. Serving over one thousand people per summer, Waldemar has always settled for nothing less than the best. The tradition of simple, timeless classics nourishing our bodies, the routine of daily exercise, and the spiritual support of love and God's beauty in every word and breath—these are the essence of the success of Waldemar.

This book is a tribute to Ora, Doris, Marsha, and Meg. To their labor of love. To the very essence that makes this place so spiritually unique. There is not a Waldemar girl out there who wouldn't agree. Here's to seventy-five more years of continued growth and support and good times. Let's get cooking!

# A Well-Stocked Pantry
# and How to Use It

It is not the most important thing to have every device made for the kitchen. It is, however, important to have those tools and ingredients that will facilitate the preparation of your favorite dishes. I have included information about numerous kitchen tools, specialty ingredients, and how to choose and how to use them all! It is important to realize that there is no definitively complete list. It is only complete once you have just what you need. I encourage you not to overstock. Too many of these items will overrun your kitchen, and many ingredients have a limited shelf life. Beware of new-fangled gadgets designed to save you time. Always be certain you can return the product if it does not meet your expectations.

## COOKWARE
### Selection

If you are serious about cooking, as are most of us who enjoy eating, it is best to invest in a set of cookware that will last for the rest of your life. Copper and aluminum are the best conductors of heat. Many of us are not able to afford a whole set of copper. If it is in your budget, though, I recommend the stainless-lined versus the tin-lined. Tin is more traditional, but it requires costly maintenance, as tin will melt at around 450° F. Because of medical studies linking aluminum to degeneration of brain functions, it is important that aluminum cookware is lined with stainless steel. There are wonderful alternatives as well, such as hard-anodized aluminum. Research the market and find the variety that suits your situation. I have a hodge-podge of my favorite lines. Remember that form follows function, so choose according to your needs. I recommend a 6- to 8-quart stockpot, an 8-inch omelet skillet, a 2- to 3-quart sauté pan, and a 4-quart saucepan. These four pieces will serve most of your requirements!

### Maintenance

As with any important investment, proper care is necessary to maintain the longevity and durability of cookware. It is recommended to never wash your cookware in the dishwasher. It is best to wash in warm, soapy water and dry with a soft cloth.

## SPECIALTY COOKWARE
### Double Boiler

Many lines of cookware offer a double boiler. I have found that I prefer to use a stainless steel bowl set atop a 4-quart saucepan. This is effective for almost every need, especially in recipes that call for the melting of chocolate. Simply fill the saucepan with several cups of water, bring to a boil, and place the bowl over the hot water. The bowl should be large enough to rest on the rim of the pan. Do not fill the pan with so much water that the bowl is in direct contact with the water.

### Cast-Iron Skillet

Ideal for frying catfish or chicken and essential in making a good roux for gravy or gumbo, the best cast-iron skillet has years of seasoning. I have found some great old pans at antique stores. If you buy a new one, expect several years of proper seasoning before it takes on the smooth black finish that is so distinctive.

To care for your cast-iron skillet, rinse in warm water and wipe clean with paper towels. Rub the interior with vegetable oil and place in a warm oven (250° F) for several hours. Remove from the oven and wipe out the excess oil. You will not have to season the pan every time you use it if you don't wash with soap, as soap dries out the metal. Always dry immediately to prevent the build-up of rust. It is very effective to dry the skillet in the oven on low heat. Remove once dry.

### Crêpe Pan

The best crêpe pan I have ever used is the traditional iron design from France. It is about seven inches in diameter, with a small, angled edge. It requires seasoning, as a cast-iron skillet does. I found mine in Kerrville at the fabulous general store Gibson's, for only ten dollars. Gibson's has the best culinary tool selection that I have ever seen.

## CUTLERY
### Selection

Another important kitchen tool that deserves serious research and handling is the knife. When choosing your cutlery, look for a knife that feels balanced in your hand. Choose from one of the many quality-forged steel products that are guaranteed for life. It is well worth the investment. A nice selection includes an 8- or 10-inch chef's knife, a 3- or 4-inch paring knife, a serrated bread knife, and a 4- to 6-inch utility knife. There are many specialty blades that you may decide to add to your collection.

## Maintenance

The next step, which is as important as choosing the knife, is keeping it properly sharpened. A properly sharpened knife will be one of your best friends in the kitchen. The knife's edge will fray with use, and there is nothing more dangerous than a dull knife! It is a good idea to have the knife professionally sharpened by a reputable craftsman at least once a year. You can maintain the edge by using a sharpening steel every time you use the knife. And again, never wash your knives in the dishwasher. They will ruin.

## Storage

Always store your knives in a block or tray, which protects the steel blades. Never place loose in a drawer. Not only is this a danger to your hands, but it is detrimental to the blade.

## Sharpening Steel

This tool is an important complement to your cutlery. It is a long rod of steel with a sturdy handle. Proper daily use will assist you in maintaining a smooth, sharp, and balanced knife edge. To use, run the blade along the steel with a smooth motion several times on each side.

## BAKEWARE

I like to have a pair of each type of bakeware piece. In other words, two jellyroll pans, two cookie sheets, two 9 x 9-inch square cake pans, two 8-inch round cake pans, two cooling racks, two 12-count muffin tins, two springform pans, and two 9 x 13-inch baking pans. You get the idea. My reasoning is simple. The times I have had only one, I really needed two. I prefer to invest in a higher quality product as well. I like the clean baking of stainless steel. The "air-designed" baking products never seem to work consistently for me. I always use parchment paper on my bakeware. It produces consistent results, preserves the quality of the pan, and makes cleanup easier.

## FOOD PROCESSOR

This is a wonderful piece of equipment. It can chop, mince, purée, knead dough, emulsify a dressing, and grate cheese, carrots, or potatoes. It is one of the most versatile tools in the Waldemar kitchen. There are several sturdy and relatively economical models on the market. If you consider its usefulness, a food processor is a worthwhile investment.

## HEAVY-DUTY STAND MIXER

Another investment that can dig deep into the pockets. But again, if you plan on doing substantial baking it is a wonderful asset. There are several recipes, such as the Black Bread, page 64, which are very heavy and can burn out the motor on a handheld mixer. A stand mixer gives you the control and freedom to beat egg whites or whip cream, or mix cake batter or cookie dough. It simplifies the process of kneading bread dough as well. The Waldemar kitchen has a model that is large enough to hide in! Each summer, the Charm Class takes a tour through the kitchen. This is the item that gets the most "oohs," "ahhs," and "wows" every time!

## BLENDER

Perfect for creating a smooth sauce, chopping ice for summer coolers, or even for emulsifying dressings such as the Caesar Dressing, page 25, or Mayonnaise, page 36, this item has a more limited repertoire than the food processor. It does, however, have the indispensable property of simplicity. What is a kitchen without a blender?

## FRUIT RIPENER

This is an ingenious contraption made of clear plastic and shaped like a very large inverted apple with breathing holes on the top and bottom. It has been an invaluable tool in my kitchen for over fifteen years. Available in some culinary supply stores and priced at around twenty dollars, this is a must-have for those of you who value perfectly ripened, soft summer fruits such as peaches, plums, avocados, mangoes, and even pears. It takes only a few days, and a good trick to speed the process along is to put a ripe fruit in with the unripe. The only caution is to be mindful that the produce will ripen quickly. If forgotten, it will over-ripen and begin to rot. Also, never let moisture build up in the bottom, as this leads to premature rot and can be an invitation to those pesky little fruit flies.

## SALAD SPINNER

This contraption is rather bulky and will take up quite a bit of space, but it is well worth it if you eat a lot of salad. It is so important to properly wash your lettuce, and equally important to dry it to prevent premature rot. A salad spinner greatly simplifies this task. It is a large plastic bowl that contains a removable basket. The top has a handle that controls a gear. As you turn the handle, the basket spins, thus creating a velocity that throws the water off the lettuce! I suggest washing a head of lettuce the day you purchase it. Line a plastic bag with several paper towels and fill with the washed and dried lettuce. It will keep for at least a week. You can also use this method of preparation with herbs such as cilantro, watercress, and arugula.

## Box-Stand Grater

This little metal box has serrated perforations on all four sides. You can grate soft cheese, such as Cheddar, Monterey Jack, or mozzarella using the large holes. Hard cheeses like Parmesan, Romano, and hard ricotta can be grated on the medium holes. The smallest perforations are perfect for grating citrus peel. The fourth side has sharp horizontal slits for slicing items such as potatoes, apples, or jicama. Be careful not to knick your fingers in using it, though, as the perforations are very sharp.

## Measuring Cups and Measuring Spoons

Every kitchen needs measuring cups and measuring spoons. Without them, it is impossible to properly prepare many recipes. Glass cups are for measuring liquids, and stainless steel cups are for measuring dry ingredients. As for measuring spoons, I prefer the heavy-duty ones that will stand up to proper use and maintenance. The lighter-weight metals can become bent, which may affect your ability to properly measure.

## Citrus Juicer

I prefer the ridged, pointed, wooden juicer, but many people like the convenience of a juicer set into a bowl. The electric version is also handy when making large quantities of fresh citrus juice. But any of these will do the trick. Choose the one that will be most convenient for you. It is important to use fresh citrus juice rather than the store-bought variety, no matter how you squeeze it!

## Lemon Zester

A decent little tool that strips the outer skin from a citrus fruit into thin, tender pieces. It is the skin of the fruit that has the strong essence of oil that perfumes so many sweet as well as savory dishes. It does not give as potent a result as the grated peel, but zesting is effective nonetheless.

## Utensils
### Whisk

A useful tool for multiple tasks. Look for a whisk with a sturdy, comfortable handle.

### Rubber Spatula

I like the spatula with a scoop-like head and a rubber handle instead of the flat-head design. It seems to clean a bowl more thoroughly, which is its main purpose, after all. I have two spatulas in my kitchen, one for savory dishes and one for sweet dishes, each marked appropriately. Rubber will absorb the fragrance of the foods it comes into contact with. Imagine using the same spatula for your chocolate mousse as for roasted garlic mayonnaise.

## Metal Spatula

Another tool by the same name, but this sturdy version with a flat metal head is ideal for flipping flapjacks or turning quesadillas on the grill.

## Wooden Spoons

No kitchen is complete without a variety of good wooden spoons. I prefer to do all stovetop cooking with wooden spoons, and many classic cookbooks recommend using wood over metal. As the spoon ages with use, it will deepen in color and the wood will become seasoned and smooth.

## Pastry Brush

Another tool of which I recommend having two—one for sweet and one for savory. Properly cared for, these will last several years. However, once they begin to readily lose their bristles, replace them!

## Sieve

This is a wonder for many different straining jobs. Select one with a good-size stainless steel head capacity, as well as one for smaller jobs.

## Rolling Pin

Every baker has at least one rolling pin. And every baker will tell you which design he or she prefers. I personally like the smooth rod with no handles. It is convenient and easy to clean. But many like the ease of the rolling pin that turns on a handle with ball bearings. In the past, I have used a smooth-sided drinking glass with success!

## Flour Sifter

It is best to sift flour once before measuring and again before baking. Use a sifter that is large enough to contain at least four cups of dry ingredients. A sifter is also wonderful for combining dry ingredients—such as flour, sugar, baking powder, baking soda, salt, and spices—evenly!

## Pastry Blender

This is a brilliant tool that I use often in my baking. It has a wooden or metal handle with eight thin steel prongs curved like a "U" attached. It cuts cold, hard butter into flour mixtures with very little effort. It also seems to produce lighter and flakier results than the other option of using two dinner knives to cut the butter in a back-and-forth motion. If you don't have one, and enjoy baking, I recommend spending a few dollars and adding it to your culinary tool collection. You will wonder why you haven't gotten one before, but you can thank me later!

## Pastry Crimper

This tool, a small wheel on a handle, is used to cut dough with a decorative zigzag finish. Simply roll the crimper across the dough and cut into strips with a lovely edge.

## Food Mill

The food mill has now been replaced by the modern convenience of the food processor. I have one that I use for several sauces, such as the tomato sauce for pasta or pizza, page 87. It is no longer a standard in a well-equipped kitchen, but many cooks will tell you that it is by far the better tool.

## Cookie Press

This is an ingenious contraption used to press cookie dough or other firm dough through a metal plate to create shapes. It is essentially a tube-shaped metal container fitted on one end with a detachable metal plate that has a cutout shape or pattern in the center. The other end has a twist-seal handle that controls the amount of dough pressed through. You can find a cookie press at any good culinary store. It is a wonderful addition to your pantry if you do a lot of baking.

## Garlic Press

This is a useful gadget that has gained popularity in the last twenty years because of the ease it affords in preparing garlic—no more garlic-scented hands! If you want to purchase one, look for the design that has the cleaner permanently attached to the body. The detachable variety can become garbage in your disposal or simply get lost in a drawer. I have found that it is best to use pressed garlic in dressings. I prefer not to sauté pressed garlic, as it burns very quickly. It is best to finely mince garlic when sautéing.

A note on removal of the strong scent of garlic from your hands and breath. Fresh lemon oil is the best neutralizer I have found to remove garlic odor from you hands. Simply squeeze the rind of a lemon in your hands. Some people swear by whole coffee beans for counteracting garlic breath. I prefer to chew a bit of parsley, followed by a sip of fresh lemon juice. Finish by chewing a sprig of fresh mint.

## Ginger Grater

This is one of my favorite tools. It looks like a miniature porcelain washboard. It has little points on the face of the tool. Simply hold it by the handle and rub a piece of ginger across the points. The grater will separate the useable pulp and juice from the very fibrous material. Discard the fiber strands, and use the ginger pulp in sauces, soups, dressings. It is inexpensive and can be found at any good culinary supply store.

## Potato Peeler

A necessary component of any kitchen, you will find as many varieties of peelers as vegetables to use it on. Owing to its efficiency, I recommend the variety with a swivel blade and a comfortable handle. It is designed to peel using a smooth, back-and-forth motion. It is important to note, however, that many of the nutrients present in vegetables are found in the skins. I prefer to buy organic vegetables when they are available and to leave the skins on. Be sure to wash all vegetables thoroughly. If you must buy commercial produce, peel away! Most of the pesticides also reside in the skins.

## Instant-Read Thermometer

Priced at around ten dollars, this is an invaluable tool for checking the readiness of meats and breads. Stay away from the digital-read versions, however, as they are less durable with the use of water and regular wear and tear.

## Candy Thermometer

If you make much candy, this thermometer is essential. It usually has the major stages for candy, from the soft-ball stage to the hard-crack stage, printed on the gauge. The best candy thermometer I have used has a clip on the side that holds the thermometer to the pan. If you use the more traditional glass of cold water to test the candy, remember to always use a clean glass of water each time you check the doneness.

## Mortar and Pestle

A small bowl (mortar) with high sides and a curved bottom, and a sturdy tool (pestle) with a rounded end. This little set is indispensable for grinding rubs or making pesto by hand. If you have a food processor, you will be able to do everything you could do with a mortar and pestle. But it is a classic tool. Many ethnically oriented kitchens have some version of the mortar and pestle on hand. Sometimes being in touch with the food during preparation is more gratifying.

## Measuring Table

This handy reference table will help you in preparing the recipes. It is a good resource for learning these measurements.

Dash = scant ⅛ teaspoon of dry ingredients
3 teaspoons = 1 tablespoon
2 tablespoons = 1 ounce = ⅛ cup
2 ounces = ¼ cup
5⅓ tablespoons = ⅓ cup
8 ounces = 1 cup
16 ounces = 2 cups = 1 pint = 1 pound
32 ounces = 4 cups = 1 quart
128 ounces = 4 quarts = 1 gallon

# Beginnings

## Starters, Soups, and Salads

# The Dining Hall

*"Blessed is he who finds his work"*

Nestled in the verdant hills along the sparkling waters of the Guadalupe, Camp Waldemar for Girls is a place of incredible beauty, filled with memories that run as deep as the history of the area. Ora Johnson, Waldemar's founder, had a vision of what her camp should be like. Calling on the skill and expertise of one of San Antonio's finest architects, she had the dining hall built to help fulfill that vision. The construction was completed just before her death in 1931. We here still firmly believe that her loving presence is everywhere. It is hard to imagine Waldemar without numerous stories of Aunt Ora in the dining hall. We believe that she resides here still, in some form of love, to protect this great building.

The dining hall is hardly a typical camp mess hall. It is a majestic, three-story structure large enough to serve all of the campers and counselors on the first floor! We currently serve about 380 women and girls per meal. The second floor is the location of the infirmary and several bedrooms currently used for counselors in the summer. During the off-season, these bedrooms are elegantly decorated in a Hill Country style for the conference business. The third floor was built as a dance floor and was named the W. T. Johnson Ballroom in honor of one of Ora's brothers. At one time, ballroom dancing was taught and enjoyed!

The dining hall was built by the German stonemason Ferdinand Rehberger, a master of his trade. The interior and exterior were constructed with the finest details, using materials found at Waldemar and the surrounding area. Honeycomb rock, a type of limestone named for its perforations, lines the interior of the Junior Dining Room. It resembles a massive cave wall, and the work is so precise that it is difficult to find the seams between the rocks. A unique asymmetrical fireplace, constructed of fragments of fossilized coral and other beautiful rocks, warms the room in the winter. Two similar fireplaces do the same in the Senior Dining Room. This larger, more interior room contains wonderful symbols of times past. The fireplace and the performance stage are set with geodes and crystals inset with lights to create an effect of glittering elegance found only at Waldemar, Camp for Girls. In contrast to the natural, rustic style of the room, the tables are set with Waldemar china and silver. The girls are served family-style while they learn proper manners and table etiquette.

Imagine experiencing your first taste of Cheese Soufflé, page 89, or Crêpes Suzette, page 148, while listening to the camp orchestra play. The setting, the meal, the music, all produce a serenade for the senses. And this is only the beginning of the bounty of wonderful memories our campers carry home with them and keep throughout their lives. It is one of the reasons that so many girls who started attending camp in 1926 have sent their daughters, granddaughters, and great-granddaughters back to Waldemar. The magic of the camp lives in the hearts and memories of all who have ever been to Waldemar.

# Starters

## Guacamole

Makes about 2½ cups

There are as many versions of guacamole as there are people who eat it. This is essentially the recipe made during the off-season by Hector Campos. He is the assistant to the chef and a true guacamole master. Guacamole is a mainstay for any Tex-Mex menu. Serve with chips for an appetizer, or as an accompaniment to any style of fajitas or quesadillas.

4–6 medium avocados, ripe
1 small roma tomato, finely diced
1 tablespoon white or red onion,
    finely diced

½ serrano pepper, finely diced
½ lemon, juiced, seeds removed
1 teaspoon salt (or to taste)

Slice the avocados lengthwise down the center. Remove the pits and reserve for later. Scoop out the pulp and put it in a bowl. Mash lightly with a fork. We like it with a more natural texture, but you may wish to mash it until it is smooth. Add the tomato, onion, and serrano, and stir to mix. Stir in the lemon juice and salt to taste. Serve immediately. If you want to store it before serving, put the pits back into the guacamole and cover it with plastic wrap. Press the plastic wrap so that it adheres to the top of the dip. The pits act as a natural preservative, and the plastic prevents oxygen from turning the avocado brown.

# Hummus

Makes 2 cups

Hummus is a dip found on many Mediterranean and Middle Eastern menus. It is a newer addition to our repertoire, and it fulfills the need for a vegetarian option on our buffets. It is delicious served with baked pita chips, or in a pita pocket with sliced tomatoes, cucumbers, and fresh cilantro.

1 16-ounce can cooked chickpeas, drained and rinsed
2–4 cloves garlic, minced
½ teaspoon cumin
3 tablespoons fresh lemon juice, plus 1 tablespoon lemon juice as optional garnish

3 tablespoons tahini (sesame butter)
1 tablespoon extra virgin olive oil
Dash of cayenne pepper
Fresh parsley or cilantro, to garnish

In a food processor fitted with a steel blade, purée the chickpeas with a tablespoon of water until a smooth paste is formed. Stir in the garlic, cumin, lemon juice, and tahini, and continue to purée until a creamy consistency is attained. Put in a shallow bowl and smooth the top, making a shallow well in the center with the back of a spoon. Mix the cayenne and the oil together. Drizzle over the hummus, allowing it to pool in the center. Sprinkle a small bit of finely minced garlic in the center with the oil. Sprinkle dish with 1 tablespoon fresh lemon juice and add chopped parsley or cilantro for a garnish. Serve cold or at room temperature. Keeps in the refrigerator covered for three to five days.

# Mango Salsa

Makes about 2½ cups

Light and fruity, with a suprising bite, this is a great dip to serve with chips, or as an accompaniment to any grilled fish. I also like it with Shrimp Fajitas, page 139.

1 large cucumber, peeled, seeded, and chopped
1 cup mango flesh, chopped
½ jalapeño, seeded and chopped
2 tablespoons green onions, chopped
2 tablespoons red onion, chopped

¼ cup tomatoes, chopped
1 clove garlic, minced
½ lime, juiced
2 tablespoons fresh cilantro, coarsely chopped
Salt to taste

Toss the cucumber, mango, jalapeño, green onions, red onion, tomatoes, and garlic. Sprinkle the lime juice over the mixture and stir to coat. Adjust the flavor with salt. Refrigerate for at least 30 minutes. Toss with the cilantro just before serving.

# Corn Salsa

David Johnson, Waldemar's chef from 1995 to 1996, made this dish and served it at the end-of-camp Big Picnic as an accoutrement with fajitas. It is wonderful. It is a little spicy, but it provides a nice flavor contrast to most any Tex-Mex dish. It makes a delicious salad to serve with Chicken and Green Chili Enchiladas, page 124, and a splendid garnish with black beans and rice.

2 cups frozen corn
    (one 16-ounce package)
½ cup red onion, diced the
    size of corn
½ jalapeño, finely minced

1 clove garlic, minced
1–2 tablespoons fresh lime juice
Salt to taste
½ cup chopped cilantro,
    loosely packed

Place corn on a baking sheet and roast at 350° F for 5 to 10 minutes or until corn is plump and hot. Do not over-roast, or the corn will dehydrate. Remove from oven and place in a mixing bowl. Add the onions, jalapeños, garlic, and lime juice. Add salt to taste. Stir well. Let mixture sit in the refrigerator for at least 2 to 4 hours to allow the flavors to marry. Add the cilantro just before serving. Stir to combine. Serve immediately.

You can make this up to three days in advance, but add the cilantro just before serving.

# Black Bean Salsa

More substantial than the other salsas, this one can not only be a dip for chips or an accompaniment to any Tex-Mex dish, but also can be used as a filling for Vegetarian Burritos (recipe follows).

1 cup black beans, cooked
    (1 can drained and rinsed)
1 cup corn kernels, cooked
½ teaspoon jalapeño, minced
1 clove garlic, minced
¼ cup red onion,
    finely chopped

2 cups roma tomatoes,
    finely chopped
1–2 tablespoons lime juice
1 teaspoon salt (or to taste)
1 tablespoon olive oil
⅓ cup cilantro, chopped,
    loosely packed

In a medium mixing bowl, toss together the black beans, corn, jalapeño, garlic, red onion, and tomato. Stir in the lime juice and olive oil. Adjust seasoning to taste with salt. Let marinate for 2 to 4 hours in the refrigerator. Stir in the cilantro just before serving. May be served either cold or at room temperature.

Store in the refrigerator for up to three days, but add the cilantro just before serving.

# Vegetarian Burrito

Lay one 12-inch warmed flour tortilla on a flat work surface. Place ½ cup Black Bean Salsa (previous recipe), 2 tablespoons Cheddar or Monterey Jack cheese, or other filling on the bottom third of the tortilla. Wrap the tortilla around the filling with envelope folds, as follows: Fold the left and the right sides toward the center to partially cover the filling and create a seal on the outer edges. Begin rolling the tortilla from the bottom end up. The finished effect will be that of a sealed envelope. Place the burrito seal side down. Sprinkle about ½ cup cheese over the top and bake for 15 minutes on 350° F, or until the chese is melted and browning. Serve hot with salsa and sour cream for garnish.

# Carlos' Salsa                                    Makes about 1 ½ cups

This is spicy, and can be spicier. One of my colleagues in the kitchen would make this for himself, as he ate it on everything! He made it so hot that you could feel all of your sinus passages open, and that you just received a week's worth of vitamin C in one spoonful. He felt that we "gringos" were incapable of eating it as spicy as he would. Well, he was probably right. You can adjust the heat by altering the number of jalapeños used. The minimum given below offers a pretty spicy medium-heat sauce. The five jalapeños are spicy enough for me, but you may like it hotter like Carlos does. Either way, it will definitely keep you healthy!

| | |
|---|---|
| 3–5 whole jalapeños | ½ bunch fresh cilantro, with |
| 7 roma tomatoes | most of the stems removed |
| | 1–2 teaspoons salt |

Snap the stems off the jalapeños. Place the jalapeños and 2 of the roma tomatoes in a small saucepan. Cover with water. Bring to a boil and cook until the jalapeños are soft and pale green, about 15 to 20 minutes.

Meanwhile, cut the remaining 5 tomatoes into large chunks. Rinse the cilantro and spin dry.

When the jalapeños and cooked tomatoes are done, remove from the cooking liquid. Purée in a food processor with about ¼ cup of the cooking liquid. Add the fresh-cut tomatoes, ½ cup at a time, pulsing in the processor between each addition. Once all of the tomatoes are added, pulse until the desired texture is reached. Add the cilantro, and pulse to chop. Adjust the flavor with salt to taste.

This keeps in the refrigerator, covered, for up to a week.

# Pico de Gallo

Fresh and spicy, the accompaniment of many Waldemar favorites. Made with red ripe tomatoes, finely chopped onion and serrano, fresh cilantro, and lime juice, this is a sauce to please the palate. Use the freshest of ingredients and serve the day you make it. It does not age well in storage. Always add the cilantro just before serving, as this slows the spoilage.

Serve with Quesadillas, page 10, Black Bean Nachos, page 11, grilled steak or fish, or with tortilla chips. I also love it served with breakfast tacos or over scrambled eggs.

2 tablespoons white or red onion, finely chopped
4 roma tomatoes, chopped
1–2 serrano peppers, finely chopped (remove seeds for less heat)

1 tablespoon freshly squeezed lime juice
½ teaspoon salt (or to taste)
2 tablespoons cilantro, coarsely chopped

In a non-reactive bowl, such as glass or plastic, mix the onion, tomatoes, serrano peppers, lime juice, and salt. Let sit at room temperature for about 30 minutes. Stir in the cilantro just before serving.

# Tortilla Chips or Strips

These are more gratifying than you can imagine. Homemade chips. Thick and crunchy or very light. It all depends on the thickness of your tortilla. Just right for any of the tasty salsas listed here. Yes, you can use your favorite store-bought variety, but it is fun to know how to do these. They are virtually essential, though, for the strips called for in Ellen Easley's Tortilla Soup, page 18. Be cautioned that you must get the oil very hot. If you have little ones helping you, keep them away from the oil. A grease burn can be extremely severe!

Corn tortillas, white or yellow
Vegetable oil
Salt to taste

Cut the tortillas into wedges, typically six cuts per round. In a cast-iron skillet, pour in enough oil to reach 1½ inches deep. Heat the oil to 375° F. Fry the tortillas. If the oil is not hot enough, the tortilla will absorb too much oil and be greasy. Cook until the chips begin to turn golden brown in the center, about 3 to 5 minutes. Watch the edges to prevent burning. Turn over at least once during cooking.

Remove from heat and let drain on a dry paper towel. Sprinkle with salt. Keep in an airtight container. To refresh if they get stale, toast in the oven at 350° F for 5 to 10 minutes or until crisp.

# Grilled Quesadillas

Serves 6–8 as an appetizer or 4 as an entrée

These are better than those served at most restaurants. Grilling crisps up the tortilla perfectly, releasing some of the natural sugars present in the flour. Just writing about these makes me want to go fix a batch. If you're not careful, the quesadillas will all be gone before you finish cooking them!

8 flour tortillas (8-inch rounds)
¼ cup oil

1 cup cheese, Monterey Jack, or Cheddar and Monterey Jack blend

Select a variety of fillings from the list below, or use your imagination.

OPTIONAL FILLINGS:

Grilled vegetables, such as zucchini, red bell peppers, mushrooms, and green onions, cut into matchstick-size pieces
Black Bean Salsa, page 7
Roma tomatoes, sliced
Cilantro

Jalapeño, minced
Beef or chicken fajita meat, thinly sliced, pages 111 and 128
Minced shrimp and crab meat with roasted poblano peppers, page 78

Brush one side of the tortilla with oil. Place oil-side down on a piece of foil. Place 2 tablespoons of cheese atop tortilla, followed by 1 tablespoon of assorted toppings. Add another tablespoon of cheese. Top with a tortilla and brush the top with oil. Cook over a hot grill. Each side should cook 2 to 3 minutes, or until crispy and lightly browned. Cut into wedges and serve immediately with Pico de Gallo, page 9, Guacamole, page 5, and sour cream.

# Mr. Reyes' Tortilla Wraps

Serves 2–3 per person

Homemade tortillas and good venison sausage are essential. Mr. Reyes would have it no other way. Mr. Reyes was a part of Waldemar for many years. He was a strong influence in the family of year-round employees, nicknamed Grandpa by Julie and others. His handiwork grows in the beautiful landscape of Waldemar. His untimely death in 1998 left a hole in our hearts, but his work still lives in our eyes. Everything we see has some of his strength and skill touching it. We are better for having been blessed with his loyalty and love. We are better for just having known him.

Mr. Reyes was also known for making the best flour tortillas at Women's Week. This little appetizer has become an annual tradition for our participants. We miss Mr. Reyes, but this little dish always brings a joyful tear at the memory of his wonderful gifts.

Homemade tortillas are best made with a packaged mix from your supermarket, unless you have an old family recipe. The packaged mixes are easy and taste very good. Follow the directions on the package. However, I like to add several tablespoons of lard, cut in with a pastry blender, before adding the water. You will not need to add as much water, though. This makes a much more tender tortilla.

The shaping of the tortilla is a little tricky, but it will only take a few tries to get good results. Divide the dough into equal parts. (The number will depend on how many you are making.) With the palms of your hands, roll each of the parts into a little ball. Each ball will be a tortilla. The more balls made, the smaller the tortillas will be. It is important to strive for equal portions.

Keep the dough covered with a cloth while you are not working with it. Using a rolling pin, roll the round into a flat disc about 6 inches in diameter. It should be about ⅛ inch thick. Stack the rolled tortillas together with a sheet of wax paper between each layer.

Heat a well-seasoned cast-iron skillet over medium-high heat. Cook one tortilla at a time, turning after about 30 seconds, or until the cooking side has begun to brown. Remove and wrap in aluminum foil. Keep in a warmed oven until ready to use. You also may cool the tortillas and refrigerate or freeze until ready to use. Heat up over a gas burner or a barbecue pit.

Cut the venison sausage into 3-inch pieces. Split in half and cook until heated though. Wrap each piece of sausage in a tortilla and fasten with a toothpick. Serve warm on a platter.

# Black Bean Nachos                                            Serves 4

We love to serve nachos. Easy, fun, and so tasty. Add your favorite cooked meat for a quick dinner. The fresh ingredients rival any restaurant's version of this Tex-Mex delicacy.

| | |
|---|---|
| 2 handfuls homemade corn tortilla chips, page 9, or your favorite store-bought variety | 1 teaspoon jalapeño, finely chopped |
| 1–1½ cups black beans, gently mashed with a fork | 1 cup Monterey Jack cheese |
| Ground cumin, optional | 1 cup Pico de Gallo, page 9 |
| | 2 tablespoons sour cream |
| | ½ cup Guacamole, page 5 |

Preheat the oven to 350° F. On a baking sheet lined with parchment paper, lay the chips together in a single layer, with sides overlapping. Sprinkle with half of the cheese. Stir the optional cumin into the black beans. Place the black beans in dollops on top of the chips and gently spread evenly over the chips. Evenly spread ½ teaspoon of the chopped jalapeño atop the cheese for a batch with a bite. You can omit this step if you don't want spice, or you can increase the amount of jalapeño for even more spice! Sprinkle with the remaining ½ cup of cheese.

Bake the nachos in the preheated oven for 15 to 20 minutes, or until the cheese is melted and beginning to brown. Remove from the oven and transfer to a large serving plate. Place a dollop of the pico de gallo in the center and serve the remaining pico de gallo, sour cream, and guacamole on the side.

# Artichoke and Green Chili Dip

Serves 8–12

This is wonderful and easy. It is great for a buffet to serve many people, or as a dish for brunch. Serve it with your favorite crackers, or with a toasted French baguette sliced into rounds. This is one of Jan Cannon's favorites. Jan was a camper and has worked as a counselor and Tejas sponsor for many years. She is employed full-time with Waldemar and is indispensable to the Waldemar family. It is a pretty sure thing that she will bring this dish to any staff party—we don't mind!

| | |
|---|---|
| 1 tablespoon oil | 4 cans artichoke hearts, |
| ½ cup chopped onion | packed in water |
| 1 clove garlic | 1 cup mayonnaise |
| 2 7-ounce cans chopped | 1¾ cups Parmesan cheese, |
| green chilies | freshly grated |
| | Salt and pepper to taste |

Preheat oven to 350° F. Sauté the onion and garlic in a sauté pan with the oil and ½ teaspoon salt until translucent, about 5 to 7 minutes. Remove from the heat and stir in the green chilies.

Cut the artichoke hearts into quarters. Toss in the onion/green chili mixture. Stir in the mayonnaise and 1½ cups of the Parmesan cheese. Salt and pepper to taste.

Place in a small casserole dish. Sprinkle with the remaining ¼ cup Parmesan cheese. Bake until bubbly and the cheese on top has started to brown, about 30 minutes.

Serve warm.

# Spicy Shrimp and Bacon Brochettes

Serves 4–6

This is another wonderful and easy appetizer. It will satisfy the heartiest of palettes. Although the bacon takes much longer to cook than the shrimp, the flavor and fat from the bacon penetrates the shrimp, and it is just plain good. It is not one of our heart-healthy creations, but it certainly packs a lot of flavor.

1 pound (16 to 20) extra-jumbo
    shrimp, shelled and deveined
    but with tails on
6–8 slices bacon

1 jalapeño, seeded and sliced
    into thin julienned strips
5 wooden skewers, soaked in
    water for 15 minutes

Preheat oven to 350° F.

Slice the bacon in half or into thirds. It needs to be just long enough to wrap around the shrimp, with only a small amount overlapping. Cook in the microwave for about 1½ minutes on high heat. I pre-cook the bacon because it takes so much longer to cook than the shrimp.

Slip a slice of the jalapeño into the open slit in the back of the shrimp. Fold the shrimp into a circle and wrap the bacon around it. Slide the shrimp onto the skewer, fitting 3 to 4 per skewer.

Bake for 10 to 15 minutes or until the bacon begins to crisp, turning after 5 to 7 minutes. This is also very good cooked over a hot barbecue grill.

# Cheese Straws

Makes about 5 dozen

It is best to use extra-sharp cheese. These are wonderful with the Tomato Basil Soup, page 20, or Gazpacho, page 23. Light and crisp, these will keep for several weeks in an airtight container. Also, you can make the dough and freeze a portion of it before you bake it. Simply let it defrost in the refrigerator.

1 cup softened butter
2 cups sharp Cheddar cheese, grated
1 teaspoon cayenne pepper
½ teaspoon salt

½ teaspoon dry mustard
⅛ teaspoon garlic powder
2–2½ cups unbleached,
    all-purpose flour

Preheat the oven to 400° F. Cream together the butter, cheese, cayenne pepper, salt, dry mustard, and garlic powder. Slowly add the 2 cups of flour and mix until well blended. The mixture should be fairly stiff. Add a little more flour if needed.

Put the dough into a cookie press (see page xiii) fitted with the star mold. Press the dough into 2- to 3-inch-long sticks.

Bake in the preheated oven on a parchment-lined cookie sheet for 10 minutes or until browned. Cool on a cooling rack.

# Chicken and Mushroom Phyllo Triangles

I have included two phyllo triangle recipes. These are fun to do, and relatively easy. You can use any filling you like, leaving out the cheese if desired, or adding more! Phyllo dough is available in the freezer section of any good supermarket. It requires a little special handling, as it will dry out easily. But once you get the hang of it, you will find yourself creating recipes, just for an excuse to use it.

1 tablespoon olive oil
1–2 garlic cloves, minced
½ teaspoon salt
1 tablespoon finely chopped onion
1 tablespoon balsamic vinegar
1 cup cooked chicken, shredded
1 tablespoon Sun-Dried Tomato
    Pesto, page 88
½ cup fresh mushrooms,
    coarsely chopped
1 green onion, whites and
    greens chopped

1 teaspoon fresh basil leaves,
    torn
1 tablespoon pine nuts,
    toasted and finely chopped
1 cup Monterey Jack cheese,
    grated
½ teaspoon salt, or to taste
6 sheets phyllo dough
1 stick salted butter, melted,
    cooled to room temperature.
    (It should be soft, but not
    completely liquid)

Sauté the garlic in a medium sauté pan over medium-high heat with the oil and ½ teaspoon salt until the fragrance is released, about 3 minutes. Add the onion and continue cooking until the onion is translucent, about another minute. Add the balsamic vinegar to deglaze and cook to reduce until all excess moisture has evaporated, about 3 to 5 minutes, stirring often.

Add the chicken and stir to coat with the glaze. Stir in the tomato pesto. Remove from the heat, and transfer the mixture to a bowl to cool.

Sauté the mushrooms in the same skillet with another tablespoon oil, until cooked, about 3 minutes. Stir in the green onions, and combine with the chicken mixture. Stir in the basil leaves, the pine nuts, the cheese, and salt to taste. Refrigerate until at least room temperature, about 15 minutes.

THE TRIANGLES:
(Makes 12)

Preheat the oven to 375° F.

On a large, flat workspace, lay down several pieces of plastic wrap to cover the same amount of area as the phyllo dough. The phyllo should be defrosted, covered with a sheet of plastic wrap, and then a light towel.

Have your semi-melted butter and a soft pastry brush handy before you begin. The phyllo dough feels like a silky piece of paper. As it dries, it becomes very brittle and will crack. You will need to work quickly with each sheet. But the beauty of phyllo is that if you get little cracks, which you invariably will, the process of brushing the dough with butter will "glue" it back together.

Begin by transferring a sheet of phyllo to your workspace. Gently brush on some butter, first around the edges, and then over the entire surface. Lay the next sheet on top of the first, and repeat the steps with the butter. Repeat with a third sheet.

With a pizza roller, cut the sheet into six 3-inch strips.

Place a tablespoon of the chicken/mushroom filling on the thin edge of a phyllo strip (the edge nearest you). Fold over the bottom right corner so the bottom of the strip lies along the left side, thus creating a small triangle about 2 inches long. Brush lightly with butter, and fold again. Repeat until the filling has been folded completely into a little triangular phyllo packet. Do not brush the outside with butter. Place fold side down onto a parchment-lined baking sheet with sides.

Repeat with the remaining 5 sheets of phyllo using the same steps.

Bake for about 15 minutes on 375° F, or until the phyllo begins to turn golden brown.

Serve hot!

# Spinach and Feta Phyllo Triangles     Serves 4–6

This is essentially the same recipe as the chicken and mushroom phyllo triangles with a different filling idea. As I said in the introduction, you can use any filling you like! These two recipes have a distinctively Mediterranean flavor, which is in keeping with the origins of the phyllo, but you can use Indian spices such as cardamom, curry, cumin, and cilantro, or Jamaican jerk spice. Really any flavor combination you please! The only consideration is that you will not want to use anything that has a great deal of liquid, which would prevent the phyllo from flaking up into its many wonderful, buttery layers.

| | |
|---|---|
| 1 tablespoon olive oil | 2 cups fresh baby spinach leaves, |
| 1–2 cloves garlic, minced |    rinsed and spun dry |
| ¼ cup chopped onion | ¼ cup feta cheese, crumbled |
| 1 tablespoon red bell pepper, | 1 cup Monterey Jack cheese, grated |
|    chopped | Salt and pepper to taste |

Sauté the garlic in a sauté pan over medium-high heat with the olive oil and ½ teaspoon salt until the fragrance is released, about one minute. Add the onion and red bell pepper, and continue cooking until the vegetables are soft. Add the spinach, and cook until the leaves wilt, about 5 to 7 minutes. Remove from heat and let cool. Drain liquid from spinach. Stir in the feta and Monterey Jack cheeses.

Season to taste with salt and pepper.

Use as a filling for phyllo triangles by following the steps in the preceding recipe.

# Baked Brie en Croute

Serves 6–8

Baked brie in a crust of puff pastry. This is a delightful appetizer. It has a beautiful presentation, with a sweet surprise inside. Make this for an evening dinner and friends will be impressed and delighted.

1–2 sheets of puff pastry, available in the frozen section of your supermarket
1 8-inch round of Brie, double cream

¼ cup brown sugar
½ cup pecan pieces
Egg wash (2 egg whites mixed with 1 tablespoon water)

Preheat the oven to 350° F.

On a parchment-lined cookie sheet, lay out one piece of the puff pastry. Place the Brie round in the center. Sprinkle the pecans and brown sugar over the top of the cheese. Draw the edges of the puff pastry around the cheese like a drawstring purse. Pinch to close. You may cut a thin strip of pastry from a second sheet to create a "tie" around the top. Brush the top and sides with the egg wash. Bake in the preheated oven until the crust is browned, about 15 to 20 minutes. Remove from the oven and place on a serving tray. Garnish with fresh fruit, such as strawberries, grapes, kiwi, and fresh mint. Serve with your favorite crackers or French bread rounds.

# Roasted Garlic

More than just an appetizer, this preparation for garlic can be used in so many different ways. Purée it with butter and salt to spread on bread served with a meal, or add it to mashed potatoes, soups, or pasta sauces. Your imagination is the limit! I like to do a whole batch of them. The baking time does not vary noticeably, and because of its many uses, it is a great ingredient to have on hand. Store in the refrigerator for up to two weeks.

8 bulbs fresh garlic (choose fresh, firm heads)
2 tablespoons olive oil

Salt
¼ cup water

Preheat oven to 350° F. Peel all extra paper from the garlic. Cut the stem end off the bulbs. This makes it easier, once cooked, to remove the extra skin. Place each bulb, root end down, in the roasting pan. Drizzle the oil over each bulb so that the exposed cloves are coated. Sprinkle with salt. Pour the water into the bottom of the pan. Cover with foil and roast for about an hour, or until the cloves are soft. The aroma will be like sweet, caramelized garlic. Remove from the oven and let cool enough to easily handle. Remove the outer skins. Store the garlic in an airtight container in the refrigerator.

Purée the roasted garlic to add to soups, mayonnaise, dressings, or sauces. Enjoy!

# Soups

## Chicken Stock

An essential for any good soup. I like to save onion skins, celery leaves, organic carrot trimmings, and garlic skins. I freeze them for future use in making this stock or Vegetable Stock, page 18.

12 cups water, cold
4½–5 pounds chicken with bones,
    skin on for more flavor
    (remove skin for less fat)
3 medium carrots, washed but not
    peeled, cut into 1-inch pieces

4 stalks of celery with leaves on,
    cut into 1-inch pieces
1 onion, diced large
4–6 cloves garlic, unpeeled and
    cut into halves

In a large stockpot, simmer water and chicken until the meat is cooked (about 20 minutes). Remove the chicken and let it cool just enough to handle. Remove the meat from the bones. Set the meat aside and put the bones back into the pot of water. Add carrots, celery, onion, and garlic. Add 4 cups of water. Simmer for an hour on low heat. Do not let the stock boil. Remove all meat and vegetables. Strain through a sieve. Store the chicken stock in the refrigerator for up to three days, or pour into ice cube trays and freeze. Remove from the trays and store in freezer bags for up to three months. Label and date the bags. This is a great way to always have a little fresh chicken stock on hand, ready to use.

# Vegetable Stock

This stock is an ideal vegetarian alternative to chicken stock. It is a much lighter stock, but it still enhances the flavor of any soup. It may also be added to any sauce in place of chicken stock or water. The *New Joy of Cooking* recommends that 5 cups vegetables to 6 cups water makes 3 to 4 cups stock. I have doubled the quantity, as most recipes call for 6 to 8 cups. Remember that it is important to cut all of the vegetables about the same size to ensure an even cooking time.

| | |
|---|---|
| 2 onions, peeled and sliced | 1 bay leaf |
| 2 carrots, cut into 1-inch dice | 4–6 whole black peppercorns |
| 1 bulb garlic, peeled and smashed | 3 sprigs fresh parsley |
| 4 ribs celery, sliced | 1 thin slice of lemon |
| 1 leek, the white part only, thoroughly cleaned and sliced | 12 cups water |

Simmer over medium-low heat in a large stockpot until the vegetables are tender, about 60 minutes. Strain into another container through a fine sieve, pressing the vegetables to extract as much liquid as possible. Use immediately, or let cool and refrigerate until ready to use. Keeps in the refrigerator for up to a week, or follow the suggestion in the Chicken Stock recipe (page 17) and freeze in ice cube trays.


# Tortilla Soup

Serves 4–6

This is based on Ellen Easley's favorite recipe. All of you Waldemar girls know who Ellen is, even if you never met her. Ellen was the backbone of Waldemar for over forty years, Doris Johnson's right hand, and it is to her that we owe a lot of what Waldemar is today. Many years ago, Ellen was served tortilla soup at the La Posada Hotel in Laredo, Texas. She liked it but could not find a recipe for it anywhere. So, with a lot of research and testing, she came upon essentially this one. It is wonderful and hearty—a delicious meal in itself.

| | |
|---|---|
| 2 tablespoons oil | 1½ teaspoons chili powder |
| 1 medium onion, julienned | ¾ teaspoon cumin |
| 2½ teaspoons salt | 3 cups cooked chicken, torn into pieces |
| 4–6 cloves garlic, coarsely chopped | 6 cups chicken stock |
| ½ bell pepper, green, red, or yellow, chopped | Salt and pepper to taste |
| 1 stalk celery, chopped | Corn tortilla strips, page 9 |
| ½–1 serrano pepper, chopped (optional) | ¼ cup Monterey Jack cheese |
| 4 roma tomatoes, seeded, and cut into julienne strips | 1 avocado, sliced, to garnish |
| | ½ cup cilantro, chopped |
| | ⅛ cup fresh cilantro sprigs, to garnish |

In a large 6-quart stock pot, sauté the onion with 1 teaspoon salt in the oil on medium heat until it begins to caramelize, about 15 minutes. Stir frequently to prevent burning. Add the garlic, bell pepper, celery, and serrano pepper. Continue to cook until the fragrance is released, about 3 to 5 minutes. Add the tomatoes, and continue cooking until they begin to wilt, about 5 minutes. Add the spices and stir to combine.

Stir in the chicken to coat with the other ingredients. Continue to cook the chicken for about 5 minutes.

Add the stock and simmer for 25 minutes. Stir in ½ cup chopped cilantro. Season with salt and pepper to taste.

To serve, fry corn tortilla strips, page 9, and place in the bottom of individual bowls. Sprinkle grated Monterey Jack cheese over strips. Ladle soup into bowl. Garnish with slices of fresh avocado and a sprig of cilantro. Serve immediately while hot.

# Cream of Mushroom Soup                                    Serves 6–8

A warm bowl of soup on a cold winter's night. Serve with crusty French bread and a salad of mixed greens and Dijon Vinaigrette, page 36. You can substitute wild mushrooms if you would like an earthier flavor.*

| | |
|---|---|
| 4 tablespoons butter | 4 tablespoons flour |
| 2 cloves garlic, finely chopped | 8 cups hot chicken stock |
| ½ teaspoon salt | 3 green onions, chopped |
| 8 cups fresh button mushrooms, | (about ⅓ cup) |
| coarsely chopped | ½ cup heavy cream |
| | Salt and pepper to taste |

Sauté garlic in butter with ½ teaspoon salt until fragrance is released, about 3 to 5 minutes. Add the mushrooms and sauté until cooked through, about 10 minutes. Stir often. Stir in the flour until fully incorporated. This is a thickening agent, so this is essentially the same as a roux, but requires less work. Slowly add the stock, ½ cup at a time. Stir until fully blended before each addition, until all the stock has been added. Stir in the green onions and season with salt and pepper to taste. Let simmer for 15 to 20 minutes. Stir in the cream. Garnish with green onions if desired and serve hot.

*To rehydrate the dried wild mushrooms, bring 4 cups water to a boil. Pour over 4 ounces dried wild mushrooms and let soak for 20 minutes. Remove the mushrooms from the stock and set aside. Reserve 2 cups of the stock and substitute for 2 cups of the chicken stock. Chop the mushrooms into small pieces. Add to the recipe in addition to the fresh button mushrooms.

# Tomato Basil Soup

A summer delight! You can also use golden tomatoes, now available in cans from a company centrally located here in Texas. Yellow tomatoes make a beautiful substitute when fresh, ripe roma tomatoes are no longer in season.*

1 tablespoon butter
1 teaspoon olive oil
2 cloves garlic, coarsely chopped
¼ cup shallots, minced
Dash of salt
¼ cup carrots, finely diced
¼ cup white wine, semi-sweet

7 cups roma tomatoes, peeled, seeded, and coarsely chopped (about 18 tomatoes)
2 cups stock, vegetable or chicken, pages 17 and 18
Béchamel Sauce (recipe follows)

Sauté garlic in butter and oil on medium-high heat until fragrance is released, about 3 to 5 minutes. Add shallots, a dash of salt, and carrots. Stir occasionally, about 3 to 5 minutes. Add the wine and stir, allowing mixture to reduce. Add tomatoes and stir occasionally for about 3 minutes. Cover and let simmer until tomatoes begin to break apart and turn bright orange, about 10 to 15 minutes. Stir occasionally to prevent burning. Remove from heat and purée in a blender or a food processor fitted with a metal blade, or pass through a food mill, until smooth. You will have to do this in batches. Return to heat and add 2 cups vegetable or chicken stock. Bring to a gentle boil, then reduce heat to medium low and simmer until mixture reduces and thickens. Make a Béchamel Sauce (recipe follows).

## Béchamel Sauce

2 tablespoons butter
2 tablespoons flour

1 cup milk

In a 1-quart saucepan, melt the butter. Stir in the flour to make a thick paste. Remove from the heat and slowly add the milk, about a tablespoon at a time. Stir to incorporate. The paste should be smooth and free of lumps before you add any more liquid. You should note that the paste will seize up when you begin adding liquid. This is normal. Continue to add liquid, diligently stirring between each addition. It will thin out as you go.

FINISHING:

3 cups fresh basil leaves

Salt and pepper

Stir ½ cup tomato soup into the béchamel sauce until smooth. Add another ½ cup. Continue until the sauce is the same consistency as the soup itself. Stir the béchamel mixture into the soup. Stir in ¼ cup fresh basil leaves, rinsed and torn into small pieces. Season to taste with salt and pepper. Serve immediately, or store in refrigerator for up to three days. Reheat until warm, and serve.

*To substitute yellow tomatoes, use four 28-ounce cans of golden yellow tomatoes, available at finer grocery stores. The color will remain essentially unchanged during cooking. Remove from heat and purée when the tomatoes are soft and break apart easily. Garnish with thinly sliced roma tomatoes (if available) and fresh basil springs for an elegant contrast.

# Carrot Ginger Soup

Serves 6–8

Golden and creamy, and tasty, too! This soup with sweet carrot and spicy ginger is delicious any time of year. Serve with Wilted Spinach Salad, page 28, and Monkey Bread, page 64.

6 cups chicken or vegetable stock
4 cups carrots, peeled and chopped
    (about 8 to 10 carrots)
½ onion, coarsely chopped
2 cloves garlic, coarsely chopped
½ cup celery, peeled and chopped
    (about 2 stalks)
1 bay leaf, fresh or dried

½ teaspoon sugar
1 teaspoon fresh ginger, grated*
    (about 1 inch ginger, peeled)
¼ cup heavy cream
Salt and pepper to taste
Cilantro for garnish
1 lime, cut into 8 wedges

Simmer carrots, onion, garlic, celery, and bay leaf in the 6 cups stock in a large stockpot until vegetables are tender (about 20 minutes). Remove the bay leaf and purée mixture in a blender or food processor until smooth. You will have to do this in batches.

Return to heat. Add grated ginger. Simmer for 10 minutes. Add ¼ cup heavy cream. Stir to blend. Season to taste with salt and pepper.

Ladle into bowls and garnish with cilantro and a squeeze of lime juice. Serve hot.

*See page xiii for information on a ginger grater.

# Sweet Potato Bisque

Serves 4–6

A sweet and warm soup based on leeks and sweet potatoes, this is a way to serve sweet potatoes at holiday time that will please everyone. I have served this at Waldemar's family Thanksgiving dinner for several years. It is a holiday favorite.

2 tablespoons olive oil
2 large leeks, the white part only,
    washed well, finely chopped
4–6 cloves garlic
1 cup white wine

3 pounds sweet potatoes, peeled,
    chopped into 2-inch cubes
8 cups chicken or vegetable stock
1 lime, juiced, rind finely grated
½ cup heavy cream or milk
Salt and white pepper to taste

In a large soup pot, sauté the leeks and garlic until tender, about 3 minutes. Deglaze the pan with the white wine, and simmer for several minutes. Add the sweet potatoes and the stock. Let the potatoes simmer until tender, about 45 minutes.

Purée the potatoes with the broth in a blender or food processor in batches until smooth. Return to the pot and continue cooking on low. Add lime juice and rind. Slowly stir in cream. Season to taste with salt and pepper.

# Chicken and Venison Sausage Gumbo

We love Gumbo! Gumbo is a regional soup from the state of Louisiana. It has evolved from the traditions of the African and French and their descendants who have settled there. "Gumbo" actually translates as "okra," an abbreviated version of a word from an African language called Bantu. With this in mind, gumbo clearly is not really gumbo without the okra. Okra aids in thickening the soup and imparts a subtle but irreplaceable flavor. However, if you are averse to the addition of okra, and many people are, you may add filé powder, from the sassafras plant, to your individual bowl. Never add the filé powder to the cooking pot, though, as the powder will begin to string up with cooking heat, essentially destroying the soup. Putting aside the okra debate, the most important gumbo technique is the roux. A gumbo must have a roux as deep and dark as the Louisiana Bayou. This is the most important flavor base. Traditionally, the roux could take upwards of an hour to prepare. I have included an old trick to save you time. This soup may seem like a lot of effort, but if you have ever had a good gumbo, you know it is worth it! Remember that this soup can be filled with seafood as well, such as crab meat, shrimp, oysters, and crawfish tails.

1 cup oil
1 cup browned flour*
1 onion, chopped into 3-inch dice
4–6 ribs celery, chopped into
   3-inch dice
1 bell pepper, chopped into
   3-inch dice
4–6 cloves garlic, coarsely chopped
6–8 cups chicken stock, heated

4 cups cooked dark chicken
   meat, removed from the
   bone
½ pound cured venison sausage,
   cut in half lengthwise,
   then cut into ⅛-inch slices
1 teaspoon Worcestershire sauce
½ teaspoon cayenne, or to taste
Salt to taste
2 cups sliced okra

Always begin your roux with equal parts oil and flour. I like to make this soup in a well-seasoned cast-iron Dutch oven, as it seems to hold and evenly distribute the heat. Also, you need to have all of the vegetables chopped and set by the stove before you begin. Warm the stock in another saucepan, and keep on a low simmer.

Over medium heat, in a 6- or 8-quart Dutch oven or soup pot, stir the browned flour* into the oil. Cook on medium heat, stirring continuously until the roux turns dark, dark brown in color (approximately 20 minutes if you use browned flour, or 1½ hours if you start with white flour). Do not leave the pot for any reason, as the flour will very quickly burn. If this happens, you can continue, but the flavor and texture will be altered, possibly ruined. It is best to devote this time to establishing a roux worthy of the effort!

When the roux is of the desired darkness, quickly add the onion, celery, bell pepper, and garlic. This arrests the cooking of the roux, stabilizing the color and the flavor. Stir the vegetables and cook in the roux until the fragrance of the onion and garlic is released, about 5 minutes.

Slowly stir in ½ cup of the hot chicken stock. Stir until it is fully incorporated. Continue adding the stock ½ cup at a time, until it is all combined. Add the chicken, sausage, salt, Worcestershire, and cayenne, and continue cooking for about 15 to 20 minutes. Stir in the okra. Continue to cook until the okra is tender and cooked through, another 15 to 20 minutes. Season to taste with salt and pepper. Just before serving, stir in the green onions. Serve over white or brown rice.

This soup gets better if it rests in the refrigerator overnight. It is wonderful as leftovers, and also freezes very well!

*BROWNED FLOUR:
Many regional cooks recommend making a large batch of browned flour and storing it in an airtight container. It is convenient to have it on hand, as it reduces the overall cooking time of a dark brown roux by about 75%. I recommend doing 4 cups to begin with. If you find you use it more frequently, make a larger batch, keeping in mind that the baking time will be longer.
Preheat the oven to 300° F.
Sift 4 cups unbleached flour and spread evenly onto a jellyroll baking sheet. Bake until the flour is a deep caramel brown color, about 45 minutes to an hour, stirring often. Remove from the oven and let cool. Sift the flour and store in an airtight container. Keeps for at least three months.

# Gazpacho                                   Serves 6–8

This soup is so easy and so delicious. We like to have it on hand, just for a quick lunch or a pick-me-up anytime. The vegetables offer a crunchy bite. You may like it with more or with fewer vegetables, and you can vary the amount according to preference. Serve for a luncheon with Cheese Straws, page 13.

48 ounces vegetable-tomato juice
1 28-ounce can peeled Italian tomatoes
   (with no seasoning)
½ red onion
2 cucumbers, peeled and seeded
3 stalks of celery
1 green bell pepper
2 tablespoons olive oil

3 teaspoons Worcestershire sauce
2 tablespoons lemon juice
   (about 2 lemons)
2 tablespoons red wine vinegar
Dash of cayenne pepper (optional)
Salt to taste
1 tablespoon fresh parsley

Pour the tomato juice into a large pitcher or container. Pulse the canned tomatoes in a food processor until they are coarsely chopped. Pour into a quart-sized measuring cup. Pulse-chop each of the ingredients with about ¼ of the pulsed tomatoes, pouring into the pitcher after it reaches a "roughly chopped" size. Stir in the olive oil, Worcestershire sauce, lemon juice, red wine vinegar, and optional cayenne pepper. Season to taste with the salt. Stir in the parsley and refrigerate for 2 to 4 hours or overnight, to allow the flavors to marry.
Serve chilled.

# Poblano Corn Chowder

Oh, my. This is a good one. And it is easy, too. But make it on the day that you plan to serve it. It doesn't reheat with the same texture.

1 cup onion, diced the size of
    corn kernels
2 cloves garlic, coarsely chopped
¼ cup olive oil
½ cup white wine
8 cups corn kernels
4 poblano peppers, roasted, peeled,
    seeded, deveined and chopped
    the size of corn kernels

1 cup vegetable stock
4 cups milk
1 teaspoon salt, or to taste
¼ teaspoon cumin
½ cup tomato, chopped the size
    of corn kernels (about 1
    tomato)
2 green onions, chopped
½ cup cilantro

Sauté onion and garlic with ¼ teaspoon salt in olive oil until the onion begins to caramelize, about 7 to 10 minutes. Stir occasionally to prevent over-browning. Deglaze with the white wine. Let it reduce for about 5 minutes, or until most of the liquid has been absorbed. Add the corn and poblanos, and sauté with the onions until heated through, about 7 to 10 minutes. Pour in the stock and the milk, and bring to a light simmer. Add the salt and cumin. Continue cooking on low for 15 minutes. Remove 4 cups of the soup and purée in a food processor or a blender. Combine with the remaining soup and stir in the tomatoes, green onions, and cilantro. Let simmer another 10 minutes, or until the tomatoes soften. Serve hot.

# Salads

## Caesar Salad
Serves 4 as an entrée or 6 as an accompaniment

The classic salad finds its origins not too far from Waldemar, in Tijuana, Mexico. This is by far one of the best variations we have ever had. It is a recipe contributed by Roy Spears, our celebrated former chef. We love to serve it all year long. It is superb accompanying any of the Italian-style entrées, such as the Lasagna Bolognese, page 113, or the Fettucine Alfredo, page 96. It is also a hearty entrée when paired with Tomato Basil Soup, page 20. It makes my mouth water just thinking about it! Top with fajita grilled chicken, page 128, for a meal in itself. Who needs to go out when it can be so good at home?

The dressing is traditionally mixed in the serving bowl, but we prefer to first mix in the food processor or in a mixing bowl, and then mix with the lettuce.

1 head romaine lettuce, washed, dried, and torn into bite-sized pieces
1 cup or so Homemade Croutons, page 68 (store-bought will do in a pinch)

¼–½ cup freshly grated Parmesan or Romano cheese
Freshly ground black pepper

DRESSING:
1 egg
2 cloves garlic, minced
1 tablespoon anchovy paste, or 3–4 anchovy fillets, chopped fine and smashed with the back of a spoon

1 whole lemon, juiced and strained
1 tablespoon tarragon vinegar
2 teaspoons Dijon mustard
1 cup olive oil
Salt to taste

Coddle the egg (by boiling a whole egg for 2 minutes in gently boiling water). The egg will still be very soft, but this helps to thicken the dressing, as well as to protect you from any health risks posed by raw egg. Whisk together the egg, garlic, and anchovy paste until smooth. Add the lemon juice, vinegar, and Dijon mustard. Whisk together to incorporate. Slowly add the olive oil in a steady drizzle, whisking continuously until the dressing emulsifies. Adjust the flavor with salt to taste.

Toss the lettuce, croutons, cheese, and black pepper in a serving bowl large enough to accommodate the ingredients and to properly toss the dressing over the salad. Pour about ¼ cup of the dressing and toss with the salad. Add more if desired. Serve immediately!

## Properly Dressed Green Salad                                    Serves 4–6

Just a few notes on creating a quick dressed salad. Its components are basic: fresh lettuce, vinegar, olive oil, and salt and pepper. You can add any vegetables that you enjoy in your salad, or keep it simple and serve just mixed greens. Do not toss the salad until just before serving, as the salt will wilt the lettuce within several minutes. The true secret is to imagine the leaves "kissed" with the vinegar and oil. It should not be too heavily soaked, or a soggy salad will result.

1 head of lettuce, such as red-leaf, green-leaf or Boston (aka Bibb or butter) lettuce, washed and spun dry
½ cup mixed greens

2 tablespoons balsamic vinegar
3 tablespoons extra-virgin olive oil
Salt and pepper to taste

In a salad bowl, toss the lettuce with the vinegar. Slowly drizzle the oil over the greens and toss to coat. Salt and pepper to taste and serve immediately.

## Monterrey Salad                                                 Serves 8

This is a great salad to serve with the Chicken Enchiladas with Verde Sauce, page 124. It has a sweet, tangy, crunchy bite to it. This is one we do quite frequently, for it is a colorful, flavorful accompaniment to any spicy dish!

1 head green-leaf lettuce
2 cups spinach, washed, stems removed
1 small jicama, peeled and cut into matchsticks, ⅛ inch thick and 1 inch long

1 cup red cabbage, chopped
½ red onion, sliced into thin rings
½ cup radishes, thinly sliced
2 oranges, peeled and sectioned, with membranes removed

Wash the lettuce. Spin dry, and tear into pieces about the size of the spinach. Toss with the spinach, jicama, red cabbage, red onion, radishes, and oranges in a salad bowl. Just before serving, toss with the dressing (recipe follows), or serve the dressing in a bowl for the table.

DRESSING:

¾ cup squeezed orange juice
3 tablespoons balsamic vinegar
¼ teaspoon dry mustard

3 tablespoons salad oil
Salt and pepper to taste

Mix the orange juice, balsamic vinegar, and dry mustard together. Slowly drizzle the oil in a steady stream, whisking continuously until it begins to emulsify. Season with salt and pepper to taste. Serve tossed with the Monterrey Salad.

# Baby Spinach, Walnut, and Mandarin Orange Salad

Serves 4

Baby spinach greens are a delightfully tender option to the thicker and more bitter mature leaf. They are readily available in most good produce departments. If your local greengrocer doesn't regularly stock it, ask him to! We love to serve this salad with Herb-Roasted Cornish Game Hens, page 130, and Wild Rice Pilaf, page 94. It offers a delicious contrast of flavors, sweet and nutty, to most simple meat entrées. The dressing is delicious and easy to prepare. Your family and friends will be so impressed. Our patrons certainly are!

4 cups tender baby spinach leaves
2 thin slices red onion, quartered
⅓ cup walnuts
1 radish, thinly sliced

1 tomato, quartered, seeded, and
  julienned
⅓ cup mandarin oranges, preferably the canned variety
  packed in light syrup

Wash the spinach leaves and spin or pat dry, removing as much excess water as possible. Rinse again if there is much sand left on the leaves. If you use the more mature spinach leaves, rinse at least twice, a third time if necessary. Place the greens in a serving bowl. Toss the red onion, walnuts, radish, tomato, and mandarin oranges with the spinach to evenly distribute. Toss with a light coating of the salad dressing, about ¼ cup, and place the remaining dressing into a cruet or bowl for table service. Serve immediately, as a dressed salad will begin to wilt.

DRESSING:

2 tablespoons syrup from oranges
1 tablespoon balsamic vinegar
1 tablespoon champagne vinegar
1 small clove of garlic, minced

1 teaspoon walnut oil
⅔ cup olive oil
Salt and pepper to taste

Whisk together the orange syrup, balsamic vinegar, champagne vinegar, garlic, and walnut oil in a small mixing bowl. Slowly drizzle the olive oil into the mixture in a steady stream, whisking continuously. The mixture will begin to emulsify, or thicken. Flavor with the salt and pepper, and stir to combine.

# Wilted Spinach Salad with
# Hot Honey Mustard and Bacon Dressing   Serves 4–6

This rich and hearty salad is excellent paired with Hoisin Pork Tenderloin, page 121, or with Boeuf Bourguignon, page 117. We borrowed and slightly altered this recipe from the restaurant Hudson's on the Bend in Austin, Texas.

8 cups fresh, mature spinach leaves

1 cup cherry or pear tomatoes, cut into halves

DRESSING:

¼ cup good Dijon mustard, regular or flavored

2 tablespoons champagne vinegar

2 tablespoons honey

1 cup cooked bacon, cut into small pieces

Mix the mustard, vinegar, and honey together in a saucepan. Bring to a simmer over medium heat. Stir in the bacon. Meanwhile, rinse the spinach leaves several times to remove all sand and dirt. Spin dry to remove all excess water. (The water thins out the dressing and the flavor. This is a very important consideration to the final outcome of the flavor). Toss with the spinach greens and tomatoes and serve immediately.

# Greek Salad   Serves 4 as an entrée or 6 as an accompaniment

Greek Salad is a meal in itself. Top it with Chicken Fajitas, page 128, or grilled chicken breast for a healthy, tasty, and complete family dinner. Serve with warm Pita Bread, page 65, or with pita crisps!

1 head of good lettuce, such as green-leaf, red-leaf, or red romaine, or 2 heads of Boston (also called Bibb or butter lettuce)
A handful of spring mix or mixed salad greens
1 cucumber, peeled and sliced
3–4 radishes, sliced
1 ripe beefsteak tomato, cored, halved, and cut into thin wedges

½ cup Kalamata olives
1 red onion, thinly sliced, then quartered and separated
½ bell pepper, green, red, or yellow, julienned
¼ cup feta cheese, crumbled
2 pepperoncini peppers per person

DRESSING:

2 cloves of garlic
½ teaspoon salt
4 tablespoons lemon juice

Fresh oregano, finely chopped
Fresh mint, finely chopped
½ cup olive oil

To make the salad dressing, sprinkle the salt over the chopped garlic and let sit for 15 minutes. This mellows the bitterness of the garlic and enhances its flavor. Whisk together the lemon juice, garlic, oregano, and mint in a small mixing bowl. Slowly drizzle the oil in a steady stream, whisking continuously until it begins to emulsify. Adjust the flavor with salt and pepper to taste.

Wash the lettuce and spin dry. Tear into smaller pieces, and toss in a large bowl with the spring mix, cucumbers, radishes, tomatoes, olives, red onion, bell pepper, and half of the feta cheese. Toss with the salad dressing to evenly coat. Arrange the pepperoncini around the edge of the bowl and sprinkle the remaining feta cheese over the top of the salad. Serve immediately.

# Tomato and Cucumber Salad                    Serves 4

We serve this great salad for lunch at camp at least once a term. The girls enjoy it with Tuna Salad, page 33, and warm Pita Bread, page 65. Rachael Meriwether, former camper, wrangler, counselor, and official taste tester, loves this salad! She puts it in pita bread and makes a cucumber and tomato salad sandwich.

| | |
|---|---|
| 2 large cucumbers, peeled and sliced | 6 roma tomatoes, sliced |
| | 1 teaspoon salt |

DRESSING:

| | |
|---|---|
| 1–2 cloves garlic, minced | 2 tablespoons canola oil |
| ¼ teaspoon salt | 2 tablespoons olive oil |
| 1 teaspoon Dijon mustard | Freshly ground black pepper |
| 2 tablespoons champagne vinegar | 1 tablespoon fresh mint, chopped |

Peel the cucumbers and slice in half lengthwise. Slice into half-moons, about ½ inch thick. Cut the tomatoes into essentially the same size, ½-inch-thick half-moons. Sprinkle the cucumbers and tomatoes with the salt and let sit for about 30 minutes. This enhances the flavor of the tomato and begins to marry the flavors of the two vegetables. Toss with the dressing and refrigerate for at least 2 hours. Return to room temperature before serving.

To prepare the dressing, stir together the minced garlic and the salt in a medium bowl. Let sit for 15 minutes. Stir in the Dijon mustard and champagne vinegar. Slowly whisk in the canola oil and olive oil until the mixture emulsifies. Season to taste with the black pepper and fresh mint.

# Waldemar Potato Salad

Serves 4–6

A classic southern potato salad. Wonderful with a barbecue dinner or a picnic lunch.

3 pounds (about 6 cups) red
    potatoes, cut into 1½-inch
    cubes, peeling optional
1 tablespoon apple cider or distilled
    vinegar
1½ teaspoons salt
½ cup celery
2 hard-boiled eggs, chopped
1 green onion, chopped
½ cup yellow bell peppers, chopped

1 cup black olives
2 tablespoons parsley
1 tablespoon champagne vinegar
1 teaspoon Dijon or good-quality
    flavored mustard
3 tablespoons olive oil
5 tablespoons mayonnaise,
    page 36
¼ teaspoon salt
A generous sprinkle of paprika

In a large stockpot, cover potatoes with water. Add 1 tablespoon vinegar and 1 teaspoon salt. Bring to a boil and cook until potatoes are tender. Do not overboil, or potatoes will begin to break down. Once tender, drain off hot water and immediately return potatoes to hot pan. This helps evaporate any excess water clinging to the potatoes. Sprinkle ½ teaspoon of salt over "dried" potatoes and toss to coat. Let cool slightly. Toss in celery, eggs, onion, yellow bell peppers, olives, and parsley. Whisk together the vinegar, oil, mustard, mayonnaise, and salt. Toss with the potatoes just to coat. To dress more heavily, add all the dressing. Garnish with a sprinkling of paprika. Serve chilled or at room temperature.

# German Potato Salad

Serves 4–6

This is a wonderful potato salad that bursts with earthy, robust flavor. We serve it with great success in the conference season. Cooking the potatoes with the vinegar offers a flavorful base for the dressing.

4 pounds (about 8 cups) new or red
    potatoes, cut into 1-inch cubes
3 quarts cold water
¼ cup apple cider vinegar
2 eggs, hard-boiled and coarsely
    chopped
1 bulb garlic
4 pieces bacon
1 whole onion, julienned

2 tablespoons honey
1 teaspoon Dijon mustard
1 tablespoon balsamic vinegar
¼ apple cider vinegar
2 tablespoons bacon grease
½ cup olive oil
2 tablespoons fresh parsley,
    coarsely chopped

In a large stockpot, cover the potatoes with the water. Add vinegar and bring to a simmer over medium heat. Cook until tender when pierced with a fork, about 25 to 30 minutes. While potatoes are cooking, prepare the remaining ingredients.

Hard-boil the eggs. Separate the garlic cloves from the bulb, removing as much of the excess paper as possible without taking the immediate shell from the clove. The shell helps the garlic to retain its flavor while it boils. Cover with water in a small saucepan, and boil until tender, about 15 minutes. Set aside the cooked garlic until cool enough to handle. When cool, remove the excess skin from the garlic and discard. Reserve the garlic until you are ready to make the dressing.

In a 350° F oven, cook the bacon in a baking pan until crisp, about 15 minutes. Remove from the oven and drain the meat on paper towels. Let cool for several minutes, then crumble or chop into small pieces. Reserve 2 tablespoons of the bacon fat for the dressing.

Caramelize the onions in a sauté pan over medium heat with 1 tablespoon oil. Stir the onions every few minutes. Keep an eye on them and stir more frequently the closer they are to being done to prevent burning. Cook until they begin to turn a golden brown. This process brings out the natural sugars.

To make the dressing:

In a food processor, blend the garlic, honey, and mustard to make a thick paste. Add the balsamic vinegar. Pulse to combine. With the machine on, add the vinegar in a steady stream until it has combined with the garlic mixture. With the machine still running, slowly add the bacon grease, and then the olive oil, in a steady stream, mixing until the mixture emulsifies. Season with salt to taste.

When the potatoes are done, drain from the hot cooking liquid and immediately return to the cooking pot. Toss in the bacon, onions, eggs, and parsley. Coat with the dressing. Add salt and pepper to taste. Serve warm or at room temperature.


# Tomato and Basil Salad                                        Serves 4

The taste of summer. Fresh, ripe, bursting tomatoes; the bite of basil just pulled from the stalk; and fruity olive oil and salt to draw all the flavors together. It just doesn't get any better than this! For some reason, this salad reminds me of my grandfather, Dr. English. He was Waldemar's camp doctor from 1979 through 1986. He was an avid gardener. He loved to garden, growing such wonderful things as watermelon, radishes, squash, and tomatoes. Even though he never put together this salad, its simplicity and summer freshness reminds me of him and all that is good.

6 ripe roma tomatoes
2 tablespoons fresh basil, torn into
    small pieces

1 teaspoon salt
2 tablespoons olive oil

Slice the tomatoes. Sprinkle with the salt, torn basil, and olive oil. Let sit for at least 30 minutes. Serve at room temperature.

# Asparagus and Tomato Salad                          Serves 4

This is one of the components of one of Waldemar's favorite meals. Paired with Cheese Soufflé, page 89, and Black-Eyed Peas, page 77, it is a delightful reminder of times gone by!

Asparagus (about 4–6 stalks
    per person)
1 tablespoon vinegar
2–3 beefsteak tomatoes,
    cut into ½-inch-thick slices
    (2 slices per person)

¼ cup mayonnaise
1 head Boston (also known as
    Bibb or butter) lettuce
½ teaspoon cayenne

Blanch asparagus in boiling water with vinegar. Remove once tender and bright green, about 2 to 5 minutes. Immediately plunge asparagus into a bowl filled with ice water to stop the cooking process. Be careful not to overcook the asparagus, or it will be mushy.

Wash the Boston lettuce leaves and pat dry, keeping the leaves whole. Lay a leaf of lettuce on the salad plate. Place 2 tomato slices on top of the lettuce. On each tomato, cross 2 or 3 asparagus stalks. In the center of each cross, place a tablespoon of mayonnaise, garnish with cayenne, and serve.

# Thousand Island Salad

An interesting, simple salad. The homemade salad dressing makes it! I think this has been served here since the days of U. S. and Lucille. A wonderful Waldemar classic.

2 heads Boston (also known as
    Bibb or butter) lettuce

Thousand Island Dressing
    (recipe follows)

Remove the tough outer leaves of the lettuce. Cut out the cores and cut the lettuce heads into quarters. Place 2 wedges on each salad plate, and drizzle about 2 to 3 tablespoons of the dressing over the wedges. Serve cold.

## Thousand Island Dressing

2 cups mayonnaise
1 dill pickle, about five inches long,
    finely chopped
2 eggs, hard-boiled and chopped

2 tablespoons shredded onions
2 canned pimientos, chopped
½ cup ketchup

Stir the ingredients together in the order listed. Let sit for at least an hour in the refrigerator before serving. Store in a jar in the refrigerator for up to four days.

# Waldemar Chicken Salad

Serves 4–6

Sweet red flame grapes, nutty Hill Country pecans, crunchy celery, tart apples, and savory homemade garlic mayonnaise: Waldemar Chicken Salad. One of the best!

6 cups cooked chicken
(6 breasts and 2–4 thighs)
1 cup toasted pecan pieces
1 cup red grapes, sliced into halves
½ cup apples
½ cup celery

½ cup red onion
¼–½ cup garlic mayonnaise,
page 36, or your favorite
good-quality mayonnaise
2 tablespoons of your favorite
vinaigrette (optional)

Poach the chicken in salted, gently simmering water until the flesh is cooked through, about 20 to 30 minutes. I cook the breast meat separately, as it cooks more quickly than the dark thigh meat. Remove from the cooking liquid and let cool. Remove the meat from the bones.* Cut the chicken into ½-inch cubes. Toss in a large bowl with the toasted pecans, grapes, apples, celery and red onion. Pour the optional vinaigrette and ¼ cup mayonnaise over the chicken mixture. Toss to coat with the ingredients.

I prefer a very light coating of dressing, just enough to hold the salad together, whereas Marsha Elmore loves it with lots of mayonnaise! You choose to fit your preference.

*This is a good time to cook down the cooking liquid to make a rich chicken stock for later use! Once the meat is removed from the bones, return the bones to the poaching liquid and continue to simmer until the liquid has reduced by half. Cool and pour into ice cube trays. Once frozen, remove the cubes from the tray and store in a freezer bag, label, and date. Now you have 1-ounce portions of rich homemade chicken stock to enhance many dishes!

# Tuna Salad

Serves 4

Tuna is so good, and so good for you. This is a delightfully fresh version, using honey and cardamom to sweeten the flavor.

¼ cup garlic mayonnaise, page 36
⅛ teaspoon cardamom
1 teaspoon honey
1 12-ounce can chunk tuna, water-
packed, drained, and rinsed
½ cup tart apples such as Granny
Smith, McIntosh or Braeburn,
finely chopped into ¼-inch dice

¼ cup red onion, cut into ¼-inch
dice
1 rib celery, cut into ¼-inch dice
1 green onion, finely chopped
Salt and pepper to taste

In a small bowl, whisk the mayonnaise, cardamom, and honey together. Set aside. Toss the tuna, apples, red onion, celery, and green onion together in a medium mixing bowl. Pour the dressing over the tuna mixture and toss to coat. Refrigerate for at least 15 minutes. Serve on a bed of lettuce, or as a sandwich.

# Mediterranean Pasta Salad

Serves 6–8

Pasta salad is a great way to substantiate a quick, light lunch. Kids love it, and you will, too! This one incorporates rich, savory ingredients borrowed from the sun-ripened landscape of the Mediterranean. If you like spice, I invite you to toss some cracked red pepper in with the ingredients!

1 pound gemelli pasta, or your
    favorite short pasta
1½ cups roma tomatoes,
    chopped into ¼-inch dice
½ teaspoon salt
1 tablespoon olive oil
2 tablespoons Basil Pesto,
    page 88
4–5 tablespoons Sun-Dried Tomato
    Pesto, page 88

½ cup feta cheese
½ cup olives, coarsely chopped
    (Kalamata, Niçoise, or
    mixed variety)
Salt to taste
¼–½ teaspoon cracked
    red pepper (optional)
2 tablespoons parsley, chopped

Cook the pasta until *al dente*. Meanwhile, sprinkle the tomatoes with ½ teaspoon salt and let sit until the pasta is done. Remove pasta from the cooking liquid and immediately toss with the basil pesto and sun-dried tomato pesto. Stir in the tomatoes, feta cheese, and olives. Adjust the flavor with salt and toss with the optional cracked red pepper. Refrigerate for several hours to allow the flavors to marry with the pasta. Toss with the parsley just before serving. Serve cold or at room temperature.

# Tomato and Pesto Pasta Salad

Serves 4–6

Another cold and flavorful summer salad. Serve at your next luncheon with Cheese Straws, page 13, and a cup of Gazpacho, page 23. You can also serve this warm. Simply toss the pesto and tomatoes with the pasta while it is still hot, garnish with some freshly grated Parmesan or Romano cheese, and serve immediately!

1 pound penne pasta
3 cups roma tomatoes,
    cut into ¼-inch dice
1 teaspoon salt
1 tablespoon red wine
¼ teaspoon cracked red pepper
    (optional)

2–3 tablespoons Basil Pesto,
    page 88
1 tablespoon olive oil
Salt and pepper to taste

Cook the penne in amply salted water until *al dente*. While the pasta is cooking, chop the tomatoes and sprinkle 1 teaspoon salt over them. Pour the red wine and the optional cracked red peppers over the tomatoes, toss, and let the mixture sit until the pasta is done. Drain the pasta and rinse under cold water to stop the cooking. Toss the pesto with the pasta. Pour the tomato mixture and the olive oil in with the pasta and toss to distribute. Season with salt and pepper to taste. Refrigerate for at least 15 minutes. Serve cold or at room temperature.

# Asian Soba Noodle Salad

Serves 4–6

This delightful summer salad has a distinct Asian flavor. It makes a wonderfully refreshing accompaniment. Soba noodles are available in most health or gourmet stores. I prefer the buckwheat variety. Its rich earth color creates a nice background for the deep reds and greens of the red pepper and cilantro!

½ pound soba noodles
1 red bell pepper, julienned into
    ½-inch-long sticks
1 cucumber, peeled, seeded, and julienned into ½-inch-long strips
4 green onions, chopped
    (about ⅓ cup)
⅓ cup cilantro

½ teaspoon minced jalapeño
    (optional)
4 tablespoons soy sauce
4 tablespoons rice wine vinegar
1 inch ginger
½ teaspoon toasted sesame
    seed oil
1 tablespoon sesame seeds, toasted

Cook soba noodles in boiling, salted water until tender, about 7 to 10 minutes. Meanwhile, toast sesame seeds in a skillet over medium-high heat. Keep seeds moving every 20 seconds or so, by shaking the pan over the heat.

Drain and rinse the pasta with cold water to stop the cooking. Put the noodles in a mixing bowl and add the bell pepper, cucumber, green onion, cilantro, and (optional) jalapeños. Stir to mix. Whisk together the soy sauce, rice wine vinegar, ginger, and toasted sesame seed oil. Pour over the noodle mixture. Stir to coat the noodles. Refrigerate for two hours. If refrigerating longer, do not add the cucumber and cilantro until a few hours before serving. Just before serving, toss the toasted sesame seeds in with the mixture.

# Coleslaw

Serves 6–8 as an accompaniment

Cold sliced cabbage tossed with a sweet dressing. This is a favorite with picnic lunches, fried chicken, and good rolls. Soak the cabbage in ice-cold water for at least an hour before tossing to get a refreshingly crisp salad.

1 tablespoon apple cider vinegar
1 tablespoon sugar
2 tablespoons canola oil
¼ cup garlic mayonnaise,
    page 36
½ head green cabbage, shredded
    (about 4 cups)
¼ head red cabbage, shredded
    (about 1½ cups)

1½ cups carrots, grated
1 tablespoon red onion, julienned
    very thin and cut into
    ½-inch "sticks"
½ jalapeño, seeded (optional)
2 green onions, sliced thin

Add sugar to vinegar. Let stand for 3 minutes until sugar dissolves. Whisk in the oil until mixture begins to emulsify. Whisk in the mayonnaise until smooth. In a bowl, toss together the cabbage, carrots, red onion, jalapeño, and green onions. Pour the dressing over salad and toss to coat. Serve immediately. This salad will begin to wilt if it sits too long!

# Homemade Mayonnaise

Makes 1 cup

There is nothing that speaks to quality better than homemade mayonnaise. If you appreciate the quality, it is worth the extra effort. But store-bought is so entrenched in today's market that many may not remember the mystique of homemade mayonnaise. This is for Lucille Bishop Smith (see page 104) and the days when these details were necessities.

For an extra-good batch of flavor, add 2 to 4 tablespoons roasted garlic purée, page 16, to the egg. Other variations include adding 1 tablespoon Ancho Chile Purée, page 39, or a combination of ½ teaspoon curry powder, ¼ teaspoon cumin powder, and ¼ teaspoon cardamom powder.

| | |
|---|---|
| 2 large egg yolks | ½ tablespoon white wine vinegar |
| 2–4 tablespoons roasted garlic purée (optional), page 16 | ½–1 tablespoon lemon juice, freshly squeezed |
| ¼ teaspoon dry mustard | 1 cup light vegetable oil |
| ¼ teaspoon salt | |

In a medium bowl, whisk together the eggs with the roasted garlic purée (if desired), the dry mustard, and the salt. Slowly add the vinegar and lemon juice, steadily whisking until evenly blended. Very slowly, add the oil a few small drops at a time. Whisk continuously and steadily. As the mixture begins to thicken, you may add the oil more steadily, but be sure to whisk all of the oil in completely before adding more. The mixture will be thick and creamy. A wonderful and versatile dressing!

You can make this in a food processor using a plastic blade. Substitute 2 tablespoons whole egg whisked together and 1 large egg yolk in place of the 2 egg yolks.

Use immediately. Homemade mayonnaise will not keep.

# Dijon Vinaigrette

Makes about ¾ cup

The better the quality of the ingredients, the better the outcome! This principle is never more true than when making a simple salad dressing. The ingredients marry to create something wonderful. This dressing is known as the "housewife's dressing" in France, because it is so common. It is easy to prepare and is delicious tossed with your favorite salad greens, or drizzled over fresh tomatoes and served as an accompaniment to a simple entrée, such as grilled Cornish game hen, page 129.

| | |
|---|---|
| 1 tablespoon good-quality Dijon mustard | 1 tablespoon shallots, finely minced |
| 2 tablespoons white wine vinegar | Salt and freshly ground pepper to taste |
| ½ cup olive oil | |

In a small bowl, whisk the mustard and vinegar together until smooth.

Slowly drizzle the olive oil into the mustard and vinegar mixture, whisking continuously. The mixture will emulsify, thereby holding the oil and vinegar together and reducing separation. Stir in the shallots, and salt and pepper to taste. Allow dressing to sit for 30 minutes before serving in order for the flavors to blend.

# Fruit Salad                                            Serves 6–8

The secret to a great fruit salad is ripe, bursting-with-flavor fruit. It is best to select fruit that is in season. Ask your greengrocer what is available. Try to select a variety of colors, as the presentation will elicit many "oohs" and "ahs." We love to prepare a watermelon basket. This is a dramatic yet functional centerpiece that is fun to do!

Choose a variety of seasonal fruit. Figure on about 1 cup of fruit per person. Select your favorite fruits from the list below.

Strawberries, quartered
Watermelon, cantaloupe, honeydew
    or other variety of melon, balled
Peaches and/or nectarines, sliced
Red and/or green grapes,
    stemmed and left whole
Oranges and/or grapefruit, peeled and
    sectioned, with the membranes
    removed

Blueberries, rinsed
Blackberries, rinsed
Pineapple, peeled, cored, and cut
    into 1-inch cubes
Kiwi, peeled and cut into
    2-inch cubes

1–2 tablespoons fresh lemon juice

Toss the fruit in a bowl together with the lemon juice. Serve in a colorful bowl or in a watermelon basket. To make a watermelon basket, set the whole watermelon on a large, flat cutting board. The watermelon should rest on its flattest side so that it doesn't roll. Measure about a quarter of the way down from the top of the melon and mark this point with a permanent marker, for reference. Draw a handle in the center of the top of the watermelon down to the ¼ distance mark. The handle should come down about the same distance on both sides, and it should be at least four inches thick, as it will break if it is too thin. To make the body, connect the ends of the handle by drawing a wave or razor pattern across the watermelon's length, keeping even with the ¼ distance mark. Using a short, sharp knife, carefully cut along the marked lines. Be careful not to cut off the handle! With a melon baller, remove all of the fruit from the inside of the watermelon to use in the salad. Cut decorative patterns along the edges with a small paring knife. Fill with fruit and serve on a platter accompanied by Poppyseed Dressing, page 38.

# Green Goddess Dressing

Makes 2 cups dressing

This is a recipe taken from *Lucille's Treasure Chest of Fine Foods* (see page 38). She gives credit to a San Francisco chef who created it for the famous actor George Arliss in honor of his performance in the stage version of *The Green Goddess*. It is a wonderful and unique reminder of times gone by!

1½ cups mayonnaise
4–5 anchovies
1 green onion
2 tablespoons parsley

1 tablespoon fresh tarragon
2 tablespoons chives
2 tablespoons tarragon vinegar

Put the mayonnaise in a medium mixing bowl. Mince the remaining ingredients and add to the mayonnaise. Whisk in the tarragon vinegar, and let stand for 30 minutes in the refrigerator to allow the flavors to blend. Serve as the dressing in chicken salad or over your favorite salad of mixed greens.

# Poppyseed Dressing

Makes 3 cups

This is traditionally served with Fruit Salad, page 37. It also makes a fine dressing for Coleslaw, page 35, producing a very sweet version.

2½ cups salad oil
1¼ cups sugar
2 tablespoons grated onion
1¼ cups distilled vinegar

1 tablespoon salt
2 tablespoons Dijon mustard
½ cup poppyseeds

Combine all the ingredients in a medium mixing bowl. Beat on high speed until thoroughly mixed. Chill. When ready to serve, shake or stir well. Keeps in the refrigerator for up to two weeks.

# Sweet and Sour Vinaigrette

Makes 1½ cups

The flavor of this dressing will suprise you. The corn syrup imparts sweetness, the garlic and ginger supply a little "bite," and the tamari and rice wine vinegar add tanginess. Tamari is a stronger version of the more accessible soy sauce. I have tried both, and tamari has a better flavor. I purchase mine at the local health food store. Serve with mixed salad greens to accompany fish or poultry.

4 tablespoons tamari sauce
¼ cup rice wine vinegar
¼ cup light corn syrup
6 cloves garlic, minced

1–1½ inch fresh ginger, grated
¾ cup canola oil
Salt and pepper to taste

In a blender, purée all ingredients except the oil until well mixed. Slowly add the oil in a steady stream while blending until the mixture emulsifies. Adjust to taste with salt and pepper.

# Ancho Chili Purée

Makes about ½ cup

This recipe relies simply on rehydrating dried peppers and puréeing with a little of the soaking liquid. This process can be used for essentially any dried pepper. The list of available dried peppers in the Southwest is extensive, and they are inexpensive and have a relatively long shelf life. So stock up and add this ingredient to your favorite salad dressings, such as ranch dressing, or include it in soups, sauces, or chili. Its versatility is limitless.

4–6 dried ancho chili peppers              2 cups boiling water

Cover the dried chilies with boiling water and let sit for about an hour. Remove from the water and peel, stem, and seed the pepper. Purée in a blender or food processor with about ½ cup of the rehydrating liquid until smooth. Store in the refrigerator covered for about three days, or freeze in ice cube trays for up to three months.

# Early On

## Breakfast Foods and Breads

# Food in the Early Days

In compiling this book, I ran across some old letters written in 1929. A young camper named Elizabeth wrote to her "Nana" about many of her experiences here at camp. She wrote about a "sunrise breakfast on Sunday morning and Sunday service out in the open" and of the "joyful news at having fried chicken at lunch." I found it amazing that in every letter I read she mentioned the meals. For example, she wrote, "I am eating spinach now, and enjoying it quite a lot!" Imagine a child commenting on spinach! Campers have delighted their families for several generations by writing of the good food they are experiencing.

The 1929 brochure regards mealtime as an important ingredient to good health. The following is the script published in this early catalog:

## Cuisine

The dining room will be under the supervision of Miss Sadie Oliver, an experienced dietician and graduate of the College of Industrial Arts. She is ably assisted by a staff of experienced cooks and waiters.

The head cook, Will Hicks, who made the camp famous for its cooking last summer, will return. He has had several years experience as head chef on dining cars.

Fresh fruits and vegetables are secured from neighboring farms. Milk, butter, and cream are delivered daily from a certified dairy. An abundant supply of fresh, wholesome food, attractively prepared, is served. Both the milk and water supply have been tested and approved by the State Health Department.

With these sentiments established early on, it has remained a consistent philosophy throughout the years. We have always striven to acquire the most competent culinary director and the freshest produce. Prepared with the utmost attention to health and flavor, the food has always been an important part of the camp experience for both the campers and the camp!

# Breakfast Foods

## Cream Waffles

Breakfast at Waldemar—warm and cozy, enduring and endearing. It is, for many, the most important meal of the day. We like to imagine waffles at every meal. Waffles for lunch? For dinner? For a mid-afternoon snack? Why not? These are that good! Top with powdered sugar or your favorite maple syrup. Fresh berries are wonderful, and for a really special occasion (like tomorrow), why not put a sprinkling of chopped pecans or blueberries in the batter? Many of you know that there is nothing better!

| | |
|---|---|
| ½ cup unsalted butter, melted | 1 tablespoon sugar |
| 2 cups flour | 2 eggs |
| 4 teaspoons baking powder | 1¾ cups milk |
| ¾ teaspoon salt | 1 tablespoon vanilla |

Melt the butter in a microwave or a small saucepan. In a small bowl, sift together the flour, baking powder, salt, and sugar. Set aside. Whisk together the eggs, milk, and vanilla in a mixing bowl. Add the sifted dry ingredients to the egg/milk mixture. Stir until it is free of lumps. Stir in the melted butter.

Make according to the waffle iron's directions or cook as a pancake in a lightly buttered sauté pan. Flip the pancake when small bubbles begin to appear, about 3 minutes. Cook another 2 to 3 minutes on the other side and remove from heat. Serve hot!

Lucille Smith wrote in her *Treasure Chest* (see page 104) of a trade secret regarding pancakes:

Butter a shallow baking dish and keep close to the right of your cooking area for convenience.

As your cakes are cooked, place them in serving stacks, and in rows.

When all the cakes are done, butter the tops and cover with aluminum foil.

When you are ready to serve, place the covered pan in a hot oven for 5 minutes. It will delight your family that you baked and can now enjoy pancakes with them!

# Migas for Two

Migas! Julie Menges, this is for you! David Johnson, food director for two years, made the best migas, and Jules, Waldemar office manager for over twenty years, still asks for them! This is a close approximation. We have served it for 450 at one time. It almost seems a challenge to make them for just one or two people! You can easily multiply out as the size of your family or gathering prescribes, but the cooking time will increase with more ingredients.

1 tablespoon butter
¼ teaspoon garlic, finely chopped
½–1 jalapeño, seeded and finely chopped (If you prefer, you can leave this out altogether for no spice, or you can leave the seeds in for a considerably hotter dish)
1 tablespoon roma tomato, seeded and chopped

Dash of salt
1 corn tortilla, cut or torn into small pieces
3 eggs, lightly beaten
1 tablespoon cheese, Cheddar or Monterey Jack, or a blend of the two
1 teaspoon cilantro, rinsed and coarsely chopped
4 flour tortillas

In a sauté pan, melt the butter and sauté the garlic with ½ teaspoon salt until it releases its fragrance, about a minute. Add the jalapeño and cook quickly with the garlic, stirring often for another minute. Add the tomatoes and a dash of salt. They should sizzle in the heat of the pan. Toss with the garlic and the jalapeño. Add the corn tortilla pieces and cook until they begin to soften in the heat. Add the eggs and cook, stirring consistently, until soft scrambled, about 3 minutes. Stir in the cheese and the cilantro. Cook for another minute to melt the cheese.

Serve with hot flour tortillas and salsa.

# Omelets

Serves 1

There are as many ways to prepare an omelet as there are people to eat them. I have been told by many guests of the Waldemar Bed & Breakfast that my omelets are the best ever! I am flattered by the comments, and I am excited to share my secrets. The first secret is that I always sauté the filling ingredients. There is nothing worse than a cold, crunchy vegetable surrounded by melting cheese and soft scrambled egg. The second secret is to use a well-seasoned or a non-stick sauté pan. The third trick is that I gently push the egg toward the center of the pan, allowing the uncooked egg to flow over onto the hot pan, thus creating a firmer center onto which I place the cheese and vegetables.

My "rolled" omelet is essentially a three-fold omelet. However, I have found that I prefer the "half-moon" omelet, with just a single fold. It allows for more cheese!

This is such a wonderful, hearty breakfast, but try it for dinner, too! It is just as filling, a quick meal, and deliciously complemented with a salad of mixed greens and Dijon Vinaigrette, page 36.

2–3 eggs or 4 egg whites*
¼ cup grated cheese such as Monterey
    Jack, Cheddar, or a blend of the two;
    Swiss, Gruyère, Gouda, goat cheese,
    Edam, or one of your favorite
    creamy-when-melted cheeses

1 tablespoon sautéed vegetables for
    a 2-egg, and 2 tablespoons for
    a 3-egg omelet

Choose from the list of ingredients below and combine as you wish:

Julienned tomatoes
Caramelized onions
Sliced mushrooms
Julienned red, yellow, or green
    bell peppers
Julienned zucchini or squash

Avocado slices
Fresh herbs, such as basil, cilantro,
    dill, tarragon
Sliced green onion
Crumbled bacon

To prepare the vegetables, sauté in a tablespoon of butter or oil with ¼ teaspoon salt until heated and wilted, about 3 to 5 minutes. Set aside. Have all of your ingredients ready to use before you begin. Omelet-making is a rapid process, and the egg will not wait once you begin cooking.

To prepare the omelet, gently whisk the eggs to break the yolk. You can add a teaspoon of the fresh herbs, the green onion, or a teaspoon of the crumbled bacon. Do not overbeat. Melt a teaspoon of butter in an 8-inch sauté pan. Pour off the excess oil. Quickly pour the egg into the hot pan. It is important that the pan be very hot. Let the egg cook for about 30 seconds so that it begins to set on the bottom. With a spatula, gently push the egg from the edge to the center. The uncooked egg will flow over onto the hot pan and begin to set. This process gives the center a firmer base to hold the weight of the cheese and vegetables. Once the egg has almost completely set, sprinkle half of the cheese over the top. Put the vegetable filling over one half of the omelet. Sprinkle the remaining cheese, and gently fold the egg half over the vegetable half. Let cook for a minute to melt the cheese. Carefully flip over to cook the other side, and serve immediately. Enjoy!

*Many people prefer to subtract the health risks of egg yolks from their diet. If you want to make an egg white omelet, use the same technique as for preparing the regular omelet. However, the egg whites need to be well whisked before pouring into the hot pan. Also, as a base, the egg whites are not as firm, so be careful not to overload with cheese and vegetables.

# Breakfast Fruit Tart                                      Serves 8

Based on the simple combination of puff pastry, fresh summer fruit, and sweet cream cheese, this recipe evolved, oddly enough, as an alternative to birthday cakes. My brother, Stan, was the dining room supervisor for camp several years ago. He volunteered to make all of the birthday cakes for the campers for the summer. He designed some really beautiful cakes. This birthday treat was created as a collaborative effort for a counselor, and it was a hit, even though it isn't a cake! I expanded the recipe, which is delightfully simple, and have served it with just as much success for breakfast. And as further endorsement, Marsha Elmore, Waldemar owner and former director, exclaimed that this is the *best* fruit tart she has ever had! It is beautiful and colorful on a buffet. When available, I like to use edible flowers as part of the design. Your family and friends will love this one.

The recipe calls for puff pastry. It is available in the freezer section at any good market. It is an excellent product and offers consistent results. However, if you live near a bakery or specialty market that sells all-butter puff pastry, by all means, this is the ideal alternative to the more time-consuming homemade variety.

| | |
|---|---|
| 2 sheets puff pastry | Assortment of fresh fruits, such as: |
| ¼ cup cinnamon sugar (¼ cup sugar to 1 tablespoon ground cinnamon) | raspberries, blueberries, strawberries, kiwi, peaches, nectarines, or blackberries |

FOR THE FILLING:

| | |
|---|---|
| 2 tablespoons softened cream cheese or Neufchâtel cheese | 1 tablespoon sugar |
| Zest of 1 lemon | ½ teaspoon vanilla |
| | ½ cup heavy whipping cream |

Preheat the oven to 350° F. To assemble, lay one of the puff pastry sheets onto a parchment-lined baking sheet. Cut 4½-inch-long strips from the second piece of pastry dough. Create a border around the sheet of pastry with the strips, using a little water as glue. With the tines of a fork, poke small holes over the entire surface of the pastry to prevent excessive puffing during baking. Sprinkle the cinnamon sugar evenly over the entire surface. Bake in the preheated oven until the crust is browned and flaky, about 15 to 20 minutes. Remove from the oven and let cool.

In a food processor fitted with a steel blade, blend the cream cheese with the lemon zest and sugar. Slowly add the vanilla and continue to blend. Add the cream in a slow, steady stream, and whip until it is light and smooth.

Spread this cream onto the cooled pastry crust.

With the fruit, create a fanciful design atop the cream. You can run the fruit in vertical or horizontal lines, or create an edible landscape of your favorite Waldemar spot! Or you can just lay the fruit in a random pattern, focusing on color and flavor. However you choose to design it, this will be one delicious addition to any breakfast. You can, of course, serve this for dessert or as a birthday treat!

Refrigerate for at least an hour before serving. It is best eaten the day it is made, as the crust will begin to soften. But if there are any leftovers, they will definitely be eaten within the next day or so. Keeps refrigerated for three days.

# Scones                                   Makes 8 wedge scones

These rich and flaky scones are a favorite for many of you who have shared breakfast with us here at Waldemar. Eat one plain or with butter and jam. Make these and freeze them, or take them to the office or your next social and see how many new friends you make!

| | |
|---|---|
| 2 cups flour | ½ cup unsalted butter, cold |
| ¼ cup granulated sugar | 1 large egg |
| 2 teaspoons baking powder | ½ cup heavy whipping cream |
| ⅛ teaspoon salt | 2 teaspoons vanilla |

CREAM TOPPING:

| | |
|---|---|
| ¼ cup cream | ¼ cup turbinado or other large-grain sugar |

OPTIONAL INGREDIENTS
(Add any of these to create a delicious variation):

| | |
|---|---|
| 2 tablespoons fresh rosemary, removed from the stem and coarsely chopped | 2 tablespoons toasted walnuts and 1 tablespoon cinnamon sugar (¼ cup sugar and 1 tablespoon ground cinnamon) |
| ¼ cup currants | |
| 1 tablespoon poppyseeds and 1 teaspoon grated lemon zest | 2 tablespoons of your favorite dried soft fruit, such as apples, cherries, or cranberries |

Preheat the oven to 425° F. In a medium mixing bowl, sift together the flour, sugar, baking powder, and salt. Cut the butter into small chunks and add to the flour mixture. With a pastry blender or two knives, cut the butter into the flour until it is about pea-sized. Stir in the optional addition here. In a small bowl, gently whisk egg to break it up, and add the cream and the vanilla. Make a well in the center of the flour/butter mixture and pour in the egg/cream mixture. Stir to moisten the flour with a fork. It is important that you do not over-mix in this stage, as it will make a heavy scone. The mixture should still be very dry and crumbly.

Pour the mixture onto a parchment-lined cookie sheet. Roll the sides up to gently knead the loose flour into the moist mixture. The trick is to not overhandle the mixture. Pat into a round about ½- to ¾-inch thick.

With a large knife, score the dough into eight rounds. Finish the scone by brushing the cream topping on lightly with a pastry brush and sprinkle with the turbinado sugar.

Bake for about 12 to 15 minutes and remove from the oven. Re-score the original lines and separate the wedges. Return to the oven and continue to cook until the tops are golden brown, about 5 to 10 more minutes. Serve warm.

# Blueberry Muffins
Makes 12 muffins

Tried and true, blueberry blue. These are THE best blueberry muffins ever. Sugar crumble crust on the outside, and warm, moist, wonderfulness on the inside. These definitely have that feeling of coming home, back to Waldemar, of all that is good and real.

If you can get wild blueberries, this is ideal. We are able to order IQF (individually quick-frozen) wild berries from our food purveyor, and the flavor is without comparison. Share this recipe with your church or local community group, and buy a pound of wild blueberries from their order, just to keep on hand!

½ cup unsalted butter, softened
¾ cup sugar
1 egg
2 cups sifted all-purpose flour
2 teaspoons baking powder

½ teaspoon salt
½ cup milk
1 teaspoon vanilla
2 cups blueberries

TOPPING:

½ cup sugar
⅓ cup all-purpose flour

½ teaspoon cinnamon
¼ cup butter, softened

Preheat the oven to 350° F. Prepare two muffin tins by lining with paper liners and spraying lightly with a non-stick cooking spray. In a large mixing bowl, cream together the softened butter and sugar until light, about 3 to 5 minutes. Add the egg, and beat until incorporated.

Sift the flour, baking powder, and salt together in a separate bowl. Set aside. In a third bowl, add the vanilla to the milk.

Add approximately ½ cup of the flour mixture to the creamed butter mixture. Stir it in for about 10 seconds, and add approximately ⅛ of the milk mixture. Repeat this process until all of the ingredients are just incorporated. It is very important not to overbeat the batter, or you will have lead-heavy muffins. The flour should be moist, but still a little lumpy. Scoop the batter into the prepared muffin tins. (An ice cream scoop is great to use, because you are able to get even portions for each muffin.)

To make the topping, mix all of the dry ingredients together in a small mixing bowl. Cut in the butter with a pastry blender to pea-size. Sprinkle atop the muffins, and bake in the preheated oven for about 15 to 18 minutes, or until the tops are brown and crunchy. Remove from the oven, and let cool for about 5 minutes.

Serve warm with a dab of butter!

# Pumpkin-Pecan Muffins

Makes about 18 muffins

This recipe is a favorite throughout the fall season, but I like them anytime. This recipe was frequently made by Josh and Allison Elmore and David Johnson for the Bed & Breakfast and Conference Center when they were here. Studies have shown that pumpkin and spice create a sense of euphoria. I agree. What do you think?

| | |
|---|---|
| 1 cup all-purpose flour | 1 egg |
| 1 teaspoon baking powder | ½ cup oil |
| 1 teaspoon cinnamon | ¼ cup milk |
| ½ teaspoon baking soda | 1 teaspoon vanilla extract |
| ½ teaspoon salt | 1 cup canned pumpkin |
| ½ teaspoon nutmeg | ¾ cup firmly packed brown sugar |
| ⅓ cup chopped pecans | |
| 1¼ cups quick-cook or old-fashioned oats | |

TOPPING:

| | |
|---|---|
| ¼ cup butter, softened | 1 teaspoon cinnamon |
| ¼ cup all-purpose flour | ¼ cup oats |
| ¼ cup firmly packed brown sugar | ¼ cup chopped pecans |

Preheat oven to 400° F. Prepare the muffin tins by lining with paper cups and lightly spraying with a non-stick cooking spray. Sift together the flour, baking powder, cinnamon, baking soda, salt, and nutmeg. In a mixing bowl, stir together the flour mixture, pecans, and oats.

In a separate bowl, whisk together the egg with the oil, milk, and vanilla. Stir in the pumpkin and sugar. Add to the flour/oat mixture and stir until just moistened. Fill the muffin tins ¾ full.

To make the topping, cut the butter into the flour, brown sugar, and cinnamon. Stir in the oats and pecans. Sprinkle over the muffins and bake in the preheated oven for about 15 to 20 minutes, or until the top is crusty and a toothpick comes out of the center clean. Let cool for 5 to 10 minutes. Serve warm.

# Orange Yogurt Muffins

Makes 18 muffins

The citrus tang is a great morning eye opener. I served these one year at Women's Week, and the response was fantastic. There is something about the addition of a sour milk product that enhances sweet bread. These muffins are no exception. They are light and fluffy, yet very moist. The orange glaze is wonderful. It was originally listed as an option, but I think it is a must.

| | |
|---|---|
| 2 tablespoons water | 1¼ teaspoons baking powder |
| ¼ cup grated orange zest (about 3 large oranges) | 1 teaspoon baking soda |
| | ½ teaspoon salt |
| ½ cup sugar, divided | 2 eggs |
| 5 tablespoons unsalted butter | ¾ cup plain yogurt |
| 1 teaspoon vanilla | ¾ cup milk |
| 2 cups all-purpose flour | |

FOR THE GLAZE:

1 cup powdered sugar, sifted  
2 tablespoons fresh orange juice  
2 teaspoons fresh orange zest

Preheat the oven to 375° F.

Line standard muffin tins with paper liners. Spray lightly with a non-stick cooking spray.

In a small saucepan over medium heat, combine the water, orange zest, and ¼ cup of the sugar. Cook until the sugar dissolves, about 2 minutes. Add the butter and stir until melted. Remove from the heat and stir in the vanilla. Set aside.

Sift together the flour, baking powder, baking soda, salt, and the remaining ¾ cup sugar.

In a large mixing bowl, whisk together the eggs, yogurt, milk, and the reserved orange/sugar mixture until smooth. Add the dry ingredients and stir until just moistened. Spoon the mixture into the muffin tins, about ¾ cup full.

Bake in the preheated oven about 15 to 20 minutes, or until a toothpick inserted in the center comes out clean. To make the glaze, whisk together the powdered sugar, orange juice, and orange zest until smooth. Remove the muffins from the oven and top with the orange glaze. Let cool in the pan for about 5 minutes. Serve warm.

# Breakfast Potatoes

Serves 6

This is a dish we serve every morning for our off-season guests. It is served during camp as well, and is a favorite for all, but it doesn't have to be just for breakfast. Top it with homemade salsa, page 6 and 7, or roll up with scrambled eggs in a tortilla. Or have it with a grilled steak. The possibilities are endless!

5 Idaho or russet potatoes, washed and  
    cut into ½-inch dice  
2 tablespoons olive oil  
2 teaspoons salt  
½ teaspoon cumin  
¼ teaspoon paprika  

Dash of black pepper  
½ cup onions, julienned  
¼ cup poblano pepper, julienned  
1 tablespoon fresh cilantro,  
    chopped (optional garnish)

Preheat oven to 350° F.

In a bowl, toss the cut potatoes with 1 tablespoon olive oil until well coated. Sprinkle with the salt, cumin, paprika, and black pepper. Toss to evenly distribute.

Spread potatoes evenly on a parchment-lined baking sheet. Bake for about 45 minutes, or until the potatoes are tender and golden brown.

After about 40 minutes, sauté the julienned onion and poblano pepper until they begin to wilt, about 5 to 7 minutes.

Remove the potatoes from the oven and toss with the sautéed vegetables and the optional cilantro. Serve warm with salsa or ketchup.

# Cheese Grits, Hill Country Style

Serves 4

This is a variation on a recipe that Hudson's On the Bend, the wonderful restaurant near Austin, Texas, prepared at Waldemar for a Cooking School Weekend. The idea is wonderful, chock full of tasty vegetables, spice, and lots of cheese. Or you can just add the cheese! They added crisp bacon, which is a hearty variation on this recipe.

| | |
|---|---|
| 2 cups water | 1 teaspoon yellow bell pepper |
| ½ teaspoon salt | ¼ teaspoon cumin |
| ½ cup quick grits (not instant) | ¼ teaspoon chili powder |
| 1 tablespoon red onion, chopped fine | ½ cup cheese |
| ½ teaspoon jalapeño, chopped | 2 tablespoons fresh cilantro, |
| 1 teaspoon red bell pepper | chopped |

Bring water and salt to a boil in a medium saucepan. Stir in the grits, red onion, jalapeño, red and yellow bell pepper, cumin, and chili powder. Stir to combine the spice. Continue to cook until it returns to a boil, and reduce the heat to low. Simmer until the grits have begun to thicken, about 5 minutes. Add the cheese, and continue cooking for another 2 to 3 minutes or until the desired thickness. If you like thicker grits, reduce the quantity of water. Likewise, if you like them thinner, increase the water. Stir in the cilantro as a final garnish, and serve.

# Waldemar Oatmeal

Serves 2

Josh Elmore made this for his family several years back, and his parents, Marsha and Dale, still eat it almost every morning. It is like no other oatmeal. It is ready in seconds, retains its bite, and is good for you, too! This is a recipe, however, in which you cannot substitute quick oats for old fashioned. It simply will not work.

| | |
|---|---|
| 4 cups water | 1 tablespoon vanilla |
| ½ teaspoon salt | 1 cup old-fashioned oats |

In a medium saucepan, bring the water and salt to a rolling boil. Once boiling, immediately add the vanilla and the oats. With a slotted spoon, remove the oats after about 30 seconds. This imparts just enough heat so that the oats will steam and continue to cook a little in your bowl.

Serve the oatmeal with a little brown sugar. Other toppings include plain or fruited yogurt, maple syrup, fresh berries, bananas, or peach slices.

# Waldemar Coffee Cake

Serves 8

This is by far one of my all-time favorite recipes. It is moist, crunchy, sweet, and nutty, everything I love in a cake, and it is soooooo good with coffee. I remember being served this at camp in the mornings. Those were always my favorite days. I know I don't stand alone! This is a recipe that the girls can make for their families. Let it become a family tradition in your home.

FOR THE CAKE:

- 1 cup butter, softened
- 2 cups sugar
- 4 eggs, beaten
- 4 cups sifted flour
- 1 tablespoon baking powder
- ½ teaspoon salt
- 2 cups milk
- 2 teaspoons vanilla

FOR THE TOPPING:

- 2 cups sugar
- 1½ teaspoons cinnamon
- 1½ teaspoons nutmeg
- 1 cup butter, cold
- 1 cup chopped pecans

Preheat oven to 375° F. In a mixing bowl, cream together the softened butter and sugar until light and fluffy. Add the eggs and continue to beat until mixed. In a separate bowl, sift together the flour, baking powder, and salt. Stir in the flour mixture ½ cup at a time, alternating with the milk. Add the vanilla and stir to combine.

Pour the batter into a well-greased 9 x 13-inch baking pan. Bake in the oven for 30 minutes. Meanwhile, prepare the topping. Mix together the sugar, cinnamon and nutmeg. Cut the butter into the sugar/spice mixture until it is pea-sized. Stir in the pecans and set aside.

Remove the cake from the oven. Sprinkle the topping over the cake, and return to the oven for another 15 to 20 minutes, or until the topping has melted and a toothpick inserted in the center of the cake comes out clean.

Let cool for 10 to 15 minutes. Cut into squares and serve warm.

# Waldemar Buttermilk Biscuits

Makes a dozen or so

Breakfast and buttermilk biscuits, an old Waldemar tradition. Serve with butter and jelly. Serve with sausage and gravy. Serve just because you want to be reminded of breakfast at Waldemar. Many recipes call for shortening as the fat, but I think butter makes a much flakier and lighter biscuit.

| | |
|---|---|
| 2 cups flour | 5 tablespoons unsalted butter, cold |
| 1 teaspoon salt | ¾ cup buttermilk |
| 1 tablespoon baking powder | ¼ teaspoon baking soda |
| 1 tablespoon sugar | |

Preheat oven to 450° F. Sift together the flour, salt, baking powder, and sugar. Cut in the butter with a pastry blender until it is in pea-sized pieces. Add the baking soda to the buttermilk. Make a well in the flour/butter mixture and pour the buttermilk into the well. Stir with a fork until it is just moist.

Pour the dough onto a floured work surface and lightly knead to form a dough that holds together, about 30 seconds. Pat into a round, flat dough, about 1 inch thick. Cut out with a 2-inch biscuit cutter and lay on a parchment-lined cookie sheet.

Bake in the preheated oven for about 15 to 20 minutes, or until the biscuits are golden brown on top. Remove from the oven and brush with a light coating of melted butter. Serve hot or warm. These can be retoasted the next morning and served with butter and jelly.

# Butterscotch Biscuits

Makes a dozen

This recipe is a variation on the buttermilk biscuits from Lucille's *Treasure Chest* (see page 104). These are essentially biscuits with brown sugar, but it is such a warm and tasty variation! Give it a try and delight your family with an age-old Waldemar recipe.

| | |
|---|---|
| 1 batch buttermilk biscuits, page 54 | ¾ cup brown sugar |
| ¼ cup salted butter, melted and partially cooled | |

Preheat oven to 450° F. Pat the biscuit dough to ¼-inch thickness. Brush generously with the melted butter. Sprinkle ¼ cup sugar evenly over the dough. Roll up like a cinnamon roll and cut into ½-inch thick slices.

Lay in a buttered 9 x 9-inch baking pan, cut side down. Brush the tops with a light coating of melted butter and sprinkle the remaining ½ cup brown sugar over the top.

Bake in the preheated oven for 15 minutes, or until the tops are golden. Remove from the oven and brush with another coating of melted butter. Serve hot!

# Honey Nut Rolls and
# Cinnamon Rolls

The following two recipes are variations using the recipe for Matt's Refrigerator Roll Dough, page 62. These are delicious! The warming smells of fresh baked bread mingling with sweet caramel and toasted pecans or spicy cinnamon are enough to send anyone over the edge! These are a delightful treat for special occasions such as Christmas, Thanksgiving brunch, a breakfast business meeting, Sunday after church, the next rainy day, or tomorrow morning—just because!

## Honey Nut Rolls

1 recipe Matt's Refrigerator
    Roll Dough, page 62
½ cup salted butter, melted
1 cup honey

1 cup brown sugar
½ cup chopped pecans
Caramel Syrup (recipe follows)
½ cup pecan halves

TO ASSEMBLE:

Preheat the oven to 425° F.

Roll dough to ½-inch thickness. Brush with the melted butter. Pour ½ cup of the honey over the dough. Combine the brown sugar and chopped pecans and sprinkle over the dough. Roll up as for a jellyroll. Slice into 1¼-inch rounds.

Prepare the muffin tins by spraying with a non-stick cooking spray. Put 2 teaspoons of the caramel syrup (see below) and 1 teaspoon honey in each muffin tin. Lay 2 or 3 pecan halves in the bottom of each tin with the caramel/honey mixture. Top with a slice of the dough, cut side down. Brush with melted butter and let rise until doubled in size, about 30 minutes.

Bake in the preheated oven for about 20 to 25 minutes, or until golden brown. Remove from the oven and invert immediately onto a serving plate, as the rolls will stick!

CARAMEL SYRUP:

¾ cup brown sugar
¼ cup salted butter

½ cup water

Put the brown sugar, salted butter, and water in a medium saucepan. Cook for about 5 minutes over medium heat, or until the sugar is melted. Set aside to cool.

## Cinnamon Rolls

1 recipe Matt's Refrigerator
    Roll Dough, page 62
¼ cup salted butter, softened to a
    spreadable consistency

½ cup granulated sugar
2 tablespoons cinnamon
Caramel Syrup (optional, recipe above)

TO ASSEMBLE:

Roll the dough out to ½-inch thickness. Spread with the softened butter.

Mix the sugar and cinnamon together until evenly combined, then sprinkle over the dough. Roll up as you would a jellyroll. Slice into 1½-inch thick rounds. To prepare the 9 x 13-inch baking pan, butter well or spray with a non-stick baking spray. Pour in the optional caramel. Place the cinnamon roll slices into the prepared pan, cut side down, with edges lightly touching.* Brush the tops with melted butter and set aside to rise until double in bulk, about 30 minutes. Bake in a preheated 425° F oven for about 25 minutes, or until golden brown. Remove from the oven and top with either a traditional milk glaze or fresh orange glaze.

MILK GLAZE:

| | |
|---|---|
| 1 cup powdered sugar, sifted | 1 teaspoon vanilla |
| 2 tablespoons milk | |

In a small bowl, whisk together the powdered sugar, milk, and vanilla until a smooth glaze is formal. Set aside to spread over the hot cinnamon rolls.

ORANGE GLAZE:

| | |
|---|---|
| 1 cup powdered sugar, sifted | ½ teaspoon freshly grated orange zest |
| 2 tablespoons fresh orange juice | ½ teaspoon vanilla (optional) |

In a small bowl, whisk together the powdered sugar and the orange juice until a smooth glaze is formed. Stir in the orange zest and the optional vanilla. Set aside to spread over the hot cinnamon rolls.

*You can refrigerate overnight at this point. Cover with foil. Prepare as above!

# Banana Bread                      Makes 2 small loaves or 1 large loaf

This versatile banana bread is rich and buttery. It uses buttermilk, which offers a subtle contrast to the natural sweetness of the bananas. We love to serve it for breakfast, but it is also delicious sliced and toasted for a midday snack. Make several batches and give as gifts! Its warming hospitality makes for a thoughtful housewarming or condolence gift, and everyone loves to receive it at Christmastime. Another suggestion is to serve as mini-muffins on a buffet with smoked turkey. Remember that it is best to use bananas that are browning!

| | |
|---|---|
| ⅔ cup butter, softened | 4 tablespoons buttermilk |
| 1½ cups sugar | 1 teaspoon baking soda |
| 2 eggs | 2 cups flour |
| 1 cup mashed bananas | ½ teaspoon salt |
| 1 teaspoon vanilla | 1 cup pecans or walnuts, coarsely chopped (optional) |

Preheat the oven to 375° F. In a large bowl, cream the butter and sugar until well mixed and light in color. Add the eggs one at a time and mix until just blended. Stir in the bananas and vanilla. In a liquid measuring cup, stir the baking soda into the buttermilk. In a separate bowl, sift together the flour and salt. Set aside.

Alternate adding a portion of the flour mix with the buttermilk and soda mix to the mashed bananas, stirring until just blended. Be careful not to over-mix, as this will result in a heavy bread. Stir in the nuts, if desired.

Pour into a floured loaf pan (9 x 4 x 2½ inches).

Bake in the preheated oven for 45 to 50 minutes. Let cool in the pan for 30 minutes before removing. If making muffins, line muffin tin with paper cup liners. Fill each cup ¾ full. Bake for 20 minutes in the preheated oven until a toothpick inserted in the center comes out clean. Let cool for 5 minutes before serving.

# Doughnuts
Makes 2 dozen doughnuts

This is one of Lucille Bishop Smith's recipes. The nutmeg is a wonderful nutty spice and reminds me of Sunday mornings here at Camp Waldemar. Sunday is a wonderful day at Waldemar. The day starts with extra sleep! We all get to sleep in, as Reveille is delayed for half an hour. Breakfast is served Continental style, and we all come down to breakfast in our pajamas! What a treat! And then we are welcomed with a warm, delicious delight, such as these doughnuts. There is nothing better! We get to sit anywhere and with anyone! The level of excited chatter is pleasurably deafening. Then it is off to church and anticipation of Sunday lunch. And lunch, well, that is another treat in and of itself!

| | |
|---|---|
| 3½ cups flour | 2 eggs |
| 2 teaspoons baking powder | 1 teaspoon vanilla |
| ½ teaspoon salt | 1 cup milk |
| 2 tablespoons butter | Light vegetable oil for frying |
| 1 cup sugar | |

Combine the flour, baking powder, and salt. In a separate bowl, cream the butter and sugar together until lemon-colored. Beat the eggs in one at a time. In a third bowl, add the vanilla to the milk.

Alternate adding the flour mixture and the milk/vanilla mixture to the creamed butter/sugar/egg mixture. Mix until a dough has formed, about 3 minutes.

Turn the dough onto a floured work surface. Roll lightly into a 3- or 4-inch-thick round and cut out doughnuts with a 3-inch doughnut cutter.

In a fryer or cast-iron skillet, fry the doughnuts in oil heated to 365° F.

Cook the doughnuts about 3 to 5 minutes each side, or until golden brown. Don't forget the doughnut holes, although they will take less time to cook.

Remove from the oil with a slotted spoon and let drain on paper towels.

Roll in cinnamon sugar while still warm.*

Serve immediately.

*To make cinnamon sugar, mix together 1 cup sugar and 2 tablespoons cinnamon. Stir until well blended.

# French Toast

Serves 2

This is one of those wonderful recipes that relies on old bread. What to do with all that leftover bread from the night before? Whip up a warm and wonderful breakfast treat. Top with your favorite berries, bananas, powdered or cinnamon sugar, or maple syrup. Brioche, page 61, makes a wonderful bread for this, as it is tender and sweet, even when it is dry!

4 slices day-old or stale bread
4 eggs
¾ cup milk

1 tablespoon vanilla
2 tablespoons butter

Whisk together the eggs, milk, and vanilla. Soak the bread slices in this mixture, turning once, until the bread has absorbed the mixture on both sides.

Melt one tablespoon butter in a sauté pan or skillet. Cook two slices of the milk-soaked bread until golden on one side, about 3 to 5 minutes. Turn to cook the other side until golden, about 3 minutes. Repeat with the remaining two slices. Serve immediately with maple syrup or powdered sugar sprinkled on top.

Garnish with fresh berries, if desired.

# Breads

## Waldemar Cornbread

Serves 6–8

This is one of Lucille's original recipes (see page 104). It works every time, and we just love it! It is a wonderful savory cornbread that makes a great base for the additions of cheese, green chilies, or jalapeños. We like to serve this with a hearty bowl of chili or a barbecue dinner. Leftover cornbread is wonderful split and toasted in the oven and served with a Tex-Mex omelet, or with plain ol' butter and jelly.

| | |
|---|---|
| 1 cup unbleached flour | 1 teaspoon salt |
| 1 cup yellow cornmeal | 3 eggs |
| ¼ cup sugar | 1 cup milk |
| 1 teaspoon baking powder | ¼ cup plus 2 tablespoons oil |

Preheat oven to 350° F. Sift together the flour, cornmeal, sugar, baking powder, and salt. Whisk the eggs gently. Add eggs to milk and stir to blend. Pour into the cornmeal mixture. Stir in the ¼ cup of oil until incorporated.

Pour the remaining 2 tablespoons of oil in a 10-inch cast-iron skillet or a 9 x 9-inch square baking pan. Set in oven for 2 to 3 minutes to allow the oil to heat up. Remove from the oven and immediately pour the batter in the skillet. Bake in the oven for about 20 to 25 minutes, or until the top is golden brown, the edges have pulled away from the sides of the pan, and a toothpick inserted in the center comes out clean.

OPTIONAL ADDITIONS:
    ¼–½ cup cheese—Monterey Jack, Cheddar, or a mixture of the two
    2–4 tablespoons chopped green chilies or pickled jalapeños

# Poblano Cheese Scones

I love this recipe, and so does everyone who tastes it! If you like cheese-laden breads, this is for you! It may seem daunting at first, but it is so delicious that it is worth the effort, and once you try it, you will see that it really doesn't take that much to have a wonderful bread accompaniment. We have served it with the Tomato Basil Soup, page 20, with great success. I have found that the flavor is much better when I use very sharp Cheddar, as the mild varieties just don't quite offer the same intensity of flavor!

2 poblano peppers, roasted, peeled,
    seeded, and chopped, page 78
2 cups flour
2 teaspoons baking powder
¼ teaspoon salt
Dash of cayenne pepper
½ cup unsalted butter

1½ cups grated sharp Cheddar cheese
2 tablespoons Parmesan or Romano
    cheese, grated
2 eggs
⅓ cup milk
1 egg yolk mixed with 1 tablespoon
    water (for a glaze)

Preheat the oven to 400° F. In a mixing bowl, add the flour, baking powder, salt, and cayenne pepper. Cut the butter into pieces and add to the flour mixture. Cut into the flour mixture using a pastry blender or two knives using a back-and-forth slicing method until the butter is pea-sized. Add the two cheeses and the roasted poblanos, and stir to blend.

In a small bowl, whisk the eggs and stir in the milk. Make a well in the center of the flour/cheese mixture, and add the egg/milk mixture. Stir with a fork until just moist. The mixture will still be crumbly and fairly dry.

Line a cookie sheet with a piece of parchment paper. I like to spray the parchment with a little cooking spray. Pour the scone mixture onto the parchment-lined cookie sheet. Gather up the dry mixture and lightly knead. You may have to do this several times, but be cautious not to overwork it, as this will make for a heavy scone.

Pat into a round. Score with a long-bladed knife into 6 to 8 slices. Cut all the way through, but do not separate. Brush with the egg/water mixture, and sprinkle with a little Parmesan cheese.

Bake for 15 minutes. Remove from the oven and rescore the original cuts. Separate the wedges to allow the cut edges to fully cook. Return to the oven until the scones are fully golden, about another 5 to 7 minutes.

Let cool on the sheet for 5 minutes before removing. Serve warm.

To store: Cool completely and store in an airtight container in the refrigerator for up to a week, or freeze in a zip-closure freezer bag for up to a month. Bring to room temperature before serving. Toast to reheat for best results.

# Brioche

A classic egg bread, as versatile as it is good. We don't necessarily shape it into the classic knot-on-top formation. It is gorgeous as a "loaf bread." The leftovers are wonderful to use for French Toast, page 58, or bread pudding, page 151. I love it as toast with sweet cream butter and jam, or crisped up for Homemade Croutons, page 68. The secret to a good brioche is patience. You must knead or beat in a stand mixer with a dough hook for up to 30 minutes. This helps to develop the wonderful texture that distinguishes this bread from most others.

| | |
|---|---|
| 1 package active dry yeast (1 scant tablespoon) | 3 eggs |
| ½ cup warm water (about 110° F) | 3–3½ cups all-purpose flour |
| 1 tablespoon sugar | ½ cup unsalted butter, softened, but not oily |
| 1 teaspoon salt | |

In a large mixing bowl, dissolve the yeast in the warm water. Let stand until bubbly, about 5 minutes. Whisk in the sugar, salt, and eggs. Using a stand mixer with a dough hook, slowly beat 2 cups of the flour into the yeast mixture, adding the remaining 1 to 1½ cups flour a little bit at a time until the dough pulls away from the sides and holds together somewhat. It will not be as firm as you would expect in a traditional bread, but still a bit soft. Too much flour will make a dry bread. Mix the dough in your stand mixer with the dough hook for a total of 25 to 30 minutes. After about 7 minutes, the dough should wrap itself around the hook and slap the sides of the bowl. If it does not, add about 2 to 3 tablespoons more flour. Continue to beat another 15 to 20 minutes. The timing is important, as this is what gives the bread its fine texture.

It is important to have cool, soft butter. It is also best to mash it on a cool work surface, using a dough scraper or a rolling pin. If it is too warm, it will be too oily and greasy. Add the butter slowly while beating constantly. It will break down and look like a gooey mess. This is okay. It will come together again. Beat on medium-low speed while you add the butter. Once all of the butter has been added, raise the speed to medium and beat for about 5 minutes. It should once again make a slapping sound against the side of the bowl. If it does not, add another tablespoon of flour and continue mixing. The dough should be slightly sticky. Turn it out onto a floured work surface and knead for several minutes by hand before shaping. It will be smooth and elastic, bouncing back into place when depressed with the pad of a finger.

Place in a buttered bowl, turning once to coat all sides with the oil. Cover loosely and let rise in a warm place until doubled in bulk, about 1½ to 2 hours. Punch the dough down, and let rise again until doubled in bulk. Pull the risen dough from all sides of the bowl. Place in the refrigerator and chill for about 4 to 6 hours.

TO SHAPE:
Divide the dough into thirds. Keep the remaining two thirds in the refrigerator until ready to use, working with just one piece at a time.
Divide each piece into 6 pieces and roll into balls. Place the balls in a but-

tered and floured loaf pan side by side. Cover with plastic wrap and let rise for 2 hours, or until doubled in bulk. Repeat with the remaining dough.

Preheat the oven to 375° F. Brush the loaves with an egg wash (2 eggs whisked together with 2 tablespoons water). Bake for about 30 minutes. If the bread appears to be browning too quickly, cover loosely with aluminum foil. To check for doneness, insert an instant-read thermometer from the bottom. It will read 200° F when done.

Remove from the oven and let cool slightly. Serve warm. Store in an air-tight container at room temperature for up to three days, in the refrigerator for up to a week, or in the freezer, tightly wrapped and placed in a zip-closure bag, for three months.

## Matt's Refrigerator Rolls

Makes 2 dozen rolls

Matt Nguyen Spears, son of Roy Spears, worked for Waldemar for over a dec-ade. He has since gone on to the Culinary Institute of America and holds a pres-tigious position in San Antonio with Rosemary's Catering, the largest caterer in the San Antonio area. This is a recipe originally from Lucille's *Treasure Chest* (see page 104), but Matt worked on perfecting it for the home kitchen. These are the rolls of yesteryear, hot and buttery, melt-in-your mouth good. I remem-ber these served for Sunday lunch with Fried Chicken, page 125, mashed pota-toes, page 100, green beans, and the Waldemar Jazz Band.

I have called for the use of this roll dough as the base for the Honey Nut Rolls and Cinnamon Rolls, page 55. It is one of the easiest yeast breads I have ever tried, with success guaranteed every time. This is a wonderful introduction to bread baking for all of the aspiring youngsters who wish to learn to cook. It calls for a resting/cold rise in the refrigerator for several hours before the final rise and baking. Who needs store-bought rolls when these are so good?

| | |
|---|---|
| 2 packages active dry yeast | 1½ cups butter or shortening |
| 1 cup cold water | 3 eggs, lightly beaten |
| 1 cup boiling water | 6 cups unbleached flour |
| ½ cup sugar | 1½ teaspoon salt |

Dissolve the yeast in the cold water. Let stand until ready to use, thus giv-ing the yeast time to activate. It will rise to the top of the water and be frothy.

In a stand mixer, combine the boiling water, sugar, and 1 cup butter or shortening. Stir on low speed with the paddle attachment until it cools down to 98° F. Add the beaten eggs and the yeast. Stir to blend.

Begin adding the flour and the salt, 1 cup at a time. Continue to mix on low speed between each addition.

Once all of the flour has been added, the dough will be like a shaggy mass. This is not a dough that pulls together into a form as other bread doughs do. Leave the dough in the mixing bowl, cover with plastic wrap, and refrigerate for at least two hours.

One hour or so before serving, remove from the refrigerator. Preheat the oven to 350° F. Pour the dough onto a well-floured work surface. Turn the dough to coat with the flour. Gently roll to about 1-inch thickness. Cut out with a 3-inch biscuit cutter. Place side by side on a jellyroll baking sheet that has been lined with parchment paper and a light coating of non-stick cooking spray. Brush the rolls with melted butter. Put in a warm place and let rise until doubled in bulk, about 25 to 30 minutes.

Bake in the preheated oven for 20 to 30 minutes, or until the tops are golden brown. Remove from the oven and brush with another coating of melted butter. Serve warm!

# Angel Biscuits                    Makes 2 dozen 3-inch biscuits

This is another refrigerator roll, but it is more like a biscuit than a roll. Angel Biscuits are light, flaky, and wonderful. We serve these every year for Thanksgiving. They are superb with all of the savory and sweet delicacies that crowd our plates. And if by chance there are any leftovers, we split and toast them with a little butter and jelly as a breakfast bread or, even better, for dessert. Simple, wonderful, buttery—better than heaven on earth.

| | |
|---|---|
| 1 package active dry yeast | 1 teaspoon baking soda |
| 2 tablespoons warm water, 110° F | 1½ teaspoons salt |
| 5 cups unsifted flour | 1 cup butter, cold and cut into pieces |
| ¼ cup sugar | 2 cups buttermilk |
| 3 teaspoons baking powder | Melted butter |

Mix the yeast with the warm water. Let stand about 5 minutes, or until the yeast is frothy. In a large mixing bowl, sift the flour, sugar, baking powder, baking soda, and salt. Cut the butter into the flour mixture, using a pastry blender, until it is pea-sized.

In a separate bowl, mix the yeast with the buttermilk. Make a well in the center of the flour mixture, and pour in the yeast/buttermilk mixture. Stir with a fork until the flour is just moistened. This is like regular biscuits in that if you overmix the dough, you will get heavy biscuits. Knead lightly in the bowl to bring the dough together.

Grease a clean bowl with butter. Put the dough in it and turn over to coat all sides with the butter. Cover with plastic wrap and refrigerate until ready to use. The dough will keep for at least a week.

When ready to bake, remove the amount you wish to bake from the refrigerator. Preheat oven to 400° F. Roll dough on a lightly floured work surface to about 1-inch thickness. Cut into 2-inch rounds with a biscuit cutter. Place on a parchment-lined cookie sheet and brush with melted butter. Let rise in a warm place until double in bulk, about 1½ to 2 hours. Bake in the preheated oven for 12 to 15 minutes, or until the top is golden brown. Serve immediately!

# Monkey Bread Serves 6–8

Monkey bread has pull-apart wonderfulness. I like to bake it in a bundt or a solid-bottom angel food cake pan. If the pan has a removable bottom, the butter will drip onto the bottom of your oven and make a terrible mess.

This is a delicate, dramatic, and very gratifying bread. This is one that is fun to have your little kitchen helpers assist you with. They will be delighted. The potatoes seem to love the yeast—or is it the other way around? Well, this dough has a deep richness, a delightful sweetness, and a moist lightness that complements any savory meal.

| | |
|---|---|
| 2 tablespoons yeast | 1 teaspoon salt |
| ½ cup warm water, 110° F | ⅔ cup sugar |
| 1 cup scalded milk | 2 eggs |
| 1 cup mashed potatoes | 5½ cups flour |
| ⅔ cup butter | 2 cups salted butter, melted |

Proof the yeast in ½ cup warm water. Let it stand until bubbly, about 5 minutes. In a stand mixer, stir together the milk, potatoes, butter, salt, and sugar until it cools to about 110° F. Add the yeast mixture and the eggs. Stir until well mixed. Add the flour 1 cup at a time, blending well until all of the flour is incorporated. Knead with the dough hook for about 10 minutes, or until the dough pulls together.

Remove from the mixing bowl, and put in a clean, well-greased bowl. Turn once to coat with the oil. Let rise in a warm place until double in bulk, about 1 to 1½ hours.

Punch down the dough and put on a well-floured work surface. Gently roll out to a thickness of about 1 inch. With a pizza rolling cutter, cut the dough into 2-inch squares.

Dip each square into the melted butter. Layer in the pan, overlapping the edges. Fill the pan with two complete layers.

Set aside to rise a second time, about 45 minutes, or until dough has doubled in volume.

Bake in a preheated oven for about 30 to 45 minutes, or until the bread is golden on top and an instant-read thermometer registers 200° F when inserted into the bottom. Serve warm.

# Black Bread

This is a deep, rich, heavy loaf, reminiscent of hearty German breads. It has many wonderful grains that give it a nutty flavor, and the molasses offers a pleasant sweetness. It is one of Marsha Elmore's favorites. Roy Spears developed this recipe many years ago, and we still serve it during camp and for many other occasions. This makes such a heavy dough, it is really recommended to use only a heavy-duty stand mixer with the paddle and dough hook attachments.

2½ cups lukewarm water
 (98° to 100° F)
2 tablespoons active dry yeast
½ cup black molasses
½ cup sugar
1 cup unbleached flour

3 cups whole wheat flour
1 cup dark rye flour
½ teaspoon salt
1 cup wheat bran
1 cup wheat germ
½ cup rolled oats

FOR SHAPING THE LOAVES, STIR TOGETHER:

½ cup whole wheat flour    ½ cup rolled oats

Preheat the oven to 350° F. In a stand mixer with the paddle attachment, stir together the water, yeast, molasses, and sugar for 1 minute. Let stand until it is foamy, about 5 minutes. Meanwhile, in a large bowl, sift together the unbleached, whole wheat, and rye flours, and the salt. Stir in the wheat bran, wheat germ, and oats.

Add the flour mixture to the yeast mixture, one cup at a time. Mix with the paddle until the dough gets too heavy. Then change it out for the dough hook. Continue to beat until all of the flour is incorporated. Knead for another 5 minutes on medium speed. Remove from the mixer and shape into 2 large or 4 smaller loaves. Roll each loaf in the whole wheat/oat mixture, as it is a very sticky dough. This coating will help you in handling the dough.

Place the loaves onto a parchment-lined baking sheet and let rise for about 45 minutes, or until it is double in bulk. Bake in the preheated oven for 45 minutes to 1 hour, or until the bread begins to crack at the top.

Remove from the oven and let cool for 15 minutes before slicing. Serve warm.

# Pita Bread

This is a Mediterranean flatbread. We serve it at lunch with Tuna Salad, page 33, and Tomato and Cucumber Salad, page 29. It is a great base for any sandwich. I love to fill it with Hummus, page 6, mixed salad greens, ripe red tomatoes, and crisp cucumbers. You can also cut the cooked pita into wedges and bake or fry until crispy. Use these as crackers for dip or in a salad for a tasty, crispy alternative. This is a highly versatile item!

Several notes to help you with this recipe: Distilled water seems to make a better pita. It should not be over 112° F, or it will kill the yeast. The recipe calls for you to add the salt after the flour, sugar, and yeast mixture has been well mixed. The salt may kill the yeast if added too soon. The most important note is that the thickness of each round should be $\frac{3}{16}$ of an inch. (You will probably have to use a ruler until you get the visual feel for it.) This is because if it is too thick or too thin it will not puff and separate in the center. The distinguishing characteristic of pita bread is, of course, a split center!

| | |
|---|---|
| 2½ cups bread flour | 2 tablespoons olive oil |
| 1 tablespoon sugar | 1 cup warm water (110° F) |
| 1 package active dry yeast | 2 teaspoons salt |

Place ½ cup of the flour in the mixing bowl of a stand mixer. Add the sugar, yeast, oil, and water. Beat on low for about 30 to 45 seconds. Then mix on high for 3 minutes.

Add the salt and the remaining flour ½ cup at a time, mixing on low speed until a shaggy mixture that cleans the bowl is formed. Put in the dough hook and knead for about 6 minutes. The dough should form a smooth, elastic mass. Remove from the bowl, and shape into 8 even-sized balls. Cover with plastic wrap and a damp cloth. Let rest for 20 minutes.

When ready to shape, preheat the oven to 450° F.

Working with one at a time, flatten each ball with your hands. Then roll each round to a thickness of $\frac{3}{16}$ of an inch. Achieving the right thickness is more important than making them perfectly round. Layer a piece of wax paper in between each pita round to prevent sticking.

Place 2 to 3 rounds directly on the oven rack, positioned in the middle of the oven. With a water bottle, spray a little water onto the sides of the oven and quickly close the door. This creates extra steam to help the bread puff properly. Cook for 5 to 8 minutes, or until the bread has puffed up and is beginning to brown. Do not overcook, as the dough will turn crisp and remain puffed!

Remove from the oven and let cool on a cake rack.

These are best served on the day that you make them, but you can cool them completely, wrap in foil, place in a freezer bag, and freeze for up to three months. To serve, defrost for an hour at room temperature and heat in a warm oven.

# Pizza                    Makes enough for two 10-inch pizzas

This recipe offers a crust that is chewy, yet delightfully crisp on the bottom. If your family enjoys homemade pizza, it is worthwhile to make a small investment in a baker's stone and a pizza peel or paddle. The stone withstands high heat and produces wonderfully crisp crust. The peel is essential for placing the prepared pizza onto—and removing it from—the hot stone. Make smaller pizzas, and family members can build their own. Individual pizzas are also fun for a birthday party or summer get-together menu. Serve with Caesar Salad, page 25.

FOR THE DOUGH:

| | |
|---|---|
| 1½ teaspoons active dry yeast | 2 tablespoons olive oil |
| ¾–1 cup lukewarm water, about 100° F | 2 teaspoons salt |
| 3–3¼ cups flour | Cornmeal |

In a large mixing bowl, stir the yeast into ¼ cup of lukewarm water. Let sit until the yeast begins to grow, about 5 to 7 minutes. Slowly stir in 1 cup of flour. Mix until fully incorporated. Add 1 tablespoon olive oil, ¼ cup water, salt, and another cup of flour. Stir with a wooden spoon until the flour is again blended. Repeat with the remaining water and flour. Add more flour and water only if necessary. It should be a soft, spongy dough. Pour onto a floured work surface. Knead for about 10 minutes to activate the gluten and to bring the dough smoothly together. Place in a clean bowl that has been coated with a thin layer of olive oil. Let rise, covered, in a warm place until doubled in bulk, about 2½ to 3 hours.

Punch down the dough and pour onto the work surface. Divide into two parts. Work with one at a time, keeping the remaining dough covered.

Place the baker's stone in a cold oven. Preheat the oven to 450° F.

Pat the dough into a round. With your hand, stretch and toss the dough to form it into a round shape. When it reaches the desired thickness, about ¼ inch in the center and thicker on the edges, place on a baker's peel that is generously covered with cornmeal. Brush the dough with olive oil; sprinkle lightly with salt.

Prepare the pizza with your favorite combination of toppings. (See list of suggested toppings below.) Bake for 15 to 20 minutes, or until the crust begins to turn a golden brown and the cheese is melted and browning. You may prepare the remaining dough while the first pizza bakes.

This dough also freezes well. Simply lightly oil the inside of a freezer bag. Put the dough in the bag and seal, removing as much air as possible. Keeps in the freezer for up to three months.

SUGGESTED TOPPINGS:

| | |
|---|---|
| Tomato sauce, page 87 (pulse the sauce in a food processor to make a smoother spread, and add 1 teaspoon each of dried oregano and marjoram) | Yellow onion, julienned |
| | Fresh spinach |
| | Fajita meat |
| | Artichoke hearts |
| | Ground sausage |
| Sun-dried Tomato Pesto, page 88 | Pepperoni |
| Basil Pesto, page 88 | Mozzarella cheese |
| Fresh roma tomatoes, sliced | Monterey Jack cheese |
| Fresh garlic, sliced | Feta cheese |
| Grilled vegetables, such as mushrooms, zucchini, red bell pepper, and onion | Parmesan cheese, freshly grated |

# Garlic Bread

Serves 4

The strong infusion of garlic coupled with fresh parsley and Parmesan is delicious with salad, pasta, and soup. It complements most meals. Use a good-quality French or Italian bread.

¼ cup olive oil
¼ cup melted butter
4 cloves garlic, finely minced
    or pressed
½ teaspoon salt
1 teaspoon dried oregano

2 teaspoons fresh parsley,
    finely chopped
1 loaf good French or
    Italian bread
¼ cup Parmesan cheese

Preheat the oven to 350° F.

Slice the bread into thick slices or split down the center lengthwise. Salt the garlic and let sit for about 10 minutes. Toss together the oil, butter, garlic, oregano, and parsley. Spread over the bread and sprinkle generously with the Parmesan. Place the bread onto a cookie sheet and toast until the bread begins to brown and crisp, about 10 minutes. Serve hot!

# Homemade Croutons

Makes 1½ cups croutons

A wonderful way to use up leftover bread. This is a small effort that is usually greatly appreciated. We use these croutons in our Caesar Salad, page 25.

¼ cup olive oil
2 cloves garlic, pressed
½ teaspoon dried herbs, such
    as *Herbes de Provence*, or your own
    mixture containing thyme,
    oregano, basil, marjoram,
    summer savory, or coriander

1½ cups good-quality bread,
    cut into ½-inch cubes
1 teaspoon salt

Preheat the oven to 350° F.

Mix the olive oil, garlic, herbs, and salt together. Toss together with the bread. Lay out on a cookie sheet lined with parchment paper and bake in the preheated oven for 20 to 30 minutes or until lightly toasted and crisp. Remove and let cool. Can be stored in an airtight container for several weeks.

# Accompaniments

## Vegetables and Grains

# The Guest Ranch:
# Then and Now

Waldemar is hands down one of the prettiest camps ever built. The unique stone buildings, designed by Harvey P. Smith and executed in brilliant stonemasonry by Ferdinand Rehberger, complement the pristine beauty of the location along the banks of the Guadalupe River in the scenic Texas Hill Country.

It was decided early on to make good use of this place year-round, and it was opened up for the off-season to conventions in September, and to families seeking respite from city life in the rugged hills between January and March.

Many of the early guest cabins were built with fireplaces, a sign of their intended use as winter domiciles. Ferdinand would start his day extra early when guests were present. He lit the fires in the dining hall to begin heating the large building for mealtime. Connie Reeves, a living legend in her own right, remembers some years when Doris and Ellen ran the operation alone. They managed the needs of their guests, prepared all the meals, and even lit the fires some mornings. This was a full-time project. Waldemar was like a secret destination for many years, and the guests wanted to keep it that way. They selfishly knew that if word got out, everyone would be coming to this paradise in the Hill Country. Doris kept the guest ranch open from the 1940s until the early 1950s. These were years that provided Waldemar with a fresh supply of patrons reaching far and wide across the United States.

After Marsha and Dale Elmore bought Waldemar, they hired a very talented young man, Roy Spears, to be Waldemar's chef. Because Roy lived at Waldemar year-round, the Elmores and Roy started an off-season business. This would be the first time in nearly thirty years that Waldemar had been open during the fall and winter months. Waldemar's reputation for exceptional service and wonderful meals attracted many different groups, such as corporate organizations and church groups, and became a desirable location for family reunions, private meetings, weddings, and many other events.

In 1980 a new event was created by Marsha and her best friend and co-director Carolyn Wheat. It was a week for women called Waldemar Women's Week. It has been so successful that it will celebrate its twenty-first anniversary in September 2000. As the off-season business grew, a bed and breakfast service was added. Rooms were upgraded with king beds, southwestern furnishings, and paintings—all the accoutrements of a first-class resort. Those who shared their considerable talents to make this possible were Teak and George Anne Elmore, Lori Appleton, Josh and Allison Elmore, and Marsha Elmore.

# Vegetables

## Pinto Beans

Serves 4

These are an essential accompaniment. They are delicious served *á la charra* or refried, page 76. Serve with any Tex-Mex dish, such as fajitas (see index), Chicken Enchiladas in Verde Sauce, page 124, or with rice! There are several techniques that can be employed to prevent cracking of the skin. If the beans boil continuously, or if salt is added before the beans are soft, the skin will crack. However, if you plan on cooking these for refried beans, this is not an important consideration.

8 ounces dried pinto beans
2 slices bacon (optional)
1 cup onion, chopped
2–4 cloves garlic
1 teaspoon chili powder

½ teaspoon cumin powder
3 roma tomatoes, chopped
Salt and pepper to taste
Cilantro for garnish

In a large stock pot, cover the rinsed beans with enough water to reach one-third of the way over the beans and soak overnight. You may also use the "quick-soak method" by bringing them to a boil, removing from the heat, and allowing to sit for 2 hours.

Pour off the soaking liquid and rinse the beans.

In a 4- to 6-quart stockpot, cover the beans with 6 to 8 cups cold water. Slice the optional bacon into 1-inch pieces and add to the beans. Add the onion, garlic, chili powder, cumin, and the chopped tomatoes. Simmer over medium-low heat for about 45 minutes to 1½ hours, or until the beans are softened. The cooking time depends greatly on the freshness of the dried bean. The older the beans, the longer the cooking time.

Once the beans have softened, season with salt and pepper to taste. (If the beans are salted too soon, they will break apart and become squishy.)

Garnish with the chopped cilantro and serve hot.

# Black Beans

Black beans have become the bean of choice among many Tex-Mex aficionados. We like to serve them with many of the popular Tex-Mex dishes in our repertoire. This recipe is also delicious simply served with rice. Garnish with Pico de Gallo, page 9, and sour cream. Very satisfying and warmly filling.

16 ounces dried black beans, rinsed and picked over
2 teaspoons chili powder
2 teaspoons dried ground cumin
½ teaspoon cayenne, or more, to taste
4 cloves garlic, coarsely chopped
1 medium red onion, chopped into ½-inch dice

1 poblano pepper, seeded and chopped into small dice
3 roma tomatoes, coarsely chopped
½–1 cup fresh cilantro, rinsed and coarsely chopped
Salt to taste

In a large stock pot, cover the rinsed beans with enough water to reach one-third of the way over the beans, and soak overnight. You may also use the "quick-soak method" by bringing them to a boil, removing from the heat, and allowing to sit for 2 hours.

Drain off the soaking liquid and rinse. Cover with fresh water and bring to a gentle simmer over medium heat, about 20 minutes. Add the chili powder, cumin, cayenne, garlic, red onion, and poblano. Continue to simmer for about 1½ hours, or until the beans are soft. Add the tomatoes, half of the cilantro, and salt to taste. Continue to cook until the mixture is thick and the beans are soft to the bite. Garnish with the remaining cilantro and serve hot.

# Refried Beans

This recipe is a traditional accompaniment to most Tex-Mex meals. There are those of us, of course, who prefer the *à la charra* version, which basically means that the cooked beans are served in a little of their cooking liquid. However, refried beans are a must for Chalupas, page 112.

¼ cup light vegetable oil
2 cups cooked pinto or black beans
Salt and pepper to taste

1–2 tablespoons Ancho Chili Purée, page 39
1 tablespoon fresh cilantro, coarsely chopped

Mash the beans with a potato masher. In a large skillet, heat the olive oil over moderately high heat. Add the mashed beans and cook, stirring continuously until heated through. Season to taste with salt and pepper. Add a tablespoon or two of Ancho Chili Purée for a little flavor kick. Garnish with the chopped cilantro. Serve!

# Black-Eyed Peas

Serves 4

In the southern states, black-eyed peas are served on New Year's Day for good luck. These warm and hearty beans are an essential element in one of the all-time favorite Waldemar meals. I have spoken with more women who have commented that Cheese Soufflé, page 89, served with black-eyed peas and Asparagus Tomato Salad, page 39, is the favorite classic lunch served here at Waldemar. It is certainly one of my favorites, and I always look forward to it.

Black-eyed peas cook in no time and do not require pre-soaking. You can use bacon or salt pork as a flavor enhancer, which is a traditional preparation. But they are just as good if you prefer to leave out the meat.

For a very short time in the summer, fresh black-eyed peas are available. They are a sublime treat that I always try to afford myself. Look for them in a good produce market, or ask your greengrocer if he can get them. They must, of course, be shelled, but the rhythm of the shelling process will take you back to a simpler time. Enjoy the opportunity to visit with your children, family, or friends as you work. Oddly enough, this makes them taste even better! Please note that if you use fresh beans, the cooking time is more than cut in half, and you are better off steaming the delicate beans than boiling them.

| | |
|---|---|
| 8 ounces dried black-eyed peas | 2 cloves garlic, minced |
| 2 strips bacon or 2 ounces salt pork | 1 bay leaf |
| (optional) | 1 teaspoon white vinegar |
| ½ cup onion, diced | Salt and pepper to taste |

In a medium stockpot, bring the peas and 6 cups of water to a boil and reduce the heat to low. Add the optional bacon or pork, the onion, the garlic, and the bay leaf. Continue to simmer until the peas are tender, about 45 to 60 minutes. The time will vary depending on the freshness of the dried beans; the older they are, the longer they will take to cook. Once tender, drain and reserve about 1 cup of the cooking liquid. Remove the bay leaf. Return the peas and the reserved cooking liquid to the heat and simmer with the vinegar for another 5 minutes.

Season with salt and pepper, and serve hot or warm.

# Steamed Vegetables

One of the best methods for preparing a vegetable side dish is steaming. It is quick and easy and maintains the natural goodness of the vegetable. Green vegetables, such as beans or peas, asparagus, zucchini, yellow squash, and carrots, are wonderful steamed. Use the basic instructions and adjust cooking time as necessary. It is best to steam only until *al dente*—the vegetable should still have a bite or tender crunch to it. If you overcook it, the vegetable loses some of its flavor and many of its healthful nutrients.

About ¼ to ½ cup per person of your
favorite vegetable
Garlic cloves, sliced coarsely
(optional)
Ginger root, peeled and sliced
(optional)

Fresh herbs on the stalk, such as
rosemary, tarragon, basil,
oregano, marjoram, thyme
(optional)

Clean and trim the vegetables. Slice if necessary into uniform size. This is important so that all the vegetables cook evenly.

Use a steam basket, which fits inside a saucepan. Add ½ to 1 cup water, just enough to come up ½ inch in the pan. Heat the water and the optional garlic or ginger root over medium-high heat until it is simmering. Layer the steam basket with the optional herbs and top with the vegetables. Place the steam basket in the simmering water and cover. Cook until the vegetables are *al dente*, from 7 to 20 minutes. Remove from the steam basket and serve immediately.

# Grilled Corn on the Cob
## One ear per person

1 ear of corn per person, with the
husks left on
Garlic butter (1 clove minced garlic
per 2 tablespoons butter)

Salt and pepper

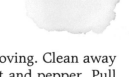

Prepare a barbecue grill. Pull back the husks without removing. Clean away the silky strands. Rub the corn with the garlic butter and salt and pepper. Pull the husks back over the corn. Microwave on high for about 5 minutes per ear of corn. Place the corn on the grill and cook, turning every 5 minutes, until the corn is tender. Remove the husks and enjoy.

# Roasted Bell Peppers

This recipe works with any peppers—green bell peppers, Holland peppers, poblano, or Anaheim peppers. A gas range works best, but you can do this over a open barbecue, or in the oven. The trick is to char the outer skin on all sides so that it blisters, then quickly place in a brown bag.

Several peppers
Culinary tongs

Brown paper bag

Using the tongs, hold each pepper over the open flame on a gas range. If grilling or cooking in the oven, brush lightly with a little olive oil.

To cook in the oven, place in a baking pan on the top rack under the broiler. Cook for 3 minutes on each side, or until the skin blisters and begins to char. Check regularly.

If cooking over a barbecue, heat the coals until very hot and white. Place the peppers onto the rack and cook. Check regularly to prevent overcooking.

Once done, remove from the heat and place in the brown bag. Close the top and let the internal heat steam the pepper for about 5 minutes. Remove from the bag and remove the skin under cold running water. If properly blistered, it should remove easily. Take off the stem and remove the seeds from the inside. Cut into strips or chop. Use as directed.

Delicious when julienned and served atop a salad or pasta, or with fajitas, pages 89, 111, 128, or 139.

# Green Beans Mediterranean                                 Serves 4

This dish is simple and very good. It combines several flavors prevalent in Mediterranean cuisine—tomatoes, capers, shallots, and a dash of red wine. It is elegant in presentation, yet still easy enough to serve for a quick mid-week dinner with roasted chicken Provençal and Rosemary-Roasted New Potatoes, page 100.

| | |
|---|---|
| ½ pound fresh green beans OR ¼ pound *haricots verts* (French green beans) | 1 tablespoon minced shallots |
| | 1 tablespoon capers, coarsely chopped |
| 4 roma tomatoes, peeled,* seeded, and diced | 1 tablespoon dry red wine |
| | 1 tablespoon olive oil |
| 1 teaspoon salt | |

To prepare the sauce, whisk together the red wine and olive oil in a small bowl. Add the minced shallots, chopped capers, and salt. Set aside.

I recommend the extra effort of peeling the tomatoes for an elegant dinner. If you are just serving this as an accompaniment to a simple family meal, it is not necessary to do this step, as it can be time consuming.

Chop the peeled and seeded tomatoes into small dice. Pour the reserved dressing over the tomatoes. Let sit for about 30 minutes at room temperature to allow the flavors to combine.

Steam the beans according to the directions on pages 77 to 78.

Serve the sauce atop the hot green beans.

*To peel tomatoes, slice a thin X in the bottom of a tomato. Cut out the stem core. Drop 2 or 3 tomatoes at a time into boiling water. Let them cook in the water for about 20 to 30 seconds. The skin will begin to split along the body of the tomato. Remove from the boiling water and plunge immediately into an ice water bath to arrest the cooking. Peel the skin from the tomato under running water. Cut in half and seed the tomato.

# Sugar Snap Peas

Serves 4

Another pea from the garden! But this one is completely edible. The "sugar" in the name is no misnomer. These are sweet! These are delicious cooked in a stir fry, steamed and chilled and added to a salad, or simply eaten raw! This recipe is essentially a flash fry, which uses the natural moisture of the fresh pea to steam with a little oil and fresh ginger and garlic. Although sugar snaps have a very short availability in the summer, this recipe is not recommended for use with frozen peas. The pea should remain crisp, and the frozen variety has already been parboiled.

| | |
|---|---|
| 16 ounces (1 pound) fresh sugar snap peas | ¼ teaspoon salt |
| 1½ teaspoons olive oil | ⅛ teaspoon sesame oil (optional) |
| 1 clove garlic, finely chopped | Salt to taste |
| ½ inch fresh ginger, peeled and grated | |

Snap off the stem end of the peas and pull the string that runs lengthwise on the inside curve of the pod. This is typically tough and fibrous. Rinse and set aside to air dry.

Heat the oil in a sauté pan over medium high heat. Add the garlic, ginger and ¼ teaspoon salt. Sauté until the garlic begins to release its fragrance, about 1 minute. Add the sugar snaps and the optional sesame oil. Sauté, tossing continuously until the peas are cooked through, about 7 to 10 minutes.

Season with salt to taste and serve immediately.

# Garlicky Collard Greens and Tomatoes

Serves 4

A fine southern tradition, although this recipe breaks away from traditional expectations. Rather than relying on hours of slow simmering with bacon, which purportedly boils away all of the bitter taste of the greens (along with all the nutrients), this recipe highlights the bitter flavor. The bitterness is balanced by the flavors of the nutty brown garlic and the acidic tomatoes. I have served these for conference groups, and many people could not believe that they were collard greens. You can use any leafy greens, such as mustard, kale, or chard, with equally good results. Try them and you'll never think of greens the same way again!

Suprisingly, this is not only a tasty accompaniment to chicken or fish, but it is also fantastic tossed with pasta and freshly grated Pecorino Romano cheese. The leftovers are great served atop a fluffy baked potato with Monterey Jack cheese.

| | |
|---|---|
| 1 bunch fresh collard or other greens, rinsed and chiffonade cut | 2 cups roma tomatoes, coarsely chopped |
| ¼ cup olive oil | 1–2 teaspoons salt, or to taste |
| 4–6 cloves garlic, coarsely chopped | |

To cut the greens in a chiffonade cut, layer the greens one atop the other, with the largest leaves on the bottom. Trim off the excess stems. Roll up the leaves in line with the stems, as for a cigar. Cut across the roll into 1-inch strips. This yields a long, narrow cut of the leaf.

In a skillet, heat the oil and garlic over medium-low heat until the garlic begins to release its fragrance, about 1 minute. Sprinkle the garlic with ½ teaspoon salt and continue cooking until the garlic turns a light golden brown, about 3 to 5 minutes. Do not leave the pan until you add the tomatoes, as the garlic may darken too much and ruin the dish. Add the chopped tomatoes immediately, and sprinkle with another ½ teaspoon salt. Cook, stirring occasionally, over medium heat until the tomatoes begin to soften, about 5 to 7 minutes. Stir in the collard greens, about ⅓ of the batch at a time. As the collards wilt, add more of the greens, continuously tossing with tongs. Once all of the greens are in the pan, cook only until they have all wilted. The whole process will take about 7 minutes. The greens will be a beautiful dark emerald green, and they will still have a little crunch. Remove from the pan and season to taste. Serve immediately. If they begin to overcook, they will become a dull olive color.

# Broccoli Etrusca                                                Serves 4

I am not really sure what the origin of this dish is. "Etrusca" refers to an ancient people of the Tuscany region of Italy. We always serve it with Caesar Salad, page 25, and Lasagna Bolognese, page 113, which is a very "Italian" meal. This is one of the best preparations of broccoli around. In keeping with our simple preparations, this dish relies largely on the natural flavor of broccoli, enhanced by garlic and a little bit of freshly grated, nutty Parmesan cheese.

This is another vegetable preparation that complements pasta well. Toss the cooked pasta with a little olive oil and the Broccoli Etrusca. Garnish with more Parmesan cheese. Enjoy!

¼ cup olive oil
6 cloves garlic, coarsely chopped
½ teaspoon salt
4 cups fresh broccoli, cut into florets

1 tablespoon water
Salt and black pepper to taste
¼ cup freshly grated Parmesan or
    Pecorino Romano cheese

In a sauté pan or a wok, heat the oil over medium-high heat. Add the garlic and ½ teaspoon salt, and cook quickly until the fragrance has been released and the garlic begins to turn brown, about 3 minutes. Add the broccoli and stir continuously until it turns a deep, bright green. Add the tablespoon of water to steam the broccoli, continuing to stir. The broccoli is done when it is *al dente*, or tender but with some resistance to the tooth, about 10 to 12 minutes.

Season to taste with salt and black pepper and toss with the Parmesan or Pecorino Romano cheese. Serve immediately.

# Asian Broccoli

Serves 4

This is another simple dish that enhances the natural beauty of broccoli. It has an Asian twist, using tamari sauce, a more concentrated and less processed version of soy sauce; freshly grated ginger; garlic; sesame oil; and sesame seeds as an optional garnish. It is delightful with the Hoisin Pork Tenderloin, page 121, and the Sweet and Spicy Mashed Potatoes, page 101.

¼ cup olive oil
2–4 cloves garlic
½ inch ginger, peeled and grated
    (optional)
4 cups broccoli florets

½–1 teaspoon tamari sauce
Dash of toasted sesame oil
½ teaspoon toasted sesame seeds
    for garnish

In a large sauté pan or wok over medium-high heat, sauté the garlic and optional ginger in the olive oil until the garlic begins to release its fragrance, about 3 minutes.

Add the broccoli and toss until it begins to turn dark green, another 3 to 5 minutes. Add the tamari and the sesame oil. Cover and continue cooking for 3 to 5 minutes, shaking the pan occasionally to prevent the broccoli from sticking. Remove from the heat and keep covered for another 5 minutes to allow the broccoli to continue steaming. Toss with the sesame seeds and serve immediately.

# Zucchini Parmesan

Serves 4–6

One of Roy Spears' creations, this is a tasty accompaniment dish. Easy to prepare and complementary to any poultry or fish dish, this is a winner all around. In drawing together the recipe selections, this one was highly requested by many Waldemar friends.

¼ cup olive oil
⅔ cup onion, chopped
2 cloves garlic, coarsely chopped
4 medium zucchini, sliced
2 tablespoons fresh parsley, chopped
1 tablespoon salt
¼ teaspoon pepper

¼ teaspoon dried oregano
¼ teaspoon dried rosemary
3 cups tomatoes, peeled and
    chopped
½ cup freshly grated Parmesan
    cheese

In a large skillet over medium heat, sauté the onion and garlic in the oil until the garlic releases its fragrance, about 3 minutes. Add the zucchini, parsley, salt, pepper, oregano, and rosemary. Cook until the zucchini is tender, about 15 minutes. Toss in the chopped tomatoes and continue to cook until the tomatoes are thoroughly heated, another 5 minutes.

Toss with ¼ cup of the Parmesan cheese. Turn onto a serving platter and garnish with the remaining ¼ cup Parmesan cheese. Serve immediately.

# Zucchini Spaghetti

Serves 4

This preparation of zucchini balances the fine texture of the tender vegetable with garlic and Parmesan and is served *al dente* alongside almost any entrée. It is superb accompanying pork, poultry, beef, or seafood. And because of its similarity to the Italian pasta for which it is named, this is a great way to prepare vegetables for more skeptical members of your family. Toss it with a Tomato Sauce, page 87 or 89, or your favorite pasta sauce, such as Basil Pesto, page 88, or Alfredo Sauce, page 96.

2 tablespoons olive oil
2–4 cloves garlic, finely chopped
4–6 zucchini

¼ cup Pecorino Romano cheese or
    Parmesan cheese
Salt and black pepper to taste

To prepare the zucchini, cut the ends off the vegetables and slice lengthwise, removing the outer flesh from the inner core of seeds and leaving the skin intact. I prefer to remove the seeds, as they tend to be mushy when cooked. Slice the remaining flesh into long, thin julienned strips, about ¼-inch wide by the full length of the zucchini itself.

In a large sauté pan or skillet, sauté the garlic with ½ teaspoon salt in the oil until it begins to release its fragrance, about 1 minute. Be very careful not to let the garlic begin to brown, as it will release a slightly bitter oil that will overwhelm the sweet and subtle zucchini.

Add the zucchini and toss gently in the garlic oil until it turns golden and tender, about 5 to 7 minutes. The zucchini should still be *al dente*, as you would cook pasta. Remove from the heat, toss with the cheese, and season to taste with salt and pepper. Serve immediately.

# Caramelized Cippoline Onions

Serves 4

These small, squat onions are available at many quality markets. Otherwise, ask your greengrocer if he can get them for you. This dish has the flavor of good onion soup. It is rich when prepared with beef stock, although a vegetarian side dish may be created by substituting vegetable stock. These are wonderful served with a simple roast tenderloin, either pork or beef.

2 cups cippoline onions
1 tablespoon olive oil
1 teaspoon salt

¼ cup white wine
2 cups beef or vegetable broth
Salt and pepper to taste

Remove the ends and the outer skins of the onions. In a skillet over medium heat, sauté the onions with the salt in the olive oil, stirring occasionally, until they begin to caramelize, about 20 to 25 minutes. Add the white wine, and cook until it reduces to a thick consistency. Add the beef stock, ½ cup at a time, cooking until it reduces. Add another ½ cup. Continue this process until all of the liquid has been added and the onions are very tender, about 20 minutes total. Season to taste with salt and pepper. Enjoy!

# Grilled Vegetable Kebabs

Serves 4–6

This fantastic summer grilled dish can be served atop Couscous with Basil, page 95, or accompanying Grilled Cornish Game Hen, page 129. You can choose any of your favorite summer vegetables. The ones listed in the recipe are a good guideline. The balsamic vinegar glaze offers a perfect enhancement—simple, healthy, delicious. Toss with Alfredo Sauce, page 96, and serve atop your favorite pasta. It is good with just about everything! I love to chop the leftovers and use as a spread on crusty French bread with smoked turkey and cheese or with freshly sliced roma tomatoes, sliced cucumbers, avocado, arugula, and smoked gouda. The possibilities are limited only by your imagination!

Wooden skewers, pre-soaked in water
    for about 15 minutes
1 cup balsamic vinegar
Button mushrooms
Cherry tomatoes
Zucchini, cut into 1-inch half moons

Red or yellow bell peppers, cut into
    1½-inch squares
Red or yellow onions, cut into 1½-
    inch squares
Whole, peeled garlic cloves
Salt and pepper

To make a balsamic vinegar glaze, simmer 1 cup balsamic vinegar until it reduces to about ½ the volume and is thick and syrup-like.

To prepare the vegetables, salt and pepper them well and let sit for 5 minutes. Slide 1 to 2 of each variety of vegetable onto your skewer. It is best to choose an arrangement and remain consistent. Brush the skewered vegetables with the balsamic reduction and grill over hot coals until the vegetables are cooked through. Some varieties will cook more quickly than others. Remove from the grill and brush lightly with the remaining balsamic reduction. Serve hot or at room temperature. See above for serving ideas.

# Spaghetti Squash

Serves 4

This is a delightful vegetable. A member of the squash family, once cooked, the flesh strings up like capellinni pasta. I love to toss it with a little butter or olive oil, freshly grated Parmesan cheese, and fresh basil, or serve it like pasta with a little tomato sauce. It is also wonderful baked with a little butter, brown sugar and cinnamon. Add this to your list of regular dinner accompaniments. Wonderful served with pork, poultry, or fish.

1 2- to 3-pound spaghetti squash
Salt and pepper to taste
2 tablespoons olive oil or melted butter
½ cup brown sugar, optional

¼ teaspoon cinnamon, optional, OR ½ cup freshly grated Parmesan cheese, optional
¼ cup fresh basil leaves, torn (optional)

Preheat the oven to 350° F. Slice the squash down the center from stem end to root end. Place the squash cut side up in a roasting pan. Sprinkle with the salt and pepper, and drizzle the oil or butter over the flesh. Turn the squash over and cook in the preheated oven for about 45 minutes. If you are using the brown sugar and cinnamon, mix together and place over the flesh of the squash after about 25 minutes. Return to the oven and leave cut side up for the remaining 15 to 20 minutes.

Once the vegetable is cooked, the flesh will be tender. Scoop the flesh out of the shell, which remains hard, and toss to separate the strands. Toss with the Parmesan and basil if preparing the more savory version. Season to taste with salt and pepper. Serve hot.

# Glazed Carrots

Serves 4

An elegant and classic accompaniment to any dish. The sugar in the dish enhances the natural sugars in carrots. This is really wonderful! You can serve the carrots cut into matchsticks or sliced on the diagonal, or use the baby carrots that are available ready-cut from your greengrocer.

1 pound carrots, peeled and cut into thin matchsticks or sliced on the diagonal (if using the baby carrots, you will need to blanch them in boiling water for about 5 minutes before proceeding with the recipe)
½ cup chicken stock or water
2 tablespoons butter

2 tablespoons brown sugar
½ teaspoon salt
½ inch fresh ginger, peeled and grated (optional), OR 1 teaspoon fresh orange zest (optional)
½ teaspoon fresh parsley, chopped

In a sauté pan with a lid, combine all the ingredients (excluding parsley) and simmer until the carrots are tender and a thick syrup has formed, about 20 minutes. Stir the carrots to coat with the syrup. Garnish with the parsley. Serve hot.

# Curried Fruit Bake

Serves 6

This is a recipe from Lucille's *Treasure Chest* (see page 104). Although it has long since been removed from the summer menu, several former campers requested that this recipe be included. Sézanne Tenor, a former camper who lived up river from the camp as a child, has many fond memories of Lucille and frequently makes this dish for guests at her home in the Rocky Mountains. It is actually one of her most requested dishes! Lucille suggested to serve with baked ham, chicken, or any other kind of meat.

| | |
|---|---|
| 1 28-ounce can fruit salad in syrup | ½ cup brown sugar |
| ½ cup maraschino cherries | 2 tablespoons cornstarch |
| 1 cup pitted black cherries | 1 tablespoon curry powder |
| 2 bananas | ½ cup melted butter |

Preheat the oven to 350° F. Drain the fruits and put in a mixing bowl. Peel and cut the bananas into small pieces and add to the bowl. Sift together the sugar, cornstarch, and curry powder. Pour the melted butter over the fruit and lightly toss in the sugar mixture. Butter a casserole dish and fill with the curried fruit mix. Bake for 40 minutes in the preheated oven. Serve hot.

# Pan-Seared Tomatoes

Serves 4

A wonderful accompaniment to fish, chicken, or steak. Serve warm atop a salad or alongside your entrée.

| | |
|---|---|
| 2–3 large and meaty beefsteak tomatoes, cut into ½-inch thick slices | 1 tablespoon olive oil |
| ½ teaspoon salt | 1 teaspoon *Herbes de Provence*, page 130 |

Place the large slices of tomatoes on a plate and season both sides with the salt, pepper, and *Herbes de Provence.* Heat the oil in a shallow skillet, and place the tomatoes in a single layer. Fry each side for about 3 minutes, or until warmed through and softened. Remove and serve immediately.

# Tomato Sauce al Fresca

Makes 4 cups

This recipe uses only the freshest of ingredients and it is not cooked. It marinates for only 30 minutes at room temperature and is ready to serve. Use the plumpest roma tomatoes, fresh garlic and basil, fruity olive oil, salt, and red wine. The size of cut used for the tomatoes will determine the use of this sauce. If tomatoes are cut fine, the sauce can be tossed with thin spaghetti or linguine. Cut thicker, it can be tossed with a shorter pasta such as penne, orrechiette, or fusili, and shaved Parmesan cheese. Omit the oil and the wine, and this is fantastic tossed with freshly steamed rice. Stir 1 cup sauce and ½ cup freshly grated Pecorino Romano cheese into the cooking pot once the rice is done and return the cover. Continue to steam for about 5 minutes. Stir and serve hot!

6–8 roma tomatoes, finely chopped
1 teaspoon salt
2 cloves garlic, finely chopped
¼ cup olive oil

2 tablespoons dry red wine
2 tablespoons fresh basil leaves,
    torn or julienned into thin
    pieces

Mix the finely chopped tomatoes and 1 teaspoon salt in a non-aluminum bowl. Set aside. For a milder garlic flavor, sauté the garlic and ¼ teaspoon salt in the oil over medium-low heat until the garlic begins to release its fragrance, about 3 to 5 minutes. Let cool to room temperature and stir in the red wine. Pour over the tomatoes and let sit at room temperature for about 20 minutes.

Toss with your favorite pasta and garnish with Pecorino Romano or Parmesan cheese.

# Cooked Tomato Sauce for Pasta or Pizza        Makes 2 Cups

This versatile, delicious tomato sauce goes well with any type of pasta. Quick and easy to make, you will find it to be a staple in your repertoire of favorite dinners. It makes a superb base for a variety of complementary additions. You can add anything from capers or olives to tuna or bacon. If you are adding an ingredient such as tuna or bacon, sauté it with the onions and garlic to cook it before adding the tomatoes. Another variation is to deglaze with about ½ cup red or white wine or any other liquor, adding a different dimension to the flavor of the sauce. Be creative! I like to double or triple the batch and freeze the remaining portion, dividing it into freezer bags in family-portion servings. This is also a great sauce for pizza. Add 1 teaspoon dried oregano to the sauce and purée the sauce until smooth. Simmer to reduce and thicken. Spread on the pizza crust and follow with your favorite toppings and cheese.

¼ cup olive oil
4 cloves fresh garlic, chopped
½ teaspoon salt
½ cup onion, chopped
Cracked red pepper to taste
    (optional)

1 28-ounce can Italian-style toma-
    toes
Salt to taste
Fresh basil leaves, torn

In a large sauté pan or skillet over medium-high heat, sauté the garlic and ½ teaspoon salt in the olive oil until the garlic releases its fragrance. Add the onion and continue to cook until it appears translucent, about 5 minutes. Stir in the optional cracked red pepper. Add the tomatoes and cut up with two knives in a back-and-forth action. Reduce the heat to low and simmer the sauce until it begins to thicken, stirring often. Add ¼ cup water and continue to cook, stirring occasionally to prevent burning. Repeat this process 3 or 4 times. The sauce will continue to thicken and develop with each successive addition and reduction.

Season to taste with salt and stir in the torn fresh basil leaves. Serve immediately or cool and store in the refrigerator for up to three days. You can also cool and freeze for up to three months.

# Basil Pesto

Makes 2 cups

A garden classic. Make a bounty of pesto and freeze the excess. Here's how: Pour the pesto mixture into an ice cube tray. Freeze until solid. Remove the 1-ounce cubes and store in a zip-closure bag for at least three months. Ah, to have homemade pesto on hand to enrich sauces, salad dressings, soups, mashed potatoes, meatloaf, or simply to toss with hot pasta. A quick meal for any season.

4–6 cloves garlic, coarsely chopped
½ teaspoon salt
1 cup pignoli (pine) nuts or walnuts
4 cups basil leaves, coarsely chopped

2 tablespoons unsalted butter, softened
½ cup olive oil
1 cup freshly grated Parmesan cheese

In a small bowl, sprinkle the garlic with the salt and let sit while you gather the remaining ingredients, at least 10 minutes.

Toast the nuts in a preheated 325° F oven until lightly browned and fragrant, about 10 minutes.

In a food processor or blender, pulse together the salted garlic, basil leaves, pine nuts, and butter. Slowly add the olive oil in a thin, steady stream while the processor or blender is on. Season to taste with salt and black pepper. Add the cheese if you are serving immediately. If you freeze the mixture, just before serving add about 1 to 2 teaspoons cheese per cube, or to taste. If you are adding to soup, leave the cheese out completely.


# Sun-Dried Tomato Pesto

Makes about 2 cups

This is another wonderful sauce that has myriad uses. It offers a rich, earthy, and complex flavor. Sun-dried tomatoes are so much more intense than fresh. This pesto is a wonderful component in a dish such as Chicken and Mushroom Phyllo Triangles, page 14, or Mediterranean Pasta Salad, page 34. Do not add cheese if you are adding the pesto to soups or sauces.

3 cloves garlic, coarsely chopped
1 teaspoon salt
2 cups sun-dried tomatoes, rehydrated
½ cup toasted walnuts

2 tablespoon olive oil
½ cup freshly grated Parmesan cheese
Salt and pepper to taste

In a small bowl, sprinkle the salt over the chopped garlic and let sit for at least 10 minutes. Toast the walnuts in a preheated 325° F oven for 10 minutes, or until lightly browned.

In a food processor or blender, pulse together the garlic, sun-dried tomatoes, and walnuts. Slowly add the oil in a steady stream and blend until the mixture binds together. Blend in the cheese and season to taste.

Add to your favorite pasta.

# Portobello Fajitas

Serves 4

This recipe is a wonderful alternative to the meat version. Portobello is a mushroom that is as large as a hand! It is a fully mature crimini mushroom, which looks like a brown button mushroom. Portobellos are thick and meaty and very easy to work with. They are a delightful meat substitute in soups, with pasta, grilled and served as a burger, or as fajitas. This dish is also delicious as an accompaniment to chicken, beef, or shrimp fajitas!

½ onion, julienned
1 poblano pepper, julienned
2 cloves garlic, coarsely chopped
2 roma tomatoes, quartered
    and seeded
½ teaspoon salt

½ teaspoon cumin
2 Portobello mushrooms, cut into
    halves, and sliced into ¼-inch
    slices
3 tablespoons soy sauce
Salt and pepper to taste

In a medium saucepan over high heat, sauté the onion until it begins to caramelize, about 10 to 12 minutes, stirring often to prevent the onion from over browning. Remove from the pan and set aside.

Sauté the poblano and the garlic until the garlic begins to release its fragrance and the poblanos have begun to wilt, about 5 minutes. Add the tomatoes to the hot pan with the garlic and poblanos. Cook until the tomatoes begin to soften. Add ½ teaspoon salt and cumin powder. Stir in the reserved onion, the Portobello mushrooms, and the soy sauce. Cook until the mushrooms begin to release their liquid, about 5 minutes, stirring continuously. Season to taste.

Serve with warmed tortillas, Refried Black Beans, page 76, sour cream, grated Monterey Jack cheese, Guacamole, page 5, and your favorite salsa.

# Cheese Soufflé

Serves 6

Light and delicious, this cheese-based soufflé is absolutely fantastic. This is a classic Waldemar dish. One of the favorite meals here includes Cheese Soufflé, page 89, Black-Eyed Peas, page 77, and Asparagus and Tomato Salad, page 32.

Don't be intimidated by this recipe. It is really not very difficult, although it tastes like it would be. It is a very impressive dish. Serve it as an entrée for a memorable evening.

Many of our campers eat their first savory soufflé here at Waldemar. Roy Spears, our chef for seventeen years, made the lightest, fluffiest soufflé ever. I have found the trick to be in the egg whites. Beat them until they are almost stiff, but before dry peaks form, and gently fold them into the cream-and-cheese mixture. It is also imperative that you use a strong-flavored cheese. We prefer sharp Cheddar. Try this and be transported back to wonderful summer days at Waldemar.

| | |
|---|---|
| 4 tablespoons butter, unsalted | 1 teaspoon Dijon mustard |
| 6 tablespoons flour | 4 drops Tabasco, optional |
| 2 cups milk | 6 egg yolks |
| 1 teaspoon salt | 8 egg whites |
| ¼ teaspoon cayenne pepper | 1 cup grated Swiss cheese |
| ¼ teaspoon Worcestershire sauce | 1 cup grated sharp Cheddar cheese |

Preheat the oven to 375° F. Prepare the soufflé dish by rubbing generously with butter and sprinkling with finely grated Parmesan cheese. Melt the butter in a skillet. Stir in the flour to make a smooth paste. Slowly whisk in the milk, 1 tablespoon at a time, until all is added and a smooth, creamy sauce has been formed. Flavor with the salt, cayenne, Worcestershire sauce, Dijon mustard, and the optional Tabasco. Bring to a boil over medium heat, stirring slowly and continuously until thick. Remove from the heat.

Beat the egg yolks one at a time into the cream mixture, stirring well until thick. Stir in the Swiss and Cheddar cheeses until melted. Whisk the egg whites until stiff, but not dry, peaks are formed. Fold ¼ of the egg whites into the sauce mixture to lighten it. Fold in the rest using a figure eight stroke.

Pour mixture into the prepared soufflé dish. Run your thumb around the edge of the inside rim of the soufflé to assist in an even rise. Prepare a hot water bath in a shallow baking pan large enough to set the soufflé dish in. Fill the baking pan with the water coming up ⅔ of the way on the soufflé dish. Bake in the hot water bath until it has risen and is golden on top, about 45 minutes to 1 hour.

Remove from the oven and serve immediately, as the soufflé will begin to fall within minutes.

# Zucchini and Onion Quiche                              Serves 6–8

Quiche has long been a staple at Waldemar. I think it was one of Roy's favorites. He certainly made outstanding quiche, and I remember loving the days that we had it for lunch. Light yet filling, this quiche always leaves you with the feeling that you were satisfied without being overstuffed.

Quiche is a versatile dish, tasty for an hors d'ouevre, brunch, lunch, or dinner. If you are preparing this for a large number of people, you can use a jelly-roll pan for the baking dish and simply cut the quiche into squares!

Serve with a garden salad tossed with the Dijon Vinaigrette, page 36.

| | |
|---|---|
| ½ batch of the basic pie crust, page 155 | 1 egg yolk mixed with 1 teaspoon water |

FILLING:

| | |
|---|---|
| 1 tablespoon butter | 1¼ cups milk |
| 2 cloves garlic, minced | ½ cup heavy whipping cream |
| 1½ teaspoons salt, divided | 2 tablespoons cornstarch |
| ¾ cup zucchini, cut into ½-inch matchsticks | ¼ teaspoon *Herbes de Provence,* see page 130 |
| ¼ cup onion, julienned | 1 tablespoon goat cheese |
| 1 tablespoon olive oil, if necessary | ½ cup grated Swiss cheese |
| 3 eggs plus 2 egg yolks | Dash of black pepper |

Preheat the oven to 375° F.

Line an unprepared 10-inch pie plate with the pastry dough and brush with the egg yolk wash. With the tines of a fork, poke several holes in the bottom of the pie dough. Bake in the oven until it begins to brown, about 10 minutes. Remove from the oven when done and set aside. It is best if you time it so that you can add the ingredients to a hot crust, as the custard will cook more evenly.

Meanwhile, prepare the filling.

Sauté the garlic with ¼ teaspoon salt in the butter until it releases its fragrance, about 2 minutes. Add the zucchini and continue to cook over medium heat until it turns bright green. Remove from the heat and set aside. Now sauté the onions with a tablespoon of olive oil. Caramelize the onions with ¼ teaspoon salt. Remove from the heat and add to the zucchini.

In a medium bowl, whisk the eggs until the yolks are broken. Whisk in the milk and cream. Sift the cornstarch into the egg/milk mixture and mix until smooth. Stir in the teaspoon salt, the *Herbes de Provence*, the goat cheese, and the black pepper.

Sprinkle the zucchini-and-onion mixture onto the bottom of the crust. Sprinkle the grated Swiss cheese over the vegetables and pour the egg/cream mixture into the crust.

Bake in the preheated oven for 45 minutes, or until the top of the quiche has set and begins to brown. Remove from the oven and let cool 15 minutes.

Cut into wedges and serve warm or at room temperature.

# Grains

## White and Brown Rice                                    Serves 4–6

White and brown rice both require an appropriate amount of water and a proper buildup of steam. White rice is the kernel with the hull mechanically removed. It is more commonly used in many varieties of cuisine than the brown rice kernel, although it is not as rich in vitamins. The brown rice requires more water and cooking time. It has a nutty flavor and a chewy texture. You can substitute brown rice for white in any of the following recipes, but please adjust the water quantity and the cooking time. You can also substitute vegetable, chicken, or beef broth for the cooking liquid, which enhances the flavor.

A QUICK TRICK TO REHEAT LEFTOVER RICE:
Bring water to a boil. Put the cold rice in a large sieve or fine mesh strainer. Pour the boiling water over the rice. Serve at once.

### White Rice

1 cup long grain white rice, such as          1 teaspoon salt
   texmati, basmati, or jasmine rice        1 tablespoon oil or butter
2 cups water

In a saucepan with a lid, bring the water, salt, and oil to a boil. Add the rice and let the mixture return to a boil. Cover and reduce heat to low. Let simmer covered for 20 minutes. DO NOT REMOVE THE LID, as this will affect the cooking of the rice. When done, remove from the heat, fluff with a fork, and serve warm!

### Brown Rice

1 cup short or long grain brown rice          1 teaspoon salt
2½ cups water                                 1 tablespoon oil or butter

The directions are the same as above. However, the cooking time increases to 50 minutes!

# Spanish Rice

Serves 4–6

This dish is a traditional accompaniment for Mexican-inspired dishes. There are many recipes that masquerade as Spanish rice, but they often bypass a very important step, namely the sauté cooking of the rice kernel itself before the addition of the cooking liquid. Julie Menges likes to use bacon grease as the cooking oil. This is a rich flavor enhancer!

| | |
|---|---|
| 1 tablespoon olive oil or bacon drippings | ½ teaspoon cumin |
| ½ cup diced onion | ½ teaspoon chili powder |
| 2 cloves garlic, finely chopped | 1 tablespoon Ancho Chili Purée, page 39 |
| ¼ teaspoon salt | 1 teaspoon salt |
| 1 cup long grain white rice | 2 cups vegetable or chicken stock, simmering |

Sauté onion and garlic with ¼ teaspoon salt in oil until the onion is translucent, about 5 minutes, stirring frequently. Add the rice and continue cooking, stirring continuously, until the rice "crackles" or "clinks" against the pan, another 5 minutes or so!

Stir in the cumin, chili powder, ancho chili purée, and salt. Quickly add the 2 cups of simmering stock. Stir to loosen the rice and bring to a boil. Cover and reduce the heat to low. Cook covered for 20 minutes. Remove the lid and fluff with a fork. Serve warm.

# Rice Florentine

Serves 4–6

This rice dish essentially blends the rich flavors of spinach and garlic, with a delicate touch of fresh basil. This is wonderful served with the Grilled Cornish Game Hen, page 129, or herb-roasted chicken.

| | |
|---|---|
| 1 tablespoon olive oil | ¼ cup fresh basil leaves, torn or finely julienned |
| 1 tablespoon butter | 1 cup rice |
| 2 cloves garlic, chopped | 2 cups hot vegetable or chicken stock |
| ½ cup chopped onion | 1 teaspoon salt |
| 1½ cups fresh spinach, finely julienned | |

In a saucepan with a lid, melt the butter with the oil. Sauté the garlic and onion until the onion is transparent, about 5 minutes, stirring frequently. Stir in the spinach and basil until they turn bright green. Add the rice and continue to cook until the rice "crackles" or "clinks" against the pan, another 5 minutes or so. Pour in the hot stock and the salt. Let the mixture come to a boil. Cover and reduce the heat to low. Cook covered for 20 minutes. Remove the lid and fluff with a fork to help distribute the greens, as they will typically rise to the top while cooking. Serve warm.

# Rice with Green Chilies

Serves 6–8

This is one of those dishes that I will always associate with Waldemar. It is rich and creamy and has a nice little bite. A very decadent side dish, it is wonderful served alongside the Chicken and Green Chili Enchiladas with Verde Sauce, page 124, and Black Beans, page 76.

| | |
|---|---|
| 2 cups cooked white rice, page 92 | 1 teaspoon salt |
| 1 7-ounce can green chilies | Pepper to taste |
| 1½ cups sour cream | 1½ cups Monterey Jack cheese |

Preheat the oven to 350° F. Mix the rice, green chilies, sour cream, salt, and pepper, and half of the cheese. Pour into a buttered casserole dish and cover with the remaining cheese. Cover tightly with foil and bake for 30 minutes. Uncover and continue baking for another 15 minutes, or until the cheese is bubbly and golden brown.

# Wild Rice Pilaf

Serves 4–6

This dish combines white rice with wild rice and a blend of herbs and garlic to create a pilaf of uncompromising flavor. It has an earthy and nutty aroma. We love to serve this with pork tenderloin or baked chicken.

The preparation is somewhat time consuming, in that the wild rice requires some advance cooking, but it is worth the extra effort. You can find wild rice in the market with specialty foods. It is not actually the same grain as rice. It was originally harvested by the native peoples who inhabited the Minnesota area. It is no longer actually harvested from the wild, but is cultivated for mass consumption, although it remains a specialty dish.

| | |
|---|---|
| 3 cups simmering chicken stock | ⅓ cup white onion, finely chopped |
| (1 cup for the wild rice | 1 cup sliced button mushrooms |
| and 2 cups for the white rice) | 1 cup long grain white rice |
| ⅓ cup wild rice | ½ cup white wine |
| 2 cloves garlic, finely chopped | |

Heat the cup of chicken stock in a small saucepan with a lid. Add the wild rice, return to a simmer, and reduce the heat to low. Cook for about 20 minutes. This preparation will partially cook the wild rice. It will continue to cook once it is added to the pilaf.

Meanwhile, prepare the rest of the ingredients for the recipe. In a medium saucepan with a lid, sauté the garlic and onion in the olive oil over medium heat until the onion is translucent, about 5 minutes. Add the mushrooms and continue cooking until they begin to soften, about 5 minutes. Stir in the long grain white rice, and stir until it begins to clink on the sides of the pan. Deglaze with the white wine. Let simmer until the wine has been absorbed. Stir in the partially cooked wild rice and its cooking liquid, and add the remaining hot chicken or vegetable stock. Add the chopped green onions and the parsley. Bring to a simmer and reduce the heat to low. Cover and cook for 20 to 25 minutes. Do not lift the lid until it has cooked for the minimum 20 minutes. If there is more liquid to absorb, return to the heat and continue to cook for another 3 to 5 minutes.

Fluff with a fork and serve hot!

# Couscous with Basil

Serves 4

Couscous is a wonderful grain. It is essentially coursely ground semolina wheat mixed with water and salt to form a dough. It is rolled into tiny balls, which are then steamed to fluffiness. Couscous is a pasta with a versatile texture and complementary flavor. Couscous available on the market in the U.S. has been precooked and only needs to be heated in boiling water or stock. It is a quick starch, ready in 5 minutes. This is a simple recipe, one that can be used as a base for your favorite spices, such as cumin, curry, or cardamom, or your favorite blend of herbs, dried or fresh! This is an ideal accompaniment to any fish or poultry dish. It is also wonderful served with grilled or roasted vegetables.

2 cups chicken or vegetable broth
½ teaspoon salt
1 tablespoon olive oil
1 10-ounce package of couscous

½ cup fresh basil leaves, torn in small pieces or cut into fine julienne strips

In a small saucepan with a lid, bring the liquid to a boil. Add the salt and olive oil. Stir in the couscous and basil. Remove from the heat, cover, and let stand for about 5 minutes. Fluff with a fork before serving. Serve warm.

# Fettucine Alfredo

WOW! This is the best Alfredo sauce ever! Not for the faint of heart, it is thick and creamy, rich and wonderful. I love to serve it over sautéed or grilled vegetables and then tossed with the fettucine. It is also wonderful to blend with Basil Pesto, page 88, or a few ounces of Gorgonzola cheese and julienned slices of tomato. The possibilities are endless.

As you will see, this recipe includes an ample amount of garlic. Some recipes don't call for quite as much of this golden gustatory treasure, but I am of the school of thought in cooking that assumes there can never be too much garlic. This is one of those dishes in which more is definitely better, although you may prefer to use less than the minimum 4 cloves of garlic. It will still be good!

2 egg yolks
2 cups heavy whipping cream
2 tablespoons butter
4–6 cloves garlic, finely chopped
1 cup Pecorino Romano cheese, finely
    grated

Salt and black pepper to taste
1 pound fettucine (or your
    favorite pasta)
¼ cup fresh basil leaves, torn
    (optional)

Whisk together the egg yolks and heavy cream. Set aside.

In a medium sauté pan over medium heat, sauté the garlic in the butter until the fragrance is released, about 3 minutes, being very careful to not let the garlic begin to brown.

Quickly whisk in the egg/cream mixture. Cook, stirring constantly with a wire whisk or a wooden spoon, until the mixture begins to thicken. Remove from the heat once the mixture coats the back of a spoon and will leave a mark if you run you finger across the spoon.

Stir in the cheese and season to taste with the salt and pepper.

Cook the fettucine according to package directions.

Stir in the torn basil leaves and serve immediately over *al dente* fettucine or your favorite pasta.

# Macaroni and Cheese

The taste of this dish signifies childhood. It is one of the summer campers' favorites. A moment of merriment surrounds macaroni and cheese; it is made of the best part of childhood. This may sound a bit romantic for a simple dish such as this, but try it for your family. Its simplicity and rich beauty have next to no equal. There are two schools of thought when it comes to macaroni and cheese. Some like to make a béchamel or cream sauce and add cheese to melt, then toss with the cooked pasta. This is similar to, but obviously much better than, the instant packages bought in stores. The other method is semi-cooked pasta tossed with an egg/milk mixture and grated cheese. It is then baked like a casserole and served piping hot from the oven. This second technique is the one we like to use. It is so good.

This recipe calls for Monterey Jack cheese, a slight detour from the more commonly used American cheese. It has such a hearty flavor and melts so creamy and smooth that I couldn't help it. You can substitute any good meltable cheese that you prefer, however.

I also list ½ cup of Pepper Jack cheese as an optional variation. You can add more, less, or none at all. But it is a fun Tex-Mex twist.

Another variation is to change the type of pasta. It is best to use a short pasta with an opening to hold sauce, or, in this case, cheese. My personal favorite is a short pasta called gnocchi (not the same as the Italian potato dumpling of the same name). It is available from most good Italian import manufacturers. Several other classic suggestions: macaroni, penne, rigatoni, gemelli, or-rechiette, or any other short, tubular pasta.

Serve macaroni and cheese as an entrée or an accompaniment. Enjoy!

1 pound macaroni, gnocchi, penne, gemelli, or your favorite short pasta
1 tablespoon olive oil or butter
4 eggs
1½ cups milk

2 pounds Monterey Jack cheese (1 pound grated and 1 pound cut into ½-inch cubes)
½ cup Pepper Jack cheese (optional)
Salt and freshly ground black pepper to taste

Preheat the oven to 375° F.

Cook the pasta for ⅔ of the recommended time on the package. Remove from the hot water and rinse with cool water to remove the extra starch.

Rub the bottom of a 9 x 13-inch pan with the butter or oil. Pour the pasta into this dish.

Whisk together the eggs and the milk. Pour over the pasta. It should come up almost to the top. Toss in the grated cheese and the cubed cheese to evenly distribute. Stir in the salt and pepper

Cover with aluminum foil, and bake in the preheated oven for 30 minutes, or until bubbling. Remove the cover and let brown for 5 to 10 minutes.

Serve hot!

# Potatoes

There are two basic types of potatoes called for in this book, boilers and bakers. The boilers have high moisture and low starch content. They are ideal for, as their name implies, boiling. They keep their shape and firm bite and are ideal for use in salads and stews. The bakers have a higher starch-to-moisture ratio. These potatoes, such as Idaho, are ideal in recipes that call for baking or roasting. Although they disintegrate when boiled too long, they are perfect for mashed potatoes, because they are so fluffy!

## Baked Potatoes                                                    Serves 4

What better accompaniment to a perfectly grilled steak? Or, as a meal in itself, it is healthy, light, and versatile. Top with traditional items, such as butter, grated cheese, sour cream, bacon, and green onions. For a new twist, add sautéed mushrooms and tomatoes with shallots and a little blue cheese. Broccoli Etrusca, page 81, with a little extra Parmesan cheese, is a fabulous topping. I love to heat up leftover vegetables tossed in barbecue sauce and smother my potato! Mmm-mmm good! Let your imagination get carried away.

> 4 baker's or Idaho potatoes,
>    1 per person

Preheat the oven to 400° F. Scrub the potato skins well and pat dry. With the tines of a fork, pierce the skin of the potato in several places to prevent a buildup of pressure during cooking, which can cause the potato to explode!

If you prefer a crispy skin, place the potatoes directly on a baking sheet and place in oven. If you prefer more tender results, rub a little oil onto the skin, salt and pepper lightly, and wrap in aluminum foil. By either method, the potato bakes for about 45 to 55 minutes. A quick squeeze of the potato is a good test. If the potato gives under the pressure, it is done. If it still seems to resist, cook a little longer. Split open down the middle and top with your favorite fixings. Serve immediately.

# Twice-Baked Potatoes

Serves 4

Kids love this. I love this. Essentially everyone I know loves this dish. It is a great way to serve potatoes, cheesy and tasty and fluffy. A great dish to have your kids jump in and help with.

2 large baker's or Idaho potatoes
1½ teaspoons salt
¼ cup grated Cheddar cheese
¼ cup grated Monterey Jack cheese
¼ cup sour cream
1 teaspoon Dijon mustard

2 tablespoons green onion,
   chopped
2 slices crisp cooked bacon,
   crumbled (optional)
Dash of cayenne pepper
¼ teaspoon of Worcestershire sauce

Preheat the oven to 400° F. Prepare the potatoes as directed for a baked potato, page 98. Remove from the oven and let cool enough to handle. Open the potato with a partial slit lengthwise down the center of the potato. With a spoon, carefully scoop out the flesh, leaving a shell about ½-inch thick, and put the potato flesh into a mixing bowl. Set the skins aside.

Mash the warm potato flesh with a fork. Stir in the salt, cheese, sour cream, Dijon mustard, green onion, optional bacon, cayenne pepper, and Worcestershire.

Fill the potato skin shells with the potato/cheese mixture, being careful not to break the skins. Place the stuffed potatoes in a baking dish and bake in the preheated oven until the cheese has melted, about 15 minutes. Serve hot!

# Oven-Baked French Fries

Serves 4

We think these taste just as good as the fried version, and they are better for you! Serve them with your next burger grill! They take less "hands-on" time than the fried version and are a lot less messy.

About 1 pound bakers's potatoes
2 tablespoons olive oil
1–2 teaspoons salt

Salt and black pepper, or cayenne
   pepper, to taste

Preheat the oven to 450° F. You can either peel the potatoes or leave the skins on. If you leave the skins on, thoroughly wash and pat dry. Slice into strips, about ⅜ inch thick. Soak covered in cold water for about 10 minutes. Drain and pat dry. Toss the potatoes with the oil and salt. Lay onto a baking sheet in an even layer. Bake on a baking sheet for 30 to 40 minutes, turning several times, until they are golden brown. Drain on a paper towel to remove any excess oil. Sprinkle with more salt to taste and black or cayenne pepper to taste. Serve warm with ketchup.

# Rosemary-Roasted New Potatoes

Serves 4–6

This is a favorite Waldemar dish. We love to serve it for camp, conferences, and special events. It is easy to prepare for large numbers and complements many entrées. We use new potatoes, fresh rosemary, a dash of olive oil, and plenty of salt and garlic. You can use dried rosemary in a pinch, but it really is not as good as the fresh. Simple and fabulous, these are served with a quick dinner of chicken or pork.

| | |
|---|---|
| 2 pounds new potatoes | 4 cloves garlic, finely chopped |
| ½ cup olive oil | 4 6-inch stalks fresh rosemary |
| 1 tablespoon salt | Dash of black pepper, freshly ground |

Rinse the new potatoes and cut into quarters. Pat dry. Toss with the olive oil, salt, chopped garlic, fresh rosemary, and freshly ground black pepper. Spread in a single layer on a parchment-lined jellyroll sheet.

Bake for 45 to 60 minutes at 375° F, or until tender and golden brown, turning every 15 minutes. Serve immediately.

# Garlic Mashed Potatoes

Serves 4–6

This preparation has become popular in the last decade as a flavorful alternative to mashed potatoes with butter and cream. The garlic purée offers a subtle taste that complements almost any dish. It is hearty yet elegant, healthy yet satisfying. Stir in some of your favorite blue cheese for a sumptuous variation. Garnish with chopped Italian parsley and paprika. It is fantastic when paired with Meatloaf, page 116, or Fried Chicken, page 125. For a homestyle look and taste, leave the skin on at least one of the potatoes. Be certain, however, that you scrub the skin well under clean water to remove any excess dirt! The recipe gives leeway in your choice of milk products. I prefer the creamier options of heavy whipping cream or condensed milk. So little is called for that the amount of added fat per serving is minimal.

| | |
|---|---|
| 6 large baker's potatoes, peeled and cut into 1-inch cubes | 4–6 tablespoons cream (you can use milk, half and half, heavy whipping cream, or condensed milk) |
| 8 cups water | 4 tablespoons butter |
| 1 tablespoon vinegar | 2 teaspoons salt |
| 1 bulb garlic, separated, excess papery skin removed | Freshly ground black pepper to taste |

Cover the potatoes with 8 cups water. Add the vinegar to the water and bring to a boil. In a small saucepan, cook the garlic cloves in boiling water for about 20 minutes, or until soft. Remove from the water and allow to cool enough to handle. Remove the garlic skins and purée the garlic in a food processor with the cream, butter, and salt. Set aside.

Cook the potatoes until tender when pierced with a fork, about 20 to 30 minutes. Drain off the water immediately from the cooked potatoes and return the potatoes to the hot cooking pot. Toss for about 30 seconds over low heat. This process evaporates any excess water that may cling to the potatoes and can make gooey mashed potatoes!

In a large bowl, mash the potatoes and the garlic purée. I like to keep a few small chunks of potato for a home-style texture! Season to taste with more salt and black pepper. Serve warm.

If you want to keep the potatoes warm until serving, or reheat, simply put in a baking dish and cover with aluminum foil. Place in a preheated 250° F oven to hold or 350° F oven to reheat.

# Sweet and Spicy Mashed Potatoes                    Serves 6–8

This combination of the classic baker's potato and the sumptuous sweet potato breaks all traditions and creates its own! This is a variation on a dish served by Hudson's on the Bend, the fabulous restaurant in Austin run by Jeff Blank and Shanny Lott. They made it for us here at Waldemar for a cooking school weekend. We have adapted it and served it for conference groups, Women's Week, and at camp. It's so good. The rich color and flavor offer a delightful contrast to a plate of greens and browns. It is just beautiful to the eye and gratifying to the palette when served with the Hoisin Pork Tenderloin, page 121, and Broccoli Etrusca, page 81. A bit sweet, a bit spicy, and altogether tasty.

Essentially, the formula is 25% sweet potato and 75% Idaho or baker's potato. Use this ratio when multiplying out for larger groups. Use the Ancho Chili Pureé, page 39, sparingly, especially if you have young children. I like things spicy and tend to favor this flavor point, but a little can go a long way toward making this dish unique!

1 pound sweet potatoes, peeled
   and cut into 1-inch cubes
3 pounds Idaho potatoes, peeled
   and cut into 1-inch cubes
1 bulb garlic, excess paper removed
4 tablespoons salted butter

2 tablespoons cream
2 ancho chili peppers, rehydrated,
   page 39
Salt and pepper to taste
1 tablespoon chopped fresh cilantro
   (optional garnish)

In a large stock pot, boil the sweet and Idaho potatoes together until tender, about 20 to 30 minutes. Meanwhile, in a small saucepan, boil the garlic cloves until tender, about 20 minutes. Purée the rehydrated chili peppers until smooth.

Once the potatoes are tender, drain off the cooking liquid and cook the potatoes over medium heat for about 30 seconds, or until the excess moisture has evaporated.

Transfer the potatoes to a large bowl. Mash in the garlic cloves. Stir in the butter and the cream until fluffy. Add half of the chili purée and check for the desired spiciness, as all of the purée may be too spicy. Season with salt and pepper to taste and garnish with the cilantro. Serve immediately.

# Waldemar Chefs

## Meats, Poultry, and Seafood

U. S. is called the "Barbecue King," and he's really king at mealtime to every girl in the junior and senior dining rooms.

# Continuing the Legacy

Among the six Waldemar chefs, there are those who stand out from the rest because of tenure, devotion, loyalty, and love of Waldemar. They are: U. S. and Lucille Smith, Robert and Bessie Munson, and Roy Spears.

## U.S. and Lucille ... Glory Days

Ulysses Samuel and Lucille Bishop Smith came to Waldemar in the late 1920s. Thus began an almost fifty-year tradition. Lucille was a working caterer in the Fort Worth area who happened to meet W. T. Johnson, Ora's brother, when she catered a party for him. With a little encouragement, this remarkable woman came to Waldemar with her husband, Ulysses Samuel Smith. U. S. was a talented culinary expert in his own right. He was known for his barbecue skills, and he was celebrated as the "Barbeque King of the Southwest" while catering for W. T. Johnson's traveling rodeo.

Lucille and U. S. had a mystique about them. U. S. was a proud man who wore a tall chef's hat and a pristinely white starched chef's coat. He seemed to command respect with each step, and people came from all around to enjoy a delicious meal. Lucille was a legend in her own right. Highly educated, she was recognized for her knowledge in home economics and was hired as the Teacher Trainer of Industrial Education of Texas in charge of House Service Training in the 1940s. Lucille published a recipe file box called *Lucille's Treasure Chest of Fine Foods*. It was in such demand that there were four printings over the next thirty years. Lucille is also noted for creating the first pre-packaged bread mix for the marketplace. Launched in 1943, "Lucille's Hot Roll Mix" set the stage for the ease in baking that we take for granted today.

We are very proud to note that Lucille Smith has been recognized as one of the top 100 Women of the Century in Texas. We consider ourselves lucky to have Lucille and U. S. as a part of our heritage and traditions. Except for two years in the early 1930s, either U. S. or Lucille or both were responsible for Waldemar's food from 1928 until the summer of 1973.

## BESSIE AND ROBERT . . . IN STEP

Lucille was succeeded in 1974 by Bessie Williams Munson and Robert Munson. Bessie was a protégé of Lucille Smith. Before coming to Waldemar, Bessie had her own restaurant, worked at Neiman Marcus under Helen Corbitt, and became a leading Fort Worth caterer. The Munsons directed the food service at Waldemar through 1979. Bessie wrote and had published her own cookbook, entitled *Bless the Cook*.

## ROY SPEARS . . . CONTINUING THE LEGACY

After Marsha and Dale bought Waldemar from Doris Johnson, they hired a young man just twenty-three years old to run the Waldemar kitchen. This young man was Roy Spears, a friend of Marsha's sons, Teak and Josh. Previously, Roy had been a counselor at Camp Stewart, where he, among other things, helped in the kitchen. He also worked at the River Hills Country Club. By accepting the Waldemar position, Roy was taking on a huge challenge with little experience. Needless to say, he proved himself again and again. In the first fifteen years, he earned his Master Chef, Five Star rating, or CCP, a level of proficiency held by fewer than 120 chefs in America at that time. His youth and enthusiasm were inspiring to all who worked with him and to all who received the blessings of his culinary talents. In 1991 Roy wrote the first *Waldemar Cookbook,* which is in its second printing. In 1995 he decided to buy his own business, which he successfully ran for three years. It is our good fortune to have Roy and his wonderful staff back with us at Waldemar.

# Meats

## Steak

Steak is served here at camp for special occasions. We have a counselor cook-out the eve of camp each term. A full spread is laid out, Texas style: steak, Baked Potatoes with all the fixin's, page 98, green salad with ranch dressing, homemade rolls, page 62, and Cherry Squares, page 154. It is a quintessential evening of food and fun.

We also have a special steak cookout for the Hilltoppers, our sixteen-year-old girls who gather together in the beginning week for their final year as campers. The cookout takes place on the evening after the Hilltoppers' ropes course, a day led by Stephanie Smith and offered to build the campers' self-esteem, sportsmanship, and cooperation. The good hearty meal shared around the campfire is a very moving and special finale, filled with laughter and camaraderie.

And the final special steak cookout is reserved for the elite riders known as Reeves' Riders First Term and Connie's Cowgirls Second Term. This is a group of girls who have passed a difficult series of tests challenging their knowledge of horsemanship and riding ability. The groups are named after the legendary Connie Reeves, horseback department head for over fifty years, who is still an active rider and counselor at the age of ninety-nine. After the new inductees are informed that they have passed the test, the riders and the riding staff, led by Elizabeth Pipkin Pohl, ride up a challenging path to the top point on Waldemar's property, called Lookout Point, also the site for Marsha and Dale's new home. There the girls enjoy a steak meal under the wide open sky, watching the sun begin to set behind the scenic Texas hills.

If that doesn't conjure up memories of wonderful times here at Waldemar, then I suggest creating your own. But one thing is certain: Steak dinners can't be beat when it comes to Waldemar and Texas traditions.

Steak, you say. That's easy. Just put it on the grill or under a broiler and cook until done. But how do you know when it is done? This is as individual as is the person cooking the meat. And then there is the question of how to season the meat. Well, this recipe is devoted solely to the preparation of steak, discussing the various cuts, cooking times, and seasoning possibilities, as well as some simple leftover suggestions.

Steak is essentially a slab of meat. Best when at least ¾-inch thick, the optimum thickness is about 2 inches. Have your butcher prepare your meat for you to the desired thickness. Obviously, the thicker the cut of meat, the longer it will take to cook. The best method for cooking a thick steak is, hands down, over a hot grill. Cook the first side until it begins to release some of its juices, turn to cook the other side, remove from the heat once done, and let sit for several minutes before serving. This resting period allows the meat's juices to redistribute evenly through the meat, enhancing the flavor and tenderness. See below for the cooking chart, based on the cut of the meat and its thickness, to achieve the desired amount of doneness.

CUTS OF MEAT:

The rib, the loin, and the sirloin are the cuts of meat ideal to use for steak.

From the rib, we get the ribs and rib-eye steak. This is a tasty steak when grilled, as the rib-eye bone releases a lot of flavor—as most dog owners know, it makes an excellent chew treat for their favorite family member.

The loin and sirloin offer much sought-after, tender meat, excellent not only for steaks, but also for roasts, stews, and more elegant presentations.

The short loin is found near the ribs. It is a muscle that runs along both sides of the backbone. The sirloin comes from the rump area. The short loin offers up the T-bone, porterhouse, and club steaks. These tend to be more tender and more mild in flavor than the sirloin, and the price generally reflects this. The tenderloin, which is also cut from the short loin, is probably the most prized cut. A long, slender piece of meat that runs along the bone, the tenderloin requires some trimming, but it is an exquisite steak when sliced.

The sirloin is probably the best deal for your money. If your supermarket has natural or organic meat, I think it is worth the extra dollar per pound, paid off in flavor. There is some question about the validity of this labeling, but the flavor is enough of a selling point for me.

SEASONING A STEAK:

**Salt and Black Pepper**: This is the classic and oftentimes the best seasoning for a good cut of meat. It highlights the natural flavor of the meat. A true purist's preference.

**Marinades**: The idea of a marinade is to simultaneously tenderize and flavor meat. Although a good cut of meat does not need much tenderizing, a good flavor can give it a unique appeal. If you are using a tougher cut of meat, it is important to marinate for at least 8 to 12 hours, or longer (see Lime Chipotle Beef Fajitas, page 111). However, if you are just looking for a little flavor, you need only soak the meat for a few hours, allowing the meat to absorb the unique flavors of the marinade.

There are several marinades used here at Waldemar. The Elmores' favorite is the product Allegro, which is made for steak, seafood, and game. It tenderizes a more muscular cut of meat and imparts a tangy and unique taste. Look for it in the meat section of your supermarket.

Another marinade that works well is one that combines Worcestershire sauce, Dijon mustard, a little olive oil, and salt and pepper. You can add spices and herbs if you like, such as cumin, chili powder, oregano, or thyme.

**Rubs**: A rub is a dry mixture of seasonings blended and "rubbed" onto the meat before grilling. The flavor is imparted to the meat during cooking. This is fun to do if your dinner has a regional or ethnic theme, such as Cajun, Tex-Mex, Indian, Jamaican, or Moroccan, just to name a few.

TESTING FOR DONENESS:

This brief chart is a good gauge for testing whether your meat is ready, based on your preference. However, if you have a thinner cut of meat, it is better to test according to the firmness of the flesh. Poke the meat, and if it is tender and yields to your pressure, it is probably rare. If it resists somewhat, it is medium. If it is firm and springy, it is probably well done.

> Rare 140° F
> Medium rare 150° F
> Medium 160° F
> Well done 170° F

# Steak Southwestern Diane                               Serves 4

This is an elegant preparation appropriate for most occasions. The "southwestern" label is due primarily to the cilantro garnish. You can omit the cilantro and use parsley and snipped chives, a more classic garnish. Use a cut of boneless meat, such as top sirloin, tenderloin, or top loin. And this is a delicious preparation for pork, such as a boneless butterfly chop. One of the main flavor points in the sauce is the brandy or cognac, which is absolutely sublime. You can use white wine if you desire (although the taste does not qualify as sublime, it is still very good).

| | |
|---|---|
| 4 boneless beef or pork* steaks, about 6 to 8 ounces each | ¼ cup brandy or cognac |
| Salt and lemon pepper | 1 tablespoon Dijon mustard |
| 4 tablespoons butter or olive oil, divided | 1 tablespoon lemon juice, freshly squeezed |
| ½ cup chopped shallots | 1 teaspoon Worcestershire sauce |
| | ¼ cup beef stock, warm |
| | ¼ cup fresh cilantro, chopped |

Season the meat with salt and lemon pepper. Sauté the meat in 2 tablespoons of the butter or olive oil until browned on both sides and cooked to desired doneness, about 5 minutes for medium rare. Set the meat aside on a warmed plate and pour off any excess liquid from the pan.

Return the pan to the heat, and sauté the shallots in the remaining butter or olive oil. Add the brandy to deglaze. Cook for several minutes, swirling the pan. Meanwhile, whisk the Dijon mustard, lemon juice, and Worcestershire sauce with the warm beef stock. Pour into the pan with the shallots and brandy. Boil for several minutes, scraping up any bits of the beef from the pan. Add the juice released by the resting meat and cilantro and stir to blend.

Pour the hot sauce over the meat and serve immediately.

*If you are using pork, it is important to note that the once firmly held belief that pork must be cooked until dry to protect you from the threat of trichinosis, a deadly parasite found in pork, has been overthrown! This deadly parasite is killed at 137° F. I think pork is perfect when the internal temperature is somewhere between 145° F and 155° F. The center is lightly rosy, and the moistness and flavor are incomparable. Use a meat thermometer to verify the internal temperature before the meat is served. Enjoy this new flavor of pork!

# Barbeque Brisket                                             Serves 6–8

This is Texas, and here in Texas, we do brisket—tender, melt-in-your-mouth brisket unrivaled in quality. And you may be surprised to learn that the oven reveals the best of a brisket, offering a moist, tender, flavorful, versatile dish. You can either sear the meat over a charcoal grill* or use a product called Liquid Smoke mixed with the BBQ sauce. Use the leftovers for chopped beef sandwiches.

There are several important factors involved in producing a juicy, tender, moist brisket. The most important one is to clean the brisket of as much fat as possible. This may take up to 30 minutes. It may seem grueling, but you will be saved the trouble of cutting away the fat when you serve the meat. The remaining factors to remember are the oven temperature and the cooking time. It is essential to slow-cook the meat for at least 35 minutes per pound. It will most likely need more time.

| | |
|---|---|
| 6–8 pounds beef brisket, trimmed of all fat | 1½ cups barbecue sauce |
| Salt and pepper to coat | ½ teaspoon Liquid Smoke (optional) |

Preheat the oven to 275° F. Trim the brisket of as much fat as possible. This will take awhile but is very important. Lightly season the meat with salt and pepper. Lay directly in a roasting pan and set aside. Mix the barbecue sauce and the optional Liquid Smoke. Pour over the meat, cover with aluminum foil, and bake in the oven for 3½ to 4½ hours (approximately 35 minutes per pound). Test the meat after the minimum time has elapsed. It should cut easily.

When done, remove from the heat and let sit for 20 minutes. Slice the meat against the grain and serve. Leftovers can be used for chopped beef sandwiches.

*If you prefer, sear the meat over a charcoal grill, about 5 minutes per side. Remove from grill and place directly into the roasting pan. Cover with the sauce and bake as directed.

# Lime Chipotle Beef Fajitas

Serves 4–6

Not simply a dish of beef, these fajitas rely heavily on the accoutrements served with them. It is, however, very important to have deliciously seasoned meat, grilled just so! We consider this a very Tex-Mex dish, and it has become a tradition here at Waldemar. During summer camp sessions, we have numerous cookouts for the older campers. Fajitas are always the favorite. Another memory of camp and fajitas. . . .

The kitchen serves a picnic lunch for the families of the campers at the end of each term. We affectionately call it the Big Picnic. We have served beef and chicken fajitas for twelve hundred guests. What a production! Try these at home for your next cookout or summer fiesta. Who needs to go out when these are so easy and tasty?

The flavor base is very tangy, utilizing lime and chipotle peppers, which are smoked jalapeños, dried and rehydrated. You can purchase chipotle peppers in adobo sauce, or if you reside in the Southwest area, you can find dried chipotle peppers and rehydrate them yourself, page 39. Beef fajitas typically use the skirt steak. This cut is preferred, although substantial tenderizing is required. For best results, marinate this dish for 12 to 24 hours, turning several times!

| | |
|---|---|
| 1–1½ pounds beef skirt steak | ⅔ cup olive oil |
| ⅓ cup lime juice | ¼ cup fresh cilantro |
| 2 tablespoons soy sauce | 1 onion, julienned |
| 1 teaspoon chipotle pepper purée | 1 bell pepper (red, green, or |
| 1 clove garlic, chopped and salted | yellow), julienned |
| ½ teaspoon salt | |

Place the meat in a heavy-duty zip-closure storage bag. Mix in a medium bowl the lime juice, soy sauce, chipotle purée, garlic, and salt. Slowly whisk in the olive oil and stir in the cilantro. Pour the marinade into the bag with the meat. Zip closed and refrigerate. You should marinate for 12 to 24 hours for best results, although I have had limited success with only 4 hours. The longer marination time helps to tenderize the meat.

To cook the fajitas, prepare an outdoor grill. While the grill is heating, caramelize the onion and bell pepper together. Deglaze with 2 tablespoons of the beef marinade, and cook until it has reduced. Set aside. Cook the meat over hot coals for about 3 to 5 minutes per side for a medium rare finish. It is a very thin cut of meat and will cook rapidly. Adjust time if you prefer it well done.

Remove the meat from the grill. Slicing across the grain, cut into ½-inch thick slices. Toss with the sautéed onions and bell peppers. Serve with the following accoutrements, wrapped in warm corn or flour tortillas.

| | |
|---|---|
| Pico de Gallo, page 9 | Refried Beans, page 76 |
| Guacamole, page 5 | Spanish Rice, page 93 |
| Shredded cheese | Sour cream |
| Salsa, pages 6 and 7 | |

# Chalupas

Ask any Waldemar girl what Saturday lunch is, and she will instantly tell you chalupas! Although I don't think this has been the Saturday lunch since the beginning of Waldemar, it has been for the last twenty to thirty years. That is a pretty good amount of time for a tradition! Chalupas are essentially seasoned meat, refried beans, shredded lettuce, chopped tomatoes and onion, shredded cheese, sour cream, guacamole, and salsa, all built upon a crispy fried flat corn tortilla. You can use all of these ingredients or just the meat, beans, and cheese. The fried tortillas are available at most supermarkets, but we fry ours here. For a lower-fat option, you can bake the tortilla on low heat in the oven until crispy. This is my favorite!

Enjoy this as a meal in itself and let it transport you to Saturdays at Waldemar!

| | |
|---|---|
| 8–12 corn tortillas | 1 teaspoon olive oil |
| 1–2 cups light cooking oil, such as corn or canola | ½ teaspoon cumin |
| | ½–1 teaspoon chili powder |
| 1 pound ground beef | 1 teaspoon tomato paste |
| ½ cup onion | ¼ teaspoon Worcestershire Sauce |
| 2 cloves garlic, chopped | Dash of cayenne pepper (optional) |
| 1–2 teaspoons salt | |

TOPPINGS:

| | |
|---|---|
| Refried Beans, page 76 | Shredded lettuce |
| Shredded cheese, Cheddar or Monterey Jack, or a blend of the two | Sour cream |
| | Guacamole, page 5 |
| Shredded lettuce | Salsa, pages 6 and 7, or your favorite store-bought variety |
| Chopped tomatoes | |

To fry the tortillas, heat the oil in a large skillet. The oil should come about 1 inch up the sides of the skillet. Heat up to about 365° F. Fry one tortilla at a time, cooking for several minutes on each side. Turn over once the edges begin to crisp. Drain on a paper towel. Set aside to cool.

To prepare the meat, cook in a skillet. Drain off the excess oil and remove the meat from the skillet. In the same skillet, sauté the onion and garlic with the salt in the olive oil until the onion is translucent. Return the meat to the skillet. Stir in the cumin, chili powder, tomato paste, Worcestershire sauce, and the optional cayenne pepper. Stir to incorporate, and continue cooking for several minutes on low, allowing the flavors to marry.

ASSEMBLY RECOMMENDATION FOR THE CHALUPAS:

Offer all of the assembly ingredients on the table in separate serving dishes and let everyone build the chalupas to their liking. The traditional order of ingredients, however, goes like this:

Fried corn tortilla, refried beans, meat, cheese, lettuce, tomatoes or pico de gallo, sour cream, and guacamole. Top with salsa, if desired.

# Lasagne Bolognese

The girls love pasta. It has become much more of a mainstay in modern diets. Several years ago, I took a casual poll, asking a variety of campers what they would like to see more of on the menu, and nine out of ten said lasagne. We in the kitchen certainly love to prepare this. It is fantastic and easy to put together ahead of time. Make this for your family, and freeze the leftovers, or eat them during the week. It is rich and satisfying, and surprisingly low in fat. You will notice the use of Monterey Jack cheese, versus the much more traditional mozzarella. Monterey Jack has so much flavor, albeit mild, and it melts beautifully. I find it rivals most of the cheeses that I have ever eaten. You certainly may use mozzarella if you prefer, however, with much the same results.

A trick we have discovered over the years is to use uncooked lasagne noodles. I recommend using an imported variety, however, as they tend to be a little less thick than the American version. The wonder of this method is that the noodles cook in the sauce, absorbing all of the delicious flavors and enhancing the final result. It also cuts down on the preparation time by about half!

There are essentially four parts to a lasagne: the noodles, the sauce, the cheese, and the binding agent, in this case the ricotta cheese. Each is equally important in making this layered Italian casserole.

Serve with Caesar Salad, page 25, and Garlic Bread, page 68.

TO MAKE THE MEAT SAUCE:

1 pound ground beef
½ pound Italian sausage
½ teaspoon fennel seed
¼ teaspoon cracked red pepper
2 tablespoons olive oil
1 cup onion, chopped
4 cloves garlic, chopped
½ cup carrot, chopped

¼ cup celery, chopped
1 teaspoon salt
½ cup white wine
1 tablespoon tomato paste
1 cup chef's-cut tomatoes*
1 bay leaf
Salt and pepper to taste

In a large sauté pan, brown the beef, Italian sausage, fennel seed, and cracked red pepper. Drain off excess liquid, remove the meat from the pan, and set aside.

Sauté the onion, garlic, carrot, and celery with the teaspoon salt in the olive oil until slightly tender, about 5 to 7 minutes. Deglaze with the white wine and simmer until reduced by half. Add the reserved meat and tomato paste. Stir to blend well. Add the chef's-cut tomatoes and the bay leaf and let simmer for about 1½ hours, stirring occasionally. Add a little water if the sauce begins to thicken and stick to the bottom, although the desired sauce should be very thick without much excess liquid. Season to taste with salt and black pepper.

*Chef's cut tomatoes are available canned in any quality supermarket. These are tomatoes that have been peeled and seeded and chopped into one-inch dice.

## TO MAKE THE RICOTTA MIXTURE:

2 cups soft ricotta cheese
1 egg
1 teaspoon salt
¼ teaspoon nutmeg
2 tablespoon freshly grated
  Parmesan or Romano cheese

½ cup Monterey Jack cheese,
  shredded
2 tablespoons fresh basil leaves,
  torn into small pieces

Whisk the egg into the ricotta cheese until well blended. Stir in the salt, nutmeg, grated Parmesan or Romano cheese, shredded Monterey Jack cheese, and the torn basil.

## TO ASSEMBLE THE LASAGNE:

2 tablespoons butter
1 package lasagne noodles
  (uncooked)

2 cups shredded Monterey Jack cheese
½ cup grated Parmesan or
  Romano cheese

Preheat the oven to 375° F. Butter the bottom of a 9 x 13-inch baking dish. Spread about ½ cup of the meat sauce in the bottom of the pan. Layer 4 to 6 noodles over the meat sauce, with the edges just overlapping. Spread half of the ricotta mixture over the noodles. Ladle on one-third of the remaining sauce and spread evenly. Sprinkle on about one-third of the Monterey Jack cheese. Repeat for the second layer. The final layer should consist of only noodles, sauce, and cheese. Sprinkle with the grated Parmesan or Romano cheese and cover with aluminum foil. Place the baking dish on a jellyroll pan and bake in the preheated oven for 45 minutes. Uncover and continue cooking for another 25 to 30 minutes or until the cheese is browned and the lasagne is bubbly. Remove from the oven and let sit about 30 minutes before serving.

# Spaghetti and Meatballs

Serves 4–6

Need I say more? A classic that brings out the child in each of us. Slender spaghetti warmly swathed with rich tomato sauce and big, beefy, yummy meatballs. This is the best. It is, needless to say, a camp favorite.

1 pound spaghetti

## FOR THE SAUCE:

1 onion, chopped
1 carrot, finely chopped or grated
1 rib celery, finely chopped
4 cloves garlic, finely chopped
¼ cup white wine vinegar

1 tablespoon tomato paste
1 28-ounce can Italian tomatoes
1 tablespoon each fresh oregano,
    marjoram, and basil,
    coarsely chopped (optional)
Salt to taste

In a large saucepan over medium-high heat, sauté the onions, carrots, celery, and garlic in the olive oil until the vegetables begin to soften. Deglaze with the vinegar. Let cook until the vinegar has reduced to half its volume. Stir in the tomato paste with the vegetables. Add the Italian tomatoes and cut into smaller pieces. Add the herbs and reduce the heat to low. Continue cooking until the sauce begins to thicken, stirring occasionally. Add ¼ cup water and continue cooking until it thickens. The sauce will turn a deep, reddish-orange color. You can continue this process as long as you desire. The longer it simmers, the richer the sauce's flavor. Continue to tend the sauce, or it will burn and stick to the bottom of the pan.

Season to taste with salt.

## FOR THE MEATBALLS:

1 pound ground beef
¼ pound ground Italian sausage
1 teaspoon salt, or to taste
Dash of cayenne pepper (optional)
2 tablespoons minced onion

1 clove minced garlic
1 teaspoon dried oregano
1 egg
1 teaspoon Worcestershire sauce
½ cup breadcrumbs

Preheat the oven to 350° F. Mix together all the ingredients. Shape into balls about the size of a golf ball. Place on a parchment-lined cookie sheet with sides, and bake for 20 to 30 minutes, or until the meat is cooked through. Remove from the cookie sheet and place into the cooked sauce. Let the sauce continue to simmer while the pasta cooks. Cook the pasta in a pot with 6 quarts of rapidly boiling water, a tablespoon salt, and a tablespoon olive oil. Cook the pasta according to the package instructions until *al dente*.

Serve the sauce and meatballs over the cooked pasta and garnish with freshly grated Parmesan cheese and freshly chopped parsley!

# Meatloaf

This is a wonderful family dish, usually large enough to serve your family and still have enough leftovers for meatloaf-and-ketchup sandwiches the following day! This version has a spicy, zesty bite and is a wonderful variation on the more traditional mixture of ground beef, breadcrumbs, and ketchup. It includes lots of finely chopped vegetables that give a refreshing crunch. (It is important to chop all of the vegetables to a uniform size, about ¼-inch cubes, to ensure consistency in texture.) I think you will find this recipe on your short list of family favorites. Serve with Garlic Mashed Potatoes, page 100, and Sugar Snap Peas, page 80, or Asian Broccoli, page 82.

2 tablespoons olive oil
3–4 cloves garlic, finely chopped
¼ cup leeks, finely chopped
  (the white bulbs only)
½ cup chopped onion
½ cup carrots, finely chopped
¼ cup celery
2 teaspoons salt, or to taste
¼ cup red bell pepper,
  finely chopped
¼ cup yellow bell pepper,
  finely chopped
¼ cup white wine

¼ teaspoon cracked red pepper
½ teaspoon cumin
1 teaspoon fresh oregano, finely
  chopped, OR ½ teaspoon dried
  oregano
3 eggs
½ cup tomato sauce, page 87, or
  your favorite Italian version
½ cup half-and-half
2 pounds ground beef
¾ pound ground breakfast sausage
1 cup breadcrumbs, finely ground
Salt and black pepper to taste

Preheat the oven to 375° F. In a medium skillet over medium-high heat, sauté the garlic in the olive oil until it begins to release its fragrance, about 1 minute. Add the leeks, onion, carrots, and celery. Sauté, stirring occasionally, for 3 to 5 minutes. Add the bell peppers and cook until they just begin to soften, about 4 minutes. Deglaze with the white wine and simmer until reduced, about 5 minutes. Stir in the cracked red pepper, cumin, and oregano. Remove from the heat and allow to cool in the refrigerator for about 30 minutes.

In a small bowl, mix together the eggs, tomato sauce, and the half-and-half. Reserve until the vegetables are cool. Stir in with the vegetables once cool.

In a large mixing bowl, mix the beef and sausage together with your hands. Add the vegetable/egg mixture and continue mixing with your hands. Add the breadcrumbs and knead into the meat mixture. It should be moist, with no loose liquid. If there is any liquid, add more breadcrumbs.

Shape into a log and place in a breadloaf pan. Cover with aluminum foil. Make a water bath by setting the loaf pan in a larger baking dish. Fill the larger dish halfway up with hot water. Place the pans in the preheated oven and cook until the meat has set and reaches 155° F on a meat thermometer, about 50 minutes. Remove from the oven and from the water bath and let sit for 20 minutes before slicing. Serve hot.

# Boeuf Bourguignon Serves 6–8

This dish reflects the rich regional flavors of Burgundy, France. It is essentially a beef stew with red wine, onions, and carrots. The secret to a tender stew is slow simmering—for at least several hours. As comfort food, this dish is unsurpassable. Put the pot on the stove on a cold winter Sunday afternoon and let the warm aroma fill the house. Serve with rice or egg noodles. One of the misconceptions about cooking with wine is that you can use a cheap bottle with no real detriment to your dish. The truth is that the better the wine, the better the dish, especially when so much of the flavor is contingent on the wine, as in this dish. A rich, robust Burgundy wine is your best option.

| | |
|---|---|
| 1 750-milliliter bottle Burgundy or good-quality red wine | 4 slices bacon, sliced into ½-inch pieces |
| 2 onions, diced | ¼ cup flour |
| 2 carrots, sliced | 2 tablespoons tomato paste |
| 1 bulb garlic, coarsely chopped | 2 cups chopped fresh tomatoes, seeded |
| 2 tablespoons fresh thyme, removed from the stem and coarsely chopped | 6 cups beef stock |
| 2 tablespoons parsley, coarsely chopped | 1 pound button mushrooms, whole, halved, or quartered depending on size |
| 3 pounds stew meat | 1 cup pearl onions, ends trimmed and peeled |
| 1 tablespoon olive oil | |

Make a marinade with the red wine, onions, garlic, thyme, and parsley. Salt and pepper the meat cubes well and pour the marinade over the meat. Let sit in the refrigerator from 4 hours to 24 hours, the longer the better. Remove the meat from the marinade and pat dry. Drain the marinade from the vegetables. Reserve the vegtables for sautéing and reserve the liquid to add to the stew.

In a large stockpot, sauté the bacon in the olive oil on low heat until it renders some of the fat, about 10 minutes. Remove the bacon and set aside, leaving the oil in the pan. Turn the heat up to medium-high, and brown the meat on all sides in batches, removing once done.

Sauté the marinated vegetables in the pan until lightly browned, about 5 minutes. Stir in the flour and continue cooking, stirring constantly. Add the meat and the tomato paste. Stir to coat. Pour in the reserved marinade and the bacon. Reduce the heat to low, and simmer for about 20 minutes, or until it begins to reduce, stirring occasionally.

Add the tomatoes. Add ½ cup of the beef stock at a time, letting it reduce for several minutes before adding more stock. Stir occasionally. Cook for about 2 hours on low, adding water if necessary. Add the mushrooms and pearl onions. Cook for another 45 minutes to an hour. The total cooking time will be about 3 hours. Serve over rice, egg noodles, or boiled new potatoes, along with a simple green salad and good crusty French bread.

# Venison Chili

Here at Waldemar, there is no debate about chili with or without beans. Being true to Texas, the state of its origin, of course chili has no beans! It is straight meat, unless you want to make a vegetarian version—then it is all beans! But this recipe is for the consumer of *carne*. Make this recipe with a tougher cut of meat, such as chuck or shoulder meat. It will simmer for a while, giving this more flavorful meat a chance to break into tender flakes when eaten.

This recipe calls for Venison stew meat, a regional delicacy. Venison is lean, with a distinct flavor. The Broken Arrow Ranch in Ingram, Texas, supplies much of the game meat for top restaurants all over the United States. If your local butcher does not stock venison, the next time you are in the Hill Country, try to pick up a few pounds of venison to have on hand.

2½–3 pounds chuck venison, cut into
    1-inch cubes
2 tablespoons flour
¼ cup olive oil
1 large onion, chopped
2–4 cloves garlic, chopped
1–6 jalapeños, chopped (seeding is
    optional and the quantity varies
    depending on the heat desired)
1 tablespoon chili powder
2 tablespoons cumin powder

1 tablespoon tomato paste
1 bottle of beer (your favorite
    brand)
1 28-ounce can of crushed tomatoes
1½ teaspoons salt
½ teaspoon cayenne
Shredded Cheddar cheese,
    to garnish
Red or green onion, chopped,
    to garnish

In a large stockpot over medium-high heat, brown the meat. Remove the meat from the pot, drain off the excess liquid, and toss with the flour. Set aside.

In the same stockpot, add the oil. Sauté the onion, garlic, and jalapeños for 5 minutes, or until the onion begins to lose its color. Stir in the chili powder, cumin, and tomato paste until evenly distributed. Add the reserved meat and slowly stir in the beer. Lower the heat and let simmer until the beer has reduced in volume by half, about 7 to 8 minutes. Add the crushed tomatoes, salt, and cayenne, and stir to combine. Continue to simmer for another 2 to 2½ hours, adding water as necessary, as it will reduce in volume as it simmers. Season to taste with salt if necessary.

Serve with rice and garnish with shredded Cheddar cheese and chopped red or green onion.

# Beef Stroganoff

A hearty meal that is one of Waldemar owner Marsha Elmore's favorites. This is her special recipe, and she was very excited to share it with all of you!

2 pounds boneless beef
    (sirloin or tenderloin)
½ cup flour
1 teaspoon salt
⅛ teaspoon black pepper
⅓ cup olive oil
½ cup onion, finely chopped

3 tablespoons butter
2 cups beef stock
8 ounces mushrooms, sliced
1 cup sour cream
3 tablespoons tomato paste
1 teaspoon Worcestershire sauce
1 pound egg noodles

Cut meat into ½-inch slices, about 2 inches long. Mix together the flour, salt, and pepper. Dredge the meat in the flour to coat. In a large skillet, cook the floured meat in the olive oil over moderate heat until brown. Remove the meat from the pan and set aside. Add the onions to the pan with 1 tablespoon butter. Sauté until soft, about 5 minutes, stirring often. Return the beef to the skillet. Add the beef stock to the pan, ½ cup at a time. Stir to blend. Cover the mixture and let simmer for about 20 minutes, or until the meat is tender.

In a small skillet, sauté the mushrooms until lightly browned. Set aside.

Once the meat is cooked, mix together the sour cream, tomato paste, Worcestershire sauce, and ½ cup of the cooking liquid. Stir until smooth. Add to the beef mixture with the mushrooms. Simmer, but do not boil. Serve over egg noodles.

# Pork with Figs and Thyme

This is one of many recipes contributed by Roy Spears. It is a delightful combination of sweet and savory, a succulent meal of transcendent flavors. Combining the richness of red wine, honey, and figs with the savory earthiness of the shallots and mushrooms, this is an unforgettable meal. We serve it here as a mainstay of quality and variety. It is that good! Serve with the Wild Rice Pilaf, page 94, and Sugar Snap Peas, page 80, or Steamed Green Beans, and of course, buttery dinner rolls, page 62.

| | |
|---|---|
| 1 750-milliliter bottle red wine | ¼ cup shallots, chopped |
| ¼ cup honey | ¼ cup red wine vinegar |
| 2 packages dried figs, stems removed, cut into quarters | 1 pound button mushrooms, sliced |
| | 1 cup roma tomatoes, chopped |
| 4 3-inch sprigs fresh thyme | ¼ cup chicken stock |
| 2 whole pork tenderloins | 2 tablespoons fresh basil, julienned |
| Salt and pepper to taste | 2 tablespoons parsley, chopped |
| 3 tablespoons olive oil, divided | Salt and pepper to taste |
| 2–4 cloves garlic, coarsely chopped | |

Preheat the oven to 350° F. In a medium saucepan, combine the red wine, honey, dried figs, and fresh thyme sprigs and simmer over medium-low heat for about an hour. Once done, strip the thyme leaves from the stems and return the leaves to the mixture. Set aside.

Season the pork tenderloin with salt and pepper to taste. In a large skillet with a tablespoon of oil, brown the pork tenderloin on all sides. Remove from the heat and lay in a roasting pan. Reserve the skillet and the pork drippings for the sauce. Place the meat in the preheated oven and cook the meat until its internal temperature reads 145° F. Remove from the oven, cover with foil, and set aside until the sauce is complete.

While the meat is baking, sauté the garlic and shallots in the remaining 2 tablespoons of oil. Cook until the aroma is released, about 3 to 5 minutes, stirring constantly. Add the red wine vinegar to deglaze, and cook until it has reduced to a thick glaze. Add the mushrooms, and continue cooking until they have wilted, another 7 minutes or so. Stir in the tomatoes, and simmer until softened. Add the chicken stock and simmer until reduced in volume and thick, about 10 minutes. Add the fig/red wine mixture. Continue cooking to desired thickness, another 10 minutes.

Slice the meat into 1-inch-thick medallions and arrange as a fan on a platter. Ladle the sauce over the meat and serve immediately. Wonderful!

# Hoisin Pork Tenderloin

Serves 6–8

Sweet and tangy, this Asian-inspired dish has received top ratings from guests here at Waldemar. The taste is so fantastic, you will be surprised at what little effort it requires. I recommend grilling. Any other method really doesn't do justice to the potential flavor. Several ingredients may be difficult to find, but most grocery stores will commonly stock them. There unfortunately aren't any common American substitutes for hoisin sauce, sesame oil, or rice wine vinegar, so if you can't locate a specific item, ask your grocer to stock it.

1 cup hoisin sauce
4 cloves fresh garlic, finely minced
1 inch fresh ginger, peeled and freshly grated
¼ teaspoon toasted sesame oil

2 tablespoons tamari or good-quality soy sauce
1 teaspoon rice wine vinegar
2 whole pork tenderloins

Whisk together the hoisin sauce, fresh garlic and ginger, sesame oil, tamari, and rice wine vinegar. Place the meat and sauce mixture in a zip-closure plastic bag and marinate overnight, or at least 4 hours.

Prepare an outdoor charcoal or gas grill, and cook the meat over hot coals, basting with the marinade and turning frequently to prevent burning, until the internal temperature reaches 145° F. Remove from the grill and let sit for 10 minutes before cutting, to allow the juices to evenly distribute. The internal heat will continue to rise. Slice into 1-inch-thick medallions and serve.

# Ham and Cheese Quiche

Serves 6–8

This is a classic brunch or luncheon offering, light yet satisfying. Best when made with Gruyère cheese, you can substitute Swiss if it is not available. Traditionally, this recipe is made in a ceramic quiche dish with low, fluted sides. If doubling this recipe for a large group, bake in a jellyroll pan and cut the quiche into squares.

½ recipe Pastry Dough, page 155
3 large eggs
1½ cups half-and-half cream
½ teaspoon salt
Dash black pepper, or to taste
Pinch of nutmeg (optional)

1 tablespoon olive oil
¼ cup chopped leek, the white part only
1 cup ham, cut into small cubes
1 cup Gruyère cheese, grated

Preheat the oven to 375° F. Lay the crust in a 9-inch pie dish. Set aside. In a medium bowl, whisk together the eggs. Add the cream, salt, pepper, and optional nutmeg. In a sauté pan, cook the leek over medium heat until it releases its fragrance. Lay the cheese in the bottom of the crust-lined quiche dish. Evenly layer the sautéed leeks over the cheese and top with the ham. Slowly pour the egg and milk mixture over the filling. Bake in the preheated oven for about 30 to 45 minutes. It is ready when the center is firm and the top is golden brown. Remove from the oven and let cool to room temperature.

# Posole: A Pork and Hominy Stew

Serves 6–8

Waldemar has always been blessed with a loyal and true staff who are competent and qualified and simply wonderful. It is more like a family than a group of employees. I was so blessed to be part of this family and to grow in respect and love for my fellow staff. This recipe is a reflection of the cultural diversity found here at Waldemar. Many of our employees have come from Mexico, our neighbor to the south, and with them they have brought a vast culture that is richly different from our own, with flavors such as spicy pasilla chili purée, hominy, green chilies, and cilantro. Serve posole for a winter meal and feel as warm and brilliant as a summer Waldemar day. Serve with an arugula salad and crusty French rolls.

1 tablespoon olive oil
¾ pound boneless pork, cut into cubes
½ teaspoon salt
3 tablespoons pasilla chili purée, page 39, divided
2 cloves garlic, coarsely chopped
1 small onion, cut into ½-inch dice
2 roma tomatoes, chopped

2 15½ ounce cans golden hominy, drained
½ teaspoon cumin
½ cup chopped green chilies, peeled and seeded
2 cups hot chicken broth
¾ cup chopped cilantro (optional)
Salt to taste

In a 4-quart soup pot, sauté the pork cubes in the olive oil. Sprinkle with the ½ teaspoon salt, and cook until the pork is brown on all sides. Stir in 1 tablespoon of the pasilla chili purée, remove from the pan, and set aside.

In the same pan, sauté the garlic and onion until the garlic releases its fragrance and the onion has softened, about 5 minutes. Add the tomatoes and cook until they soften, about 3 to 5 minutes, stirring occasionally. Return the meat to the pot. Add the hominy, cumin, remaining 2 tablespoons of pasilla chili purée, green chilies, and the chicken stock. Reduce the heat to low and simmer for about 20 minutes. Season with salt to taste.

Just before serving, stir in the optional cilantro. Store in the refrigerator for up to two days, or freeze for up to three months.

# Poultry

## King Ranch Chicken

Serves 6-8

The ultimate in chicken casseroles. The ultimate in comfort food. The ultimate in camp food. Quite simply, the ultimate Waldemar dish. This is an adaptation of the renowned King Ranch Chicken Casserole. Roy Spears makes the best version I have ever had, rich and creamy and so very good. If you have had it before, you know what I mean. If you haven't, try it. You may find that this will become a new family favorite. Serve with a good green salad, ranch dressing, green beans, and plenty of rolls. This dish freezes beautifully. Bake in a disposable foil pan. Let cool completely, cover with plastic wrap and aluminum foil, refrigerate overnight, and freeze for up to three months.

1 cup chicken stock
1½ cups chopped onion
2 10.75 ounce cans cream of chicken
   and mushroom soup
1½ cups Rotel tomatoes (liquid drained
   off before measuring)

½ cup chopped green chilies
2 cups sliced fresh mushrooms
18 small flour tortillas
4 cups cooked chicken, torn into
   bite-sized chunks
4 cups grated Cheddar cheese

Preheat the oven to 325° F. In a saucepan over medium heat, combine the chicken stock and onion. Simmer until the onion has softened, about 10 minutes. Add the cream of chicken and mushroom soup, the Rotel tomatoes, the green chilies, and the mushrooms. Stir until combined and heated through. Remove from the heat.

In a 9 x 13-inch glass baking dish, butter the bottom and sides. Lay 6 tortillas across the bottom, with the sides of the dish partially covered. Begin layering the ingredients by first spreading half of the chicken, about 2 cups, over the tortillas. Gently ladle half of the sauce over the chicken and sprinkle with half of the cheese. Repeat the layering of tortillas, chicken, sauce, and cheese. End with the remaining 6 tortillas. Cover with foil and bake in the oven for an hour. Remove the foil and continue to bake until the tortillas are crisp and the sauce is bubbling, about 10 to 15 minutes.

Remove from the oven and let sit for 15 minutes before serving.

# Chicken Enchiladas with Verde Sauce

Serves 6–8

A delightful variation on the traditional beef enchiladas. Clean and light, this is a delicious summer dish. A little spicy and full of south of the border flavors, serve this with the Monterrey Salad, page 26, and Black Beans, page 76, for an exceptional evening. Note that the recipe calls for one to two jalapeños, to be cooked whole with the tomatillos. These are for spicy heat. If you don't want a spicy dish, you can leave them out, although I feel that the spice balances the flavor.

TOMATILLO SAUCE:
- 4 cups fresh tomatillos, peeled, rinsed and quartered
- 1 small onion, chopped
- 4 cloves garlic, coarsely chopped
- 1–2 whole jalapeños, stems snapped off (optional)
- 1 chicken bouillon cube
- 1 cup fresh cilantro, chopped
- 2 tablespoons Ancho Chili Purée, page 39
- Salt and pepper, to taste

ENCHILADAS:
- 1 cup corn or canola oil
- 18 corn tortillas
- 1 small onion, diced finely
- ½ cup green chilies, diced
- ½ teaspoon cumin
- Salt to taste
- 2 cups cooked chicken meat, torn into pieces (meat from a whole fryer)
- 1 tablespoon Ancho Chili Purée (see page 39)
- ½ cup fresh cilantro, chopped
- 3 cups grated Monterey Jack cheese
- 1 ripe avocado, peeled and thinly sliced (optional garnish)

Preheat the oven to 350° F. To make the sauce, cover the tomatillos, onion, garlic, jalapeños, and the bouillon cube with 4 cups water. Bring to a boil and cook until the jalapeños are soft, about 15 minutes. Remove from the heat and purée in batches in either a food processor or a blender. Return the purée to the cooking pan and season with salt. Stir in 2 tablespoons ancho chili purée and 1 cup cilantro until combined and set aside.

To prepare the tortillas,* line a plate with paper towels. Heat the cup of oil in an 8-inch skillet. Quickly dip a corn tortilla in the oil and cook for about 15 seconds, or until the tortilla begins to curl. Quickly turn over and cook another 10 to 15 seconds. Remove to the paper towels to drain. Pat dry with extra paper towels if necessary to remove any excess oil. Repeat until all of the tortillas are soft-fried.

To prepare the filling, caramelize the onion in a sauté pan. Stir in the green chilies, cumin, and salt. Add the torn chicken and a tablespoon of ancho chili purée. Cook for several minutes to heat the chicken through. Remove from the heat. Stir in the ½ cup cilantro and 2 cups of grated cheese.

Prepare a 9 x 13-inch baking dish by spreading about 1 cup of the tomatillo-ancho sauce evenly across the bottom. To roll the enchiladas, place a long piece of plastic wrap on a clean work surface. Place a soft-fried tortilla on the surface and 2 tablespoons of the chicken and cheese filling in the center. Roll up into a long, tubular roll and place in the baking dish, seam down. Repeat with all of the tortillas, placing them closely, side by side. Evenly spread enough sauce to cover and sprinkle with the remaining cup of cheese.

Cover with aluminum foil and bake for about 30 minutes, or until the enchiladas are bubbling. Remove the foil for the last 5 to 10 minutes of baking time if you prefer the cheese to brown. Serve hot with avocado slices as a garnish.

*This process not only enhances the flavor of the tortilla, but it also stabilizes the tortilla and prevents splitting once you begin to roll the enchilada.

# Fried Chicken                                               Serves 2–4

Sunday afternoons at Camp Waldemar. I can think of no stronger memories. Do you remember those days? Ah, I can still smell the aroma of fried chicken wafting from the kitchen, filling the air with a richness resplendent with love as we walked back from the Sunday church service. Impatience for the meal ran thick as we sat on the porch or filled the spaces on the rock wall, waiting, waiting, until finally the second soupy bugle rang and the doors swung open. With brisk politeness, we scurried to the empty places, eyes fixed on the plates filled with homemade fried chicken. Prayer was sung in beautiful harmony, announcements were quickly made, and lunch was underway, a mealtime full of music from the Counselor Jazz Band.

This recipe requires a little planning and effort, and a lot of love, which I call for as a special ingredient. Only one whole frying chicken is called for, but you can expand this recipe to provide for leftovers. This is a great meal for a picnic or backyard party, or anytime for an excuse to remember Sundays at Waldemar.

1 whole fryer chicken, cut into pieces
2 cups buttermilk
4 cups warm water
½ teaspoon cayenne pepper
2 tablespoons salt
1 tablespoon black pepper
1 tablespoon Worcestershire sauce
2 tablespoons baking powder

3 cups unbleached flour
2 tablespoons salt
1 teaspoon cayenne pepper
1 tablespoon black pepper
4–6 eggs
Several ounces of love mixed in with your effort (this is a very special ingredient)
Canola oil for frying

Rinse chicken and pat dry. Remove any excess fat, keeping the skin intact, and place in a large bowl. Mix together the buttermilk, warm water, cayenne pepper, salt, black pepper, and Worcestershire sauce. Pour the marinade over the chicken and refrigerate for at least 4 hours, preferably overnight.

Pour at least two inches of canola oil into a large cast-iron skillet or Dutch oven. Heat until it reaches about 350° F on an instant-read thermometer. Prepare a rack set over a cookie sheet to drain the cooked chicken for a crispier finish. Sift together the flour, baking powder, salt, cayenne pepper, and black pepper. In a separate bowl, whisk together the eggs. Remove the chicken from the buttermilk marinade. Dip into the egg, and dredge into the flour mixture until all sides are coated. Set aside and repeat with all the chicken. Immediately fry in the hot oil until the chicken is golden brown and crispy. Remove and let drain on several layers of paper towels for a minute. Set on the roasting rack and hold in a 200° F oven until all the meat is done. Serve warm!

# Pecan-Crusted Chicken                              Serves 4

A wonderful sweet and savory dish, using the favorite Texas nut. The pecan is so versatile. It makes for an elegant crust, full of flavor, and tantalizing smells. The sauce offers the sweetness of a southern caramel sauce mixed with an Asian tang. This is an elegant dish. At Waldemar, we consider ourselves lucky, as there are many mature pecan trees that yield an annual bumper crop of the best nut in the world!

4 boneless chicken breasts
1 cup buttermilk
3 teaspoons salt, divided
½ teaspoon black pepper,
     finely ground

¼ teaspoon cayenne pepper
4 cups pecans, finely chopped

Wash and pat dry the chicken. Combine the buttermilk, 2 teaspoons of the salt, black pepper, and cayenne. Marinate the meat in the mixture for at least 4 hours.

Preheat the oven to 350° F. Mix a teaspoon of salt and pepper with the finely chopped pecans. Roll the marinated chicken breasts in the pecans and set aside on wax paper. Once all are covered, repeat the process in the pecans to fully cover.

Sauté the chicken in a large skillet with a little oil to set the pecans, about 3 minutes per side. Finish cooking the chicken in the preheated oven for another 10 to 15 minutes, or until the chicken is cooked through. Make the sauce while the chicken is cooking.

### Ginger Caramel Sauce

1 cup chicken stock
1 cup brown sugar
1 inch fresh ginger, grated
1 clove garlic, minced

½ teaspoon salt, or to taste
2 tablespoons cornstarch
4 tablespoons water
1 tablespoon fresh basil, torn

In a small saucepan over medium-high heat, bring the chicken stock, brown sugar, ginger, garlic, and salt to a boil. Lower the heat of the sauce. In a small bowl, measure the cornstarch and slowly add 4 tablespoons of water, whisking in 1 tablespoon at a time until smooth. Slowly stir ¼ cup of the sauce into the cornstarch mixture. Stir to combine and add to the remaining sauce. Continue cooking over low heat until the sauce has thickened to a syrup-like consistency. Stir in the basil and serve over the pecan-crusted chicken.

# Grilled Chicken Sandwich

This is one of those recipes that is so easy and so flavorful, you may wonder why you have never made it before. I first made these sandwiches one summer for a counselor cookout at Waldemar. They were served alongside regular beef burgers for the non-beefeaters, and they were so popular that we quickly ran out of them. Well, the next year we had plenty. The longer the chicken marinates, the better the flavor. The chicken is so good, in fact, that you needn't serve it only as a sandwich. Try serving with Grilled Vegetable Kebabs, page 84, and Rosemary-Roasted New Potatoes, page 100, for fresh summer fare.

4–6 boneless, skinless
   chicken breasts
2 cups Worcestershire sauce
1 cup brown sugar

1 teaspoon salt
½ teaspoon black pepper
¼ cup lemon juice
2–4 cloves fresh garlic, minced

Wash the chicken and pat dry. Mix together the Worcestershire sauce, brown sugar, salt, black pepper, lemon juice and minced garlic. Marinate the chicken in the refrigerator for 4 to 6 hours. Cook over a prepared grill until firm and meat reaches 165° F on a meat thermometer.

Serve on a kaiser roll with garlic mayonnaise, page 36, lettuce, tomato, Monterey Jack cheese, optional pickled jalapeños, and crisp bacon slices.

# Chicken Fajitas

Serves 4–6

Possibly more popular with the girls than the beef version, so we always serve both chicken and beef fajitas for our cookouts. This simple marinade is full of south-of-the-border flavors. Serve traditional-style with all the fixin's. Tex-Mex at its finest.

I always salt the garlic about 10 minutes prior to mixing with the other ingredients. This draws out the bitter juices and enhances the flavor.

This dish is definitely best cooked on a grill. The charcoal flavor is a very important traditional element.

| | |
|---|---|
| 4–6 boneless, skinless chicken breasts | 2 cloves garlic |
| ⅔ cup fresh lime juice | 1⅓ cup olive oil |
| ½ teaspoon cumin powder | 1 onion, julienned |
| ½ teaspoon cayenne pepper | 1 roasted poblano pepper, peeled, seeded, and julienned |
| 2 teaspoons salt | 1 tablespoon fresh lemon juice |
| 2 tablespoon honey | |

Wash the chicken and pat dry. Set aside.

In a medium bowl, whisk together the lime juice, cumin powder, cayenne pepper, salt, honey, and garlic. Slowly whisk in the olive oil. Marinate the chicken in the refrigerator for 6 to 8 hours. The longer the better!

Sauté the onions over medium heat until caramelized. Add the roasted poblano slices and 1 tablespoon fresh lemon juice. Set aside.

Cook the meat over a hot grill until firm, about 165° F on a meat thermometer. Slice into ½-inch-thick slices and toss with the reserved onion mixture. Serve with warmed corn and flour tortillas, Black Beans, page 76, Pico de Gallo, page 9, Guacamole, page 5, shredded Monterey Jack cheese, and sour cream.

# Grilled Cornish Game Hen
# with Rosemary and Lemon

Serves 4

We have served this successfully for our conference groups, and it always goes over wonderfully for an outdoor grilling party. Easy to prepare and delicious to eat, this is a summer must. You can use chicken just as successfully. Wonderful accompanied with green beans and Wild Rice Pilaf, page 94.

2 tablespoons fresh rosemary
1 tablespoon fresh parsley
2 cloves garlic, minced
2 Cornish game hens, split,
   with skins intact

4 tablespoons butter, softened
½ teaspoon salt
Salt and pepper
½ cup fresh lemon juice

Finely chop the rosemary, parsley, and garlic. Mix in with the softened butter and the salt. Wash the hens and pat dry. Spread the butter and herb mixture under the skins, seeking to cover as much of the meat as possible. Salt and pepper the skins.

Cook over a prepared charcoal grill, basting with the lemon juice regularly until the meat is firm and the juice runs clear when the meat is pierced. It should read 165° F on a meat thermometer. Serve hot!

You may also cook this dish in the oven. Preheat the oven to 350° F and roast the birds in a roasting dish for 30 to 45 minutes, or until the internal heat registers 165° F. Remove and serve hot!

Will, the Cook

# Herb-Roasted Cornish Game Hens

Serves 4

This dish is made with a mixture of herbs known as *Herbes de Provence,* commonly used in French provincial cooking. You can find this mixture ready-made at most gourmet supermarkets, but you can make you own mix with just as much ease. The recipe is included. Serve with Garlic Mashed Potatoes, page 100, and Pan-Seared Tomatoes, page 86.

| | |
|---|---|
| 2 Cornish game hens, split | ¼ cup olive oil |
| 4 tablespoons butter, softened | Salt and pepper to taste |
| 2 cloves garlic, minced | ¼ cup *Herbes de Provence* |
| ½ teaspoon salt | (recipe below) |

Preheat oven to 350° F. Rinse the birds and pat dry. Set aside.

Mash the butter, garlic, and salt together to form a paste. Spread this mixture under the skins of the hens. Rub the skins with olive oil in. Sprinkle on the salt and pepper and rub into the skins to evenly distribute. Lightly pat the herb mixture onto the skins of the chicken to cover. Bake on a roasting pan in the preheated oven until the meat is firm and the juices run clear when pierced, about 35 to 40 minutes.

### Herbes de Provence

Please note that this is only one combination of herbs available. Others include summer savory, lavender bay leaves, and/or parsley.

| | |
|---|---|
| 1 tablespoon dried thyme | 1 tablespoon dried oregano |
| 1 tablespoon dried marjoram | ¼ teaspoon white pepper |
| 1 tablespoon dried rosemary | ¼ teaspoon dried coriander |
| 1 tablespoon dried tarragon | |

Mix together and store in an airtight container.

# Spinach-Stuffed Chicken

Serves 4

David Johnson made this one year for the conclusion of Mother-Daughter Weekend on Mother's Day. I thought it was perfect. A tangy, savory, colorful blend of flavors and textures. Serve with Rice Florentine, page 93, Glazed Carrots, page 85, and dinner rolls, page 62.

| | |
|---|---|
| 6 chicken thighs, skins on | ¼ cup loosely packed fresh |
| 2 tablespoons olive oil | basil leaves |
| 2 cloves fresh garlic, finely chopped | 8 ounces goat cheese |
| 1 tablespoon salt, divided | 1 tablespoon walnut oil |
| 8 ounces baby spinach leaves | 3 tablespoons fresh lemon juice |

Preheat the oven to 350° F. Wash the chicken and pat dry. Sauté the garlic with ½ teaspoon salt in the olive oil until it begins to release its fragrance. Add the spinach and basil and cook until it is bright green and wilted, about 3 to 5 minutes. Remove from the heat. Spoon 2 tablespoons of goat cheese under the skin and spread evenly. Then layer the wilted spinach and basil under the skin of each chicken. Salt and pepper the outside of the chicken.

Whisk together the walnut oil, lemon juice, and the remaining ½ teaspoon of salt. Baste over the chicken.

Bake in the oven for 30 to 40 minutes, basting with the walnut oil/lemon juice vinaigrette every 10 minutes. When ready, the chicken should be firm and the juices should run clear when pierced. The meat thermometer should read 165° F.

# Chicken and Asparagus Crêpes                 Serves 6–8

A light summertime favorite. I have included a recipe for homemade crêpes, which are a challenge only for the first two or three crêpes. After you get the hang of the thickness and timing, they are extremely gratifying to make. If you decide to make them at home, I highly recommend purchasing a traditional crêpe pan (see page viii). But if you need to save time, you can usually find crêpes in the frozen section of any good market. This recipe is very mild and is a good start for savory crêpes. It is an elegant dish that appeals to most palettes. Serve with a dressed salad of mixed greens, page 26, and steamed asparagus.

## Crêpes

| | |
|---|---|
| 2 eggs, beaten | Pinch of salt |
| 1 cup milk | 1 tablespoon butter, melted |
| 1 cup all-purpose flour | |

To make the crêpes, whisk the eggs and milk in a mixing bowl. Gradually whisk in the flour and salt until a smooth consistency. Add the melted butter and whisk until smooth. Set aside for 30 minutes to allow the batter to thicken. To cook, heat your skillet on high heat. Melt a small amount of butter. Add about ¼ cup of batter, just enough to very thinly cover the bottom of the pan. Cook for about a minute. Remove from the pan and repeat with the remaining batter. Layer a piece of wax paper between each crêpe. Set aside until ready to roll.

SAVORY FILLING:

| | |
|---|---|
| 2 cups cooked chicken, chopped | 2 teaspoons salt |
| 2 cups asparagus, cooked until tender | 4 cups Cheese Sauce (recipe follows) |
| 2 tablespoons minced onion | Several sprigs fresh parsley, chopped |

Preheat the oven to 350° F. Place the chicken, asparagus, and onion in a food processor with ½ cup of the sauce. Purée until smooth.

In a 9 x 13-inch glass baking dish, spread about 1 cup sauce thinly on the bottom. Place 2 tablespoons of the chicken-asparagus mixture into each crêpe and roll like a cigar. Place the rolled crêpe seam side down, and repeat until the pan is filled. Cover with the remaining sauce and bake uncovered for 20 to 30 minutes, or until brown and bubbling.

## Cheese Sauce

This sauce begins with a classic béchamel or white sauce. It gains its distinctive flavor from the rich cheese.

½ cup unsalted butter
½ cup flour
4 cups milk
Salt and pepper to taste

1 teaspoon Dijon mustard
½ cup Parmesan cheese
¼ cup Swiss or Gruyère cheese

Melt the butter in a saucepan. Stir in the flour until fully blended. Slowly add the milk, about 1 ounce at a time. Stir in with each addition until absorbed. The mixture will clump when you first add the milk. As you continue adding the milk, however, it will smooth out to a velvety sauce. As it begins to smooth out, you can add the milk in larger quantities.

Stir in the mustard and cheeses until melted. Adjust the flavor with salt and pepper.

# Chicken Pot Pie                                   Serves 4–6

A simple and enduring classic. A favorite with the summer campers. Treat your family to the warm richness of this wonderful, hearty dish. The recipe calls for chicken, but it can be made with equal success using leftover turkey. It also gives directions for poached chicken, using the poaching liquid in the cream sauce. You can substitute with 4 cups of leftover chicken, cubed, and canned chicken stock. Rather than using pie crust, this top-crust-only pot pie uses puff pastry. This product is available in the freezer section of your favorite grocery store. It puffs up in multiple buttery layers, a crisp and tantalizing beginning to a wholesome family meal.

1 whole fryer chicken, in pieces
    (yields about 4 cups
    poached chicken meat)*
6 cups cold water
4 tablespoons butter
½ cup all-purpose flour
2 cups liquid from poaching chicken
    or chicken stock*
1½ cups whole milk
Salt and pepper to taste
2 tablespoons olive oil
2–4 cloves garlic, finely chopped

½ teaspoon salt
1 onion, cut into ½-inch dice
2 carrots, cut into ½-inch dice
2 celery stalks, cut into ½-inch dice
¼ cup white wine
8 ounces mushrooms, sliced
¾ cup green peas
1 tablespoon fresh Italian parsley,
    chopped
1 sheet puff pastry
Egg wash (1 tablespoon cold water

TO ASSEMBLE THE POT PIE:

Preheat oven to 350° F. In a 4-quart saucepan, melt the butter over medium heat. Stir in the flour until well mixed and cook for a minute, stirring constantly. Remove from the heat and slowly stir in the 2 cups of chicken stock until smooth. Return to the heat and whisk in the milk, stirring constantly until the mixture thickens to coat the back of a spoon. It should be the consistency of cream gravy. Season with salt and pepper to taste. Stir in the chicken pieces and set aside.

In a sauté pan, sauté the garlic and ½ teaspoon of salt in 1 tablespoon of the olive oil until the fragrance is released, about 3 to 5 minutes. Add the onion, carrots, and celery. Cook until the vegetables begin to soften, another 5 to 7 minutes. Deglaze with the white wine, and let simmer until the liquid has reduced. Remove from the pan. Sauté the sliced mushrooms in the remaining tablespoon of olive oil until they soften, about 3 minutes. Add the sautéed vegetable mixture, the sautéed mushrooms, the peas, and the Italian parsley to the creamed chicken mixture.

To prepare the cooking dish, lay the puff pastry on a clean work surface lined with plastic wrap. Invert a three-quart baking dish onto the puff pastry and cut out an inch away from the bowl's edge, following the shape of the bowl. Fill the bowl with the creamed chicken mixture and lay the crust on top, being careful not to stretch the dough. Pinch the edges of the crust as you would a pie. To make a decorative border, you can cut out leaves or twist together long, 1-inch-wide strips to form a braided border. Brush the pastry with the egg wash. Bake in the preheated oven on the middle rack until the crust is firm to the touch and golden brown, between 40 and 50 minutes.

*TO POACH THE CHICKEN:

In a large stockpot, cover the chicken with 6 cups cold water. Bring to a low simmer and poach until the chicken is done, or when liquid runs clear when pierced. Remove from the poaching liquid and set aside until cool enough to handle. Remove the meat from the bone and return the bones to the poaching liquid. Cut the meat into bite-sized chunks and set aside. Continue cooking the poaching stock until the liquid has reduced and the color is a rich golden yellow, at least 30 minutes. The longer it simmers the better. This is a step that can be done a day in advance. Discard the skin and bones. Reserve 2 cups of the poaching liquid for the next step. The remaining stock can be frozen in an ice cube tray reserved for this purpose. Once frozen, remove and store in a labeled and dated zip-closure plastic freezer bag. These 1-ounce cubes are perfect for enhancing many dishes.

# Chicken Spaghetti

Serves 6–8

This dish of comfort food combines simplicity with flavor, and was Marsha Elmore's mother's favorite. Serve with a simple green salad and Monkey Bread, page 64. This is a perfect way to use leftover chicken or turkey.

1 pound spaghetti or vermicelli pasta
3 cups cooked chicken or turkey meat, torn into bite-sized pieces
4 cloves garlic, chopped
1 cup onion, chopped
½ cup celery, chopped
1 teaspoon salt
8 ounces button mushrooms, coarsely chopped

1 ounce cognac, brandy, sherry, or whiskey (your preference)
½ cup green onions, chopped
2 cups Chicken Cream Sauce (see recipe below)
3 cups grated Monterey Jack cheese
1 cup freshly grated Parmesan cheese, divided
Salt and pepper to taste

Preheat oven to 350° F. Dot the bottom of a 9 x 13-inch baking dish with several tablespoons of butter.

Cook the pasta according to the package directions until *al dente*. Drain and run under cold water to stop the cooking. Return to the cooking pot.

In a sauté pan over medium heat, cook the garlic, onion, celery, and 1 teaspoon salt until they release their fragrance and soften. Add the chopped mushrooms, and continue cooking until they have wilted. Deglaze with the spirits. Remove from the heat.

Stir the Chicken Cream Sauce (recipe follows), the chicken, the sautéed vegetables, the green onions, the grated Monterey Jack cheese, and ½ cup of the Parmesan cheese together with the pasta. Pour the mixture into the baking dish and cover with the remaining Parmesan cheese.

Bake for 25 to 30 minutes in the preheated oven. Serve hot.

## Chicken Cream Sauce

2 tablespoons butter
3 tablespoons flour
2 cups chicken broth, warmed

1 cup milk
Salt and pepper to taste

In a saucepan, melt the butter. Stir in the flour until smooth. Stir constantly for about 5 minutes over medium heat. Slowly add the chicken broth, about 1 ounce at a time. Stir vigorously until the liquid is absorbed. Please note that the sauce will initially seize up as you add the liquid. This is normal. Continue adding the liquid until the sauce begins to thin out, stirring constantly. When all of the stock has been added, stir in the milk and heat over medium heat until it thickens to coat the back of a spoon. Salt and pepper to taste. Use as directed.

# Seafood

## Pan-Fried Salmon Filets with Dijon-Shallot Glaze

Serves 4

This is a classic dish served for many conference groups. It is an easy-to-prepare, tasty, healthy dish. Complement with steamed asparagus and salad with mixed greens and Dijon Vinaigrette, page 36.

4 salmon filets
1 teaspoon salt
½ teaspoon celery salt
1 teaspoon ground coriander
1 teaspoon paprika

2 tablespoons Dijon mustard
2 shallots, sliced
½ cup dry sherry
Salt to taste

Preheat the oven to 350° F. Mix the salt, celery salt, ground coriander, and paprika together. Rub onto both sides of the salmon. Pan fry in a non-stick or well-seasoned cast-iron skillet until both sides are seared, about 2 minutes per side. Remove from the pan and place on a parchment-lined baking sheet. Repeat with all of the fish. Bake in the preheated oven for about 15 minutes, or until the fish is firm and flakes apart.

To make the sauce, add the shallots to the hot skillet and cook for several minutes. Deglaze the pan with the sherry. Stir in the mustard, and continue cooking until the sauce has reduced. This is a thick sauce to be spread atop the cooked salmon. Set aside.

# Salmon Croquettes

Roy Spears makes the best salmon croquettes. These have been a favorite among many Waldemar girls for as long as I can remember. Freeze any leftovers and serve by defrosting and heating in the oven. Serve with a salad of mixed field greens and accompany the croquettes with Tartar Sauce, page 137, and Spicy Tomato Cocktail Sauce (recipe follows).

| | |
|---|---|
| 2 cans flaked salmon | ½ cup milk |
| ¾ cup onion, finely chopped | 3 eggs, beaten |
| ½ cup celery, finely chopped | ½ cup breadcrumbs |
| 1 tablespoon flour | 3 cups cornmeal |
| Dash of cayenne pepper | 1 teaspoon pepper |
| 2 teaspoons salt, divided | 2 cups canola or light corn oil |

Drain the salmon well. Mix salmon, onion, celery, flour, cayenne, and 1 teaspoon salt. Blend in the milk and eggs. Add the breadcrumbs and stir to incorporate. Let sit for 15 minutes to allow the moisture to absorb.

In a separate bowl, stir together the cornmeal, 1 teaspoon salt, and pepper.

To shape the croquettes, scoop about 2 tablespoons of salmon mixture into the cupped palm of your hand. Shape into a domed, oblong shape, curved on the top and flat on the bottom. Roll in the cornmeal mixture and set aside on a wax-paper-lined surface.

To cook, heat about 2 cups of light corn or canola oil in a skillet to about 365° F. Cook 3 to 5 croquettes at a time, being careful not to crowd the pan, as this will cool the oil and the croquettes may absorb too much grease. Cook until golden brown on all sides, about 5 to 7 minutes total. Remove from the oil and drain on a layer of paper towels. Hold in a 200° F oven until all croquettes have been cooked. Serve with tartar sauce and cocktail sauce. Enjoy!

## Spicy Tomato Cocktail Sauce
Make this for any fried or boiled seafood meal.

| | |
|---|---|
| ½ cup ketchup | 1 jalapeño, finely chopped |
| ½ cup chili sauce | (optional) |
| ¼ cup fresh horseradish, grated | Fresh lemon juice and |
| 1 tablespoon red onion, finely chopped | hot pepper sauce to taste |

Stir together all ingredients and serve. Will keep covered in the refrigerator for up to a week.

# Crab Cakes

Serves 6 (2 per person)

I love crab cakes. These are so tasty and so easy to make. Serve with corn on the cob and oven-baked potatoes, page 99. I also like to serve them atop a salad of bitter greens. It is important to note that some here in Texas like to top these with ranch dressing. The zippy twang is perfect. Mix a little chipotle-pepper purée into the ranch for a south-of-the-border twist. But I still prefer the zest of a good tomato cocktail sauce. These are best served immediately.

1 pound lump crabmeat,
    twice picked over
1 tablespoon olive oil
1 tablespoon onion, finely chopped
1 tablespoon red bell pepper, finely
    chopped
1 teaspoon minced garlic
1 cup mayonnaise
1 teaspoon Dijon mustard
Pinch of cayenne or dash of pepper
    sauce

Salt and pepper to taste
1 egg, lightly beaten
¾ cup cracker crumbs, divided
1 cup fresh breadcrumbs, lightly
    toasted
¼ teaspoon salt
Dash of black pepper, freshly
    ground
1 tablespoon oil
1 tablespoon butter

Gently sauté the onion, bell pepper, and garlic in the olive oil until tender and fragrant. Set aside.

In a medium bowl, stir together the mayonnaise, Dijon mustard, cayenne or pepper sauce, and salt and pepper. Stir in the crab and the reserved sautéed vegetables. Gently fold in the egg and ¼ cup of the cracker crumbs.

Mix the breadcrumbs, the remaining cracker crumbs, and ¼ teaspoon salt and a dash of freshly ground black pepper. Form the crab mixture into 8 round cakes. Gently pat one at a time into the breadcrumb mixture to evenly coat. Set aside on a piece of wax paper.

Heat the oil and butter in a skillet over medium-high heat. Cook the cakes, being careful not to overcrowd in the pan. Cook each side at least 5 minutes until golden on each side.

## Tartar Sauce

1 cup mayonnaise
1 tablespoon minced shallots
2 teaspoons minced sour pickle
1 tablespoon minced sweet pickle

½ teaspoon fresh lemon juice, or to
    taste
Dash of cayenne pepper (optional)
1 teaspoon fresh parsley, chopped,
    as a garnish

Stir all of the ingredients together. Serve cold. Keep covered in the refrigerator for up to a week.

# Shrimp Creole

Ohhh, child! This is the best recipe ever. I think many recipes fail to begin with that ever important base of Creole cooking—the roux. The roux enriches the flavor, heightening the experience. Refer to the recipe for Chicken and Sausage Gumbo, page 22, for directions on browning flour. This makes all the difference in the world when it comes to time. Serve this dish with brown or white rice. And don't forget your smile. You in Louisiana now, child!

1 pound large shrimp, shelled and deveined
5 tablespoons browned flour (see page 23)
5 tablespoons oil
1½ cups onion, diced
1 cup green bell pepper, diced
¾ cup celery, chopped
2–4 cloves garlic, chopped
1 tablespoon tomato paste
½ cup white wine

2½ cups shrimp stock (made from boiling the shrimp shells in salted water for about 20 minutes)
2 cups chef's cut tomatoes
1 bay leaf
1 teaspoon salt, or to taste
¼ teaspoon cayenne pepper, or to taste
¼ cup chopped green onions, for garnish

In a cast-iron Dutch oven, make a roux with the browned flour, stirring continuously until a deep caramel color is reached. (See pages 22–23 for more details on making a roux.) Quickly add the onion, bell pepper, celery, and garlic, and stir until the vegetables begin to soften, about 5 minutes. Stir in the tomato paste until blended. Pour in half of the white wine and stir until smooth. Add the remaining wine, stir until smooth, and begin adding the shrimp stock, ½ cup at a time, stirring to blend well between each addition. It is important to note that if you add the liquid too quickly, the sauce may be lumpy rather than velvety smooth. Add the chef's cut tomatoes, the bay leaf, salt, and cayenne pepper, and simmer over medium heat for about 30 minutes. The sauce should be thick and flavorful. Season to taste with salt if needed. Add the shelled and deveined shrimp, and simmer until the shrimp turn pink and opaque. Serve over cooked rice and garnish with green onions.

# Shrimp Fajitas

A light and refreshing adaptation of the traditional beef or chicken fajitas, this recipe is a winner. The shrimp need to marinate for only 30 minutes, a fraction of the time required for heavier meats. I prefer to grill these on skewers, but they are just as good if they are pan-grilled. Serve with the usual accompaniments of flour and corn tortillas, homemade Pico de Gallo, page 9, Guacamole, page 5, shredded lettuce, grated cheese, and sour cream. These are also great with the splash of flavor from Mango Salsa, page 6. Serve these hot off the grill. Shrimp do not hold their heat for long and if overcooked will become rubbery in texture.

1 pound large shrimp, peeled and deveined
⅓ cup fresh lime juice
3 tablespoons honey
½ teaspoon puréed chipotle peppers in adobo sauce*
2 cloves garlic, minced (2 additional cloves garlic, coarsely chopped, if pan grilling)
1 teaspoon salt

1 onion, julienned
2 roma tomatoes, quartered and seeded
1 poblano pepper, roasted, peeled, seeded, and cut into julienne strips
1–2 tablespoons lemon juice, or the juice of half a lemon
¼ cup fresh cilantro, for a garnish
1 tablespoon olive oil, if pan grilling

Whisk together the lime juice, honey, chipotle purée, garlic, and salt. Stir in the cilantro and pour over the shrimp. Let marinate in the refrigerator for 30 minutes to an hour. Meanwhile, prepare the grill and all of the accompaniments.

While the shrimp are marinating, sauté the onion in a skillet over medium-low heat until it begins to caramelize. Add the tomatoes and the julienned poblano strips to the pan, and cook until the tomatoes wilt, about 5 minutes. Squeeze half a lemon (about 1 to 2 tablespoons lemon juice) into the mixture, stir in the fresh cilantro, and set aside.

If cooking on the grill, soak wooden skewers in water for 20 minutes. Thread the shrimp onto the skewers, 4 to 5 per skewer, and grill until pink and opaque, turning once, about 2 minutes per side. Be careful not to overcook, as the shrimp will become rubbery! Toss with the onion/tomato/poblano mixture. Serve immediately.

If you are cooking in a pan, heat a separate skillet, preferably a cast-iron skillet, with a tablespoon of olive oil. Sauté the coarsely chopped garlic until the fragrance is released, about 2 minutes. Remove the shrimp from the marinade and add to the hot pan. Cook, tossing frequently until the shrimp has cooked, about 5 minutes. Add the onion/tomato/poblano mixture, and toss to combine. Serve immediately.

*Chipotle peppers in adobo sauce are available in most markets in the Latin food section. If you cannot find them, Ancho Chili Purée, page 39, is an acceptable substitute.

# Asian Stir-Fried Shrimp and Linguine　　　Serves 4–6

Another David Johnson specialty. This delicious dish is light and refreshing, a very healthy all-in-one meal. Serve with Garlic Bread, page 68, and mixed field greens salad with vinaigrette. This is best cooked in a wok, a sharply angled pan traditionally used in Asian cuisine that allows for quick cooking at a high heat. The result is a crisp, full-of-flavor finish. It is important to get the wok very hot and to have all of the ingredients ready before you begin. Do not leave the pan once the cooking starts, as this will cook fast!

1 pound medium shrimp, peeled and
　　deveined
6 quarts water
1 tablespoon salt
1 tablespoon olive oil
½ cup carrots, angle cut
2 tablespoons peanut or olive oil
4 cloves garlic
½ cup onion slices, julienned
½ cup bok choy
½ cup fresh sugar snap peas
1 inch fresh ginger, peeled
　　and grated

½ cup dry sherry
2 cups Vegetable Stock, page 18, or
　　shrimp stock (see page 138)
1 pound linguine pasta
2 tablespoons water
1 tablespoon cornstarch
1 tablespoon soy sauce
Salt and white pepper to taste
1 cup loosely packed whole fresh
　　basil leaves

Bring 6 quarts of water with a tablespoon salt and a tablespoon olive oil to a boil. Drop the carrots in to blanch. Cook for 4 to 6 minutes, or until lightly tender. Remove from the hot water and set aside. Save the water to cook the pasta.

In a wok, heat the peanut or olive oil until it is very hot but not smoking. Add the shrimp and cook until they begin to turn pink. Quickly remove from the wok. Add the garlic and onions. Tossing quickly and continuously, cook until the onions begin to brown around the edges. Add the bok choy, blanched carrots, sugar snap peas, and grated ginger. Toss the vegetables for a minute and deglaze with the dry sherry. Let simmer until the sherry has reduced. Remove from the pan. Add the shrimp or vegetable stock and bring to a simmer. At this point, begin cooking the pasta. It should be *al dente* when the sauce is ready, about 8 minutes.

Make a cornstarch paste by adding 2 tablespoons of water to 1 tablespoon of cornstarch and blending until smooth. Stir slowly into the simmering sauce. Cook until the mixture begins to thicken. Add the cooked vegetables and shrimp and soy sauce and continue to cook, allowing the shrimp to cook. Salt and pepper as needed. Stir in the fresh basil leaves and toss with the hot pasta. Serve immediately.

# Grilled Shark Kebabs with
# Cilantro Pesto and Orange Balsamic Glaze     Serves 4

This is a delightful meal, full of summer flavors. The sauce is tantalizing, sweet, and poignant, balancing the savory, sea-fresh flavors of the grilled shark. Shark is the ideal fish to use, as the flesh is firm and clean tasting. It is complemented by the summer tang of fruits such as nectarine, pineapple, firm mango, or strawberries. I prefer ripe nectarine, but all are delightful. Serve the kebabs with Couscous with Basil, page 95, or atop a plate of mixed field greens.

4 shark steaks, cut into
    1½-inch cubes
1 bunch cilantro
2 cloves garlic
4 green onions
1 tablespoon olive oil
Salt to taste

1 yellow onion, cut into
    1-inch cubes
About 2 cups fresh summer fruit,
    such as nectarines, pineapple,
    mango, or strawberries
4 oranges, sliced into ½-inch rounds

Place the cubed shark in a gallon-size zip-closure bag. Make a paste by puréeing the cilantro, garlic, and green onions together, slowly adding the olive oil to bind the sauce. Season with salt to taste. Pour the paste into the bag with the shark, and let marinate for at least an hour. Prepare the sauce below.

To make the kebabs, prepare an outdoor grill. Use either metal skewers or wooden skewers soaked in water for about 20 minutes. Thread an onion slice onto a skewer, followed by a piece of shark, a cube of fruit, a slice of onion, a piece of shark, and a slice of orange. Repeat until the skewer is full, leaving about an inch open at the end of the skewer. Grill until the meat has cooked through, about 6 to 8 minutes, turning every 3 minutes to cook all sides. Glaze with the Orange Balsamic Glaze (below), and serve with the extra sauce on the side.

## Orange Balsamic Glaze

8 ounces orange juice,
    freshly squeezed
2 tablespoons balsamic vinegar
½ cup brown sugar

2 cloves garlic, minced
¾ cup olive oil
Salt to taste

In a small saucepan, reduce the orange juice, balsamic vinegar, and brown sugar at a slow boil over medium-high heat. Reduce by about a third, stirring occasionally, about 7 to 10 minutes. Remove from the heat, stir in the garlic, and slowly whisk in the olive oil to create an emulsion. Season to taste with salt. Serve warm atop the grilled shark kebabs, or as a warm dressing for mixed salad greens.

# Fried Catfish

Serves 4

This Texas classic is also a Waldemar classic, and surprise!—it's a Guadalupe River delicacy.

I remember a year when a fisherman set his lines prior to camp. When he pulled the lines, he found catfish no less than three feet long. I didn't know they could grow so large! The counselors enjoyed a catfish fry of immense proportions that year. How many of them knew that the fish came from our river, I'm not certain. But they definitely enjoyed the meal!

Some may regard catfish as too plebian for a refined palate, but I assure you that this recipe is as fine as any meal. The tang of the mustard, the sweet flesh of the catfish, and the perfect crisp of the crust combine to present a delightful dish for any table. This is the quintessential southern fry. Serve with Tartar Sauce, page 137, and cocktail sauce, page 136. Garlicky Collard Greens and Tomatoes, page 137, and cornbread, page 58, make perfect accompaniments.

| | |
|---|---|
| 1 pound catfish filets or nuggets | 2 cups oil for frying |
| ⅓ cup prepared yellow mustard | 2 cups yellow cornmeal |
| 2 tablespoons warm water | 1 tablespoon salt |
| ⅛ teaspoon cayenne pepper | 1 tablespoon black pepper, finely |
| 1 tablespoon Worcestershire sauce | ground |

Mix together the mustard, water, cayenne, and Worcestershire sauce. Marinate the catfish for 4 to 6 hours, or overnight.

In a cast-iron skillet, heat about 2 cups oil to between 280° F and 300° F. Be careful not to heat the oil too high, as the fish crusts will cook too fast and burn!

Stir together the cornmeal, salt, and black pepper. Dredge the fish through the cornmeal, making certain all of the fish is coated. Fry in the hot oil for about 5 to 7 minutes, or until the crust is golden brown, turning at least once. Remove from the oil and drain on several layers of paper towels. Keep warm in a 200° F oven until all the fish is cooked. Serve warm.

# Fried Shrimp

Serves 4

Almost every child will offer a smile of incredible gratitude at the mention of fried shrimp for dinner. This is an all-time favorite for the girls here in the summer. Serve with oven-fried potatoes, page 99, and Coleslaw, page 35.

1 pound extra-large shrimp
    (12 to 14 shrimp)
½ cup buttermilk
1 teaspoon salt
1 cup toasted breadcrumbs
1 cup cracker crumbs

1 teaspoon salt
¼ teaspoon cayenne pepper
¼ teaspoon white pepper
2 eggs, lightly beaten
2 cups oil for frying

Clean the shrimp, removing the shells and the veins, but leaving the tails on. Whisk together the buttermilk and salt, and soak the shrimp in this mixture for about 20 minutes. Toss together the breadcrumbs, cracker crumbs, salt, cayenne, and white pepper. Remove the shrimp from the buttermilk, and dip in the lightly beaten eggs. Dredge through the crumb mixture. Heat the oil in a cast-iron skillet with at least 2-inch-high sides. Fry the shrimp until the crust is golden brown, about 7 minutes. Remove from the oil, and drain on a layer of several paper towels. Serve hot!

# Grand Finale

## Desserts

# Dessert—Waldemar Style

**T**his final chapter is devoted to the grand finale of every meal—dessert. Waldemar desserts have long been the most unforgettable course of the meal. Besides being delicious, they are presented, to the delight of campers and staff, with much fanfare. This is a chapter resplendent with Waldemar memories.

Lucille and U. S. Smith created many treasured traditions, including Blarney Stones with Coffee Ice Cream, Cherry Squares, Caramel Squares, Lemon Meringue Pie, and the list goes on. Marsha and Dale brought with them an assortment of unforgettable desserts, including Mrs. Elmore's Chocolate Cake, Brownie Fudge Pie, Mrs. English's Cheesecake, and, of course, the sublime Russian Cream with Raspberry Sauce. Roy Spears expanded Waldemar's repertoire to include such elegant additions as Bananas Foster, Crème Brulée, Crêpes Suzette, and, last but not least, Lemon Baked Alaska. Treat your family and friends to the sublime, the extravagant, the traditional . . . the Dessert, Waldemar style.

# Caramel Squares

Makes 2 dozen

Golden caramel flavor surrounding crisp Texas pecans: A wonderful, easy, classic Waldemar treat. Who has ever tried these and not loved them? If you have a current camper, she will be clamoring for you to make these all the time. And you will find it an appropriate treat for any occasion.

These are a little tricky as far as gauging doneness goes. When you remove them from the oven, they will still be a bit gooey in the center, but they will not "jiggle when wiggled." As they cool, this center will firm up somewhat, although, being caramel, they do remain delectably gooey.

| | |
|---|---|
| 2 eggs | ½ teaspoon salt |
| 2 cups brown sugar, firmly packed | 1 teaspoon baking powder |
| ½ cup melted butter | 1 teaspoon vanilla |
| 1 cup plus 2 tablespoons flour | 2 cups pecans, chopped and toasted |

Preheat the oven to 350° F. Grease and flour a 9 x 13-inch baking pan. Set aside. In a large bowl, whisk the eggs together. Add the brown sugar and beat until well blended. Stir in the melted butter.

Sift together the flour, salt, and baking powder. Gradually stir into the sugar/butter mixture until evenly blended. Add the vanilla and toasted pecans. Immediately pour into the prepared baking pan and bake in the preheated oven for about 30 to 35 minutes. Remove from the oven and let cool in the pan before slicing. They will continue to cook and firm up as they cool.

Store in an airtight container for up to three days (if they last that long!).


# Lemon Squares

Makes about 3½ dozen

This is for all of you lemon lovers who believe that there should be a perfect balance between tart and sweet. Tingly lemon curd atop a buttery shortbread-like crust, topped with a sprinkling of finely dusted powdered sugar. . . . You will be reminded of sun and summer.

This recipe is a two-part process. First make the crust. While it bakes, put together the lemon curd mixture. It is important to have the curd ready to pour onto the hot crust immediately. However, if you make the curd too soon, the flour and baking powder will react with the acid and it will begin to froth, which affects the finished texture. (An important note: Always use fresh lemon rind. There would be no point if you use the dried sort.) Wash and dry your lemons. Using the fine side of a box grater, grate the rind. Watch your knuckles, and do not grate the white pith, as this is bitter.

A trick for juicing lemons. After you have grated the rind, roll the lemon on the countertop beneath your curved palm, using a bit of pressure. Slice it in half and microwave the lemon for about 30 seconds. The lemon will be ready to offer all its juice with little effort on your part!

| | |
|---|---|
| 1½ cups salted butter, softened | 4 tablespoons flour |
| ⅔ cup powdered sugar | 1 teaspoon baking powder |
| 3 cups flour | The rinds of 3 lemons, grated |
| 6 eggs | 8 tablespoons lemon juice, freshly |
| 3 cups sugar | squeezed |

Preheat the oven to 350° F. In a medium bowl, sift together the flour and sugar. Beat the softened butter in a mixer. Add the flour/sugar mixture until it comes together as a dough, being careful not to overbeat the dough. Pat dough into a jellyroll pan, spreading evenly across the bottom and slightly up the sides. With the tines of a fork, poke several holes across the surface to prevent the crust from puffing. Bake for 20 minutes, or until the crust has browned around the edges and is golden in the center.

While the crust is baking, mix together the filling ingredients, taking extra care to follow the listed order: eggs, sugar, flour, baking powder, lemon zest, lemon juice. Pour onto the hot crust and return to the oven for another 20 minutes. Remove when done. Let cool for about 15 minutes. Sift powdered sugar across the top, and continue to let sit until cool to the touch. Cut into squares and serve. Store in an airtight container for 3 to 5 days.

You can freeze these successfully by following these steps: let cool completely; do not sprinkle on the powdered sugar; wrap in single layers, using wax paper between each layer. Store in a zip-closure plastic freezer bag for up to two months. Defrost to room temperature and top with sifted powdered sugar.

# Crêpes Suzette                                                    Serves 4

An enduring classic, this dessert is believed to have evolved from a mistake made by a French master chef over a hundred years ago. Roy Spears has served this flambé dessert to great applause during camp and the off-season. For an exceptional presentation, pour the brandy atop the dish and light the flame at the table.

One batch yields about twelve 8-inch crêpes (three per person).

### Dessert Crêpes

| | |
|---|---|
| 2 large eggs | 2 tablespoons sugar |
| 1 cup milk | 1 teaspoon vanilla extract |
| ⅓ cup water | 2 tablespoons butter, melted |
| 1 cup all-purpose flour | |

Whisk together the eggs, milk, and water, and whisk to blend. In a separate bowl, sift together the flour and sugar, and stir the egg/milk mixture into the flour. Beat until smooth. Stir in the vanilla and the melted butter and cover. Refrigerate for at least an hour. Gently stir before cooking.

Cook in a hot crêpe pan. Rub the pan lightly with butter. Pour enough batter to coat the bottom of the pan. Cook for about 3 minutes, or until the crêpe is cooked through. It will be golden brown on one side. Repeat with the remaining batter. Layer the cooked crêpes atop each other, separated by a sheet of wax paper.

FOR THE SAUCE:

3 oranges, zested on the fine side of a box-stand grater
½ cup sugar
2 sticks unsalted butter
3 tablespoons orange liqueur

½ cup fresh orange juice
⅛ teaspoon salt
½ cup brandy, cognac, or orange liqueur, to flambé

In a medium saucepan over medium-high heat, melt the butter. Add the sugar and orange zest, and cook until the sugar has melted, about 5 minutes. Add the orange liqueur, orange juice, and salt, and whisk to incorporate. Continue cooking until the mixture begins to thicken to a syrup. Remove from the heat. Working with one crêpe at a time, dip into the syrup and fold in quarters, so that it looks like a triangle. Remove from the syrup and arrange on a plate, 2 to 3 per person. Pour the remaining syrup over the individual plates.

TO FLAMBÉ:

In a small saucepan, heat the brandy until warm. At the table, scoop the heated brandy in a ½-cup ladle and carefully light with a match. Pour over the plated desserts and let burn until the flame dies. Serve!

# Chocolate Mousse                                             Serves 6–8

A classic for chocolate lovers. I remember an adolescent desire of mine to make the perfect chocolate mousse. Well, this is it. Although it requires several steps, it is relatively simple, especially if you have a good stand mixer. Chocolate mousse is the perfect dessert for a special occasion, as it is best when made at least one day ahead of serving, and it makes an extra-special presentation when served chilled in individual bowls or champagne stemware.

12 ounces bittersweet or semi-sweet chocolate
1 cup unsalted butter
6 eggs, separated
2 tablespoons sugar

1 teaspoon vanilla extract
1½ cups heavy whipping cream
½ teaspoon orange liqueur, such as Grand Marnier or Cointreau

In a double boiler, melt the chocolate and butter together. Set aside to cool to room temperature.

In a separate bowl, whisk together the egg yolks and sugar until thick and light in color. Gently stir the cooled chocolate mixture and the vanilla into the egg yolks until well combined. Set aside.

With a wire whisk, whip the heavy whipping cream until soft peaks form. Fold in a spoonful of the whipped cream to lighten the chocolate. With a rubber spatula, fold in the rest of the whipping cream until it is well incorporated.

Whip the egg whites until stiff peaks form, being careful not to overwhip them, as they will separate. Gently fold a spoonful of the egg whites into the chocolate mixture to lighten it. Gently fold in the remaining whipped egg whites until well incorporated. Scrape the sides with the spatula.

The mixture will be light and airy in texture. Chill in a large serving bowl, or in individual serving bowls or champagne stemware. Chill at least 4 hours, or overnight.

Garnish with freshly whipped cream. I like whipped cream with little to no sugar, as the mousse is so rich, but if you prefer, add 2 teaspoons sugar to each pint of heavy whipping cream.

Fresh berries and a sprig of mint make an elegant garnish.

## Crème Brulée
Serves 6–8

This is the ultimate in custards. Roy Spears made this for the rehearsal dinner when Waldemar director Meg and her husband Clayton were married. This custard is in the same family as flan or crème caramel, but it is not removed from the serving dish, and the texture is not as firm. It also has a thin crust of burnt sugar on top. Hence the name, "Burnt Cream."

| | |
|---|---|
| 3 cups heavy whipping cream | ½ cup sugar |
| 8 egg yolks | 1 tablespoon vanilla |
| 2 whole eggs | 2 inches vanilla bean |

FOR THE TOP:
 ½ cup brown sugar

Preheat the oven to 275° F. Heat the cream and vanilla bean over medium heat to almost a simmer. Do not scald.

In a mixing bowl, whisk the egg yolks, whole eggs, and sugar until well blended. Add the vanilla. Slowly add the hot cream, half a cup at a time in a slow drizzle, whisking continuously. Repeat until all of the cream is added. Strain through a fine sieve to remove any cooked egg particles. Pour into 8 individual 8-ounce ramekins or a large soufflé dish.

Now prepare a hot water bath. Place all of the ramekins or the large soufflé dish in a 9 x 13-inch baking dish. Pour about 2 cups hot water into the baking dish so that the water comes at least a third of the way up the sides of the ramekins. Place in the preheated oven, and cook until the custard has set but is still a bit jiggly in the center. The ramekins will take about 40 minutes, while the large soufflé will take closer to an hour.

Remove from the oven and let cool, at least 4 to 6 hours.

Just before serving, spread a thin layer of brown sugar atop each dessert. Place under the broiler for about 5 minutes, or until the sugar has melted. Remove and serve immediately.

# Southern Comfort Bread Pudding

Serves 8

Every year while working at Waldemar during Women's Week, I always made a bread pudding—for breakfast, of all things. Judy Hillegeist, this is for you! Judy, a long-time Women's Week attendee, mentioned that she loved bread pudding and couldn't believe that we never served it. So with leftover bread, I made this for breakfast! It was the hit of the day. Serve this after a gratifying meal of Shrimp Creole, page 138. Or serve it for a brunch. Anytime, it is a wonderful, rich and easy treat.

The recipe calls for egg bread, such as Brioche, page 61, or challah. But I have also used leftovers such as cinnamon rolls, breakfast muffins, or French or Italian bread. Any good-quality bread will do!

| | |
|---|---|
| 8 tablespoons butter | ¾ cup sugar |
| 8 cups egg bread, about 1 loaf cut into 1-inch cubes | 1 teaspoon cinnamon |
| | 3 cups milk |
| ⅓ cup raisins or currants (optional) | ¼ teaspoon freshly grated |
| 3 eggs | orange peel |

Preheat the oven to 350° F. Cut butter into small pieces. Place about a third of the butter in the bottom of a 4- to 6-quart casserole dish. Place half of the bread in the dish and dot with another third of the butter. Sprinkle in half the optional raisins or currents. Repeat with the remaining bread, butter, and raisins.

Whisk the eggs and sugar until blended. Add the cinnamon, orange zest, and vanilla. Whisk to combine. Slowly add the milk, stirring to fully incorporate. Carefully pour over the bread, saturating it all. Cover the dish with aluminum foil. Place the casserole dish in a slightly larger, oven-proof dish. Fill the larger dish with hot water to make a hot water bath. Bake in the preheated oven for an hour. Remove the foil and cook for another 15 minutes. Serve warm with Southern Comfort Cream Sauce (recipe follows) or softly whipped cream.

## Southern Comfort Cream Sauce

You can use Southern Comfort, which has a subtle orange essence, or bourbon. Either one is good!

| | |
|---|---|
| 10 large egg yolks | 1 teaspoon vanilla |
| 1 cup sugar | ¼ cup Southern Comfort or bourbon |

In the top of a double boiler, whisk together the egg yolks and the sugar until lemon-colored and thick, about 7 to 10 minutes. Slowly add the vanilla and spirits and continue to stir until fully incorporated. Heat the mixture slowly, stirring constantly, over cool water until the water is boiling and the mixture is thick and creamy. Do not cease stirring until the sauce is thick, or it will cook onto the bottom of the pan. Spoon over the bread pudding and serve.

# Strawberry Shortcake

Serves 6–8

Let's get back to basics. This is as close to perfect as we can get. Perfectly simple. Perfectly fresh. Perfectly perfect. It is a scrumptious cream scone topped with fresh strawberries and freshly whipped cream. Delightful for a spring brunch.

1 recipe cream scones, page 48, cut
    with a 2-inch biscuit cutter
1 pint strawberries, sliced, plus
    1 cup whole berries to garnish
    (optional)
⅛ cup sugar

2 cups heavy whipping cream
⅛ cup sugar
1 teaspoon vanilla
8 sprigs fresh mint
Fresh edible flowers, if available

Sprinkle the sliced berries with the sugar and let sit at room temperature for about 30 minutes, or until the berries begin to release their juice and a light syrup develops. In a mixing bowl, whip the cream with the sugar until soft peaks form. Add the vanilla and continue to whip until stiff peaks have almost formed.

To serve, slice a scone through the center. Put about ⅛ cup of strawberries on the bottom half of the scone. Top with a dollop of whipped cream and another ⅛ cup of the strawberries. Arrange the top slice of the scone at a loose angle to the structure. Garnish with several whole berries, a sprig of mint, and an edible flower.

# Mrs. Elmore's Chocolate Cake

Serves 12

This is a recipe that was contributed from the annals of Dale's childhood. And it quickly became a Waldemar favorite. We have served it for almost every group, for almost every function. It is always wonderful. Serve with Blue Bell or Homemade Vanilla Ice Cream, page 164.

2 cups sugar
2 cups flour
½ teaspoon salt
½ cup buttermilk
1 teaspoon baking soda

1 cup cocoa
1 cup water
1 cup butter, unsalted
2 eggs
1 teaspoon vanilla

Preheat the oven to 400° F. Sift together the sugar, flour, and salt in a large bowl. Set aside. Measure the buttermilk in at least a 2-cup measurer and add the baking soda. In a saucepan, mix together the cocoa and water. Add the butter and heat until the butter is melted, stirring to blend. Pour over the reserved sugar/flour mixture, stirring well to blend.

In a mixing bowl, whisk the eggs until blended. Add the buttermilk mixture and the vanilla. Stir to combine with the chocolate/flour mixture.

Pour into a greased and floured 9 x 13-inch baking pan. Bake in the preheated oven for about 30 to 45 minutes. It is done when it has pulled away from the sides of the pan and a toothpick inserted in the center comes out clean. Begin to prepare the icing while the cake cooks.

## Chocolate Icing

½ cup butter
4 tablespoons cocoa
6 tablespoons milk
2 cups powdered sugar, sifted
    into a large bowl

1 teaspoon vanilla
1 cup chopped nuts, pecans or
    walnuts

In a saucepan over medium heat, melt the butter with the cocoa and milk. Whisk until smooth. Remove from the heat, and pour over the powdered sugar. Whisk until smooth, scraping the sides with a spatula to incorporate all the batter. Add the vanilla and the nuts, and stir to blend.

Once the cake is done, insert a toothpick into the cake in many places. Pour the hot icing over the hot cake. It will drip into the holes made by the toothpick. Let sit until cooled enough to touch. Serve warm with vanilla ice cream.

# Cherry Squares

First featured in *Lucille's Treasure Chest* in 1942 (see page 104), this recipe has withstood the test of time, and it is served year after year with the same fantastic results. The squares have a wonderful crisp crust and a perfectly sweet and tart sauce. Serve with a dollop of whipped cream.

Please note that the cherries must be the tart, pitted variety packed in water or juice. The recipe just isn't the same if made with sweet, dark cherries. Unfortunately, the tart kind are not always available. Ask your grocer if he can order the frozen variety. Or stock up on the canned ones when they are available in the fall.

| | |
|---|---|
| 2 16-ounce packages of frozen tart, pitted cherries, OR 3 14.5-ounce cans tart, pitted cherries packed in water | 1½ cups flour<br>1 cup sugar<br>⅓ cup softened butter |

Preheat the oven to 375° F. Drain the cherries and reserve the liquid for the sauce. Sift together the flour and sugar. Cut the butter into the flour/sugar mixture, until it resembles course meal. Do not overmix, as it will not finish with the right flavor. Press half of the crumbly dough into the bottom of a 9 x 9-inch cake pan. Spread the cherries over the crust. Top with the remaining dough and gently press to spread evenly.

Bake in the preheated oven for about 45 minutes. The crust will begin to brown and the cherries will be bubbling. Cook the sauce while the cherry squares are baking.

## Cherry Squares Sauce

| | |
|---|---|
| 2 cups cherry juice, (reserved)<br>1 tablespoon fresh lemon juice<br>⅝ cup sugar<br>3 tablespoons cornstarch | ⅛ teaspoon salt<br>2 tablespoons butter<br>1 teaspoon vanilla |

Pour the cherry juice and lemon juice into a saucepan. Sift together the sugar, cornstarch, and salt. Stir into the cherry juice. Add the butter and heat over medium heat until the butter melts and the sauce begins to thicken, about 10 to 15 minutes, stirring continuously. The sauce will be a cloudy color, but as it begins to thickens it will become clear. This is a good signal that the sauce is ready. Remove from the heat and stir in the vanilla.

Serve atop the hot cherry squares.

# Pastry Dough
### Makes enough for two 9-inch pies or 1 covered pie

The secrets to a good pie crust are to not overhandle it; to use cold butter, cold shortening, and ice-cold water; to refrigerate for at least 30 minutes before rolling out; and to make it with a little love. This is such a simple recipe, but it can be dreadfully tough if you don't employ the secrets of good pie crust making.

This recipe is actually used not only for desserts. It is also perfect for Quiche, pages 90 and 121.

Add a teaspoon of cinnamon, nutmeg, or cardamom for a particularly delightful flavor twist.

2½ cups flour
1 teaspoon salt
2 teaspoons sugar, granulated
8 tablespoons unsalted butter, chilled
    and cut into pieces

6 tablespoons solid vegetable
    shortening, cold
5–6 tablespoons ice water

Mix the flour, salt, and sugar in a medium-sized mixing bowl. Cut in the butter and shortening with a pastry blender or using knives in a back-and-forth cutting motion, until it resembles a coarse meal. Make a well in the center, and add 1 tablespoon of ice cold water at a time. Mix just enough with a fork to moisten the flour. The mixture will still be very crumbly. Pour out onto a work surface and knead, turning over several times. Wrap well in plastic wrap and refrigerate at least 30 minutes. Remove from the refrigerator and roll out to about ¼ inch thick. Use according to the recipe.

This dough will keep in the refrigerator for up to three days, or you can freeze it in an airtight, freezer-quality bag for up to two months.

# Apple Pie
### Makes one double-crusted pie to serve 8

We here at Waldemar know how to appreciate the simple things in life. And there is nothing better than hot apple pie à la mode. It is the sublimely perfect end to any meal (and it's equally good for a midday snack!). We prefer to use apples that are extra tart and firm, such as Granny Smiths. If you have a favorite apple in your area, experiment with it. You may find you prefer another variety to this one. There is an organic apple farm just about two miles up river from Waldemar. If you have organic apples available in your market, I highly recommend using them, as the flavor is much more intense.

1 recipe Pastry Dough, page 155
1 teaspoon ground cinnamon
6 apples, about 2 pounds, cored,
    peeled, and thinly sliced
¾ cup sugar
¼ cup + 1 tablespoon
    unbleached flour
½ teaspoon cinnamon

1 teaspoon fresh lemon juice
1 teaspoon vanilla
2 tablespoons butter, cut into
    small pieces
1 egg
1 tablespoon milk
2 tablespoons coarse-ground
    turbinado sugar

Preheat the oven to 425° F.

Make the pastry crust according to directions, adding ½ teaspoon of cinnamon to the recipe.

Line a deep-dish pie plate with half of the pastry. Cover and reserve the remaining amount to use for a top crust. Mix 2 tablespoons sugar and one tablespoon flour together and sprinkle evenly on the bottom crust. Set aside.

In a separate bowl, toss the apple slices together with the lemon juice and vanilla. Stir together the remaining ⅝ cup sugar, ¼ cup flour, and ½ teaspoon cinnamon, and toss with the apples. Place the apple mixture in the pastry-lined pie dish. Dot the top with the butter pieces.

Cover the pie with the remaining crust, and pinch the edges of the bottom and top together to seal. (You may want to be creative in finishing off the edges, using the tines of a fork, alternating slit-folds, or any other method you recognize as traditional.) Cut several slits in the center of the pie to allow steam to escape. Make a milk-egg wash with 1 egg and 1 tablespoon milk whisked together well. Brush over the pie and sprinkle with about 2 tablespoons coarse-ground turbinado sugar.

Bake in the preheated 425° F oven for 10 minutes. Reduce the heat to 350° F and continue baking for about 50 minutes, or until the crust is golden brown and the apple mixture is bubbling. Remove from the oven and let sit for at least 20 minutes before serving.

Best when served warm with a scoop of Homemade Vanilla Ice Cream, page 164.

# Hill Country Peach Pie     Makes one pie, enough for 8 servings

Fredricksburg, a Hill Country town about twenty miles north of Kerrville, has become renowned for its peach harvest. I must say that the juiciest, most perfect peaches I have ever had were bought from a roadside vendor while traveling through Fredricksburg. This recipe is a wonderful complement to fresh, rich peaches.

If you do not have access to organic or orchard-fresh peaches, be certain those you are using are ripe and flavorful. A good trick in choosing flavorful peaches in the market is to weigh the fruit in your hand—a ripe fruit will have some weight to it. Gently squeeze the fruit. It should give slightly to your pressure, but it will not mush. The final test is to smell the fruit. It will either have a fragrance of peach, or it won't. If the first two criteria seem to be present, but there is no smell, put it back. If there is a fragrant smell, but it still seems too firm, take it home and let it ripen in a fruit ripener or in a small brown bag at room temperature for several days. This will speed up the ripening process and produce a near-perfect fruit.

| | |
|---|---|
| 1 batch Pastry Dough, page 155 | ½ teaspoon vanilla extract |
| ½ teaspoon cinnamon | 1 tablespoon sugar |
| 4 cups fresh peaches, sliced, pits removed | 1 tablespoon flour |
| | 1 tablespoon butter, cut into pieces |
| 1 tablespoon fresh lemon juice | 1 egg white |
| ½ cup brown sugar | 1 teaspoon water |
| 1 teaspoon cinnamon | 1 tablespoon sugar |
| 3 tablespoons flour | |

Preheat the oven to 425° F. Prepare the pastry dough according to directions, adding the cinnamon to the flour before mixing. Set aside in the refrigerator for at least 30 minutes before rolling out to ¼ inch thick. Line a deep-dish pie plate with the crust, reserving the leftovers for a top crust, keeping refrigerated until ready to use. In a large mixing bowl, toss together the peaches, lemon juice, brown sugar, cinnamon, flour, and vanilla. Let stand for 10 minutes.

Sprinkle a mixture of 1 tablespoon sugar and 1 tablespoon flour on the bottom of the pie crust. Pour the peach mixture into the piecrust. Dot the top with the butter pieces. Roll out the remaining dough, and cut with a pastry crimper into long strips of crust. Weave a lattice crust for the top. Pinch the top and bottom crust edges together, and brush with a mixture of 1 egg white and a teaspoon of water. Sprinkle with a tablespoon of sugar.

Place a baking sheet on a rack below the middle rack to catch any drippings. Place the pie on the middle rack and bake in the oven for about 30 minutes. Reduce the heat to 350° F and continue cooking for another 20 to 30 minutes, or until the pie filling is thick and bubbling and the crust is a rich golden brown. Remove from the oven and let cool until room temperature. Serve with a dollop of freshly whipped cream or Homemade Vanilla Ice Cream, page 164, and taste the warmth of a Hill Country summer day!

# Buttermilk Pie

Makes one 10-inch pie

Another southern specialty. You will be hard pressed to meet a girl from Texas who does not love a buttermilk pie. And you will be even harder pressed to find one who does not have a special recipe from her grandmother or great aunt or favorite old family friend. This recipe is a traditional favorite. The simpler the better. Just mix the ingredients in the order listed. Consume with a hot cup of coffee and chicory (and with a lovely companion).

½ recipe Pastry Dough, page 155,
    lining a 10-inch pie pan
2 eggs, well beaten
1¾ cups sugar
4 tablespoons flour

1 stick melted butter
1 cup buttermilk
1 teaspoon vanilla

Sift together the sugar and flour, and mix in all the remaining ingredients in the order listed.

Pour into the unbaked pie shell and bake for an hour to an hour and 15 minutes. If the top begins to brown too quickly, you can loosely cover the pie with a piece of aluminum foil. To test for doneness, insert a dinner knife into the center of the custard. It should remain clean when removed.

Remove from the oven and let cool to room temperature. This allows the custard to continue to set up.

Serve with a hot cup of coffee and chicory, and enjoy!


# Lemon Meringue Pie

Makes one 10-inch Pie

This recipe dispels the mystery of meringue. Long a bane of the from-scratch cook, most have scratched meringue from the list, as there is nothing more disappointing than a weeping, fallen meringue. As we love this dessert at Waldemar, we feel it deserves to be attempted once again. I have some very specific suggestions that will simplify the process and that can guarantee success under most circumstances. (It is not advisable to attempt a meringue on a rainy or very humid day.)

The secret to a perfect soft meringue topping lies in the stabilization of the egg whites with the use of a cornstarch paste. Always begin with ingredients at room temperature for this pie, and it is of utmost importance that you do all of your prep before you begin even the first step. Once you begin, time will be of the essence. In other words, the soft meringue should be added atop the lemon curd while the curd is hot! By adding the meringue to the hot lemon curd, you are able to cook the underside of the meringue topping. If the curd is cold, the underside will not have a chance to cook, and it will most definitely separate. So if the phone rings, let the answering machine get the call!

½ recipe Pastry Dough, page 155

## LEMON CURD FILLING:

1¼ cups sugar
⅓ cup cornstarch
⅛ teaspoon salt
1½ cups water
½ cup lemon juice, freshly squeezed

3 teaspoons grated lemon zest, from
    approximately 5 lemons
4 egg yolks
3 tablespoons unsalted butter

## MERINGUE TOPPING:

1 tablespoon cornstarch
1 tablespoon sugar
⅓ cup water
4 egg whites

½ teaspoon vanilla
¼ teaspoon cream of tartar
½ cup very fine sugar

Preheat the oven to 350° F.

Line a pie pan with the pastry dough. Prick the bottom and sides with the tines of a fork. Line with foil and top with pie weights or beans. Bake for 15 minutes or until it has begun to brown. Remove from the oven and set aside.

Sift together the sugar and cornstarch. In a medium saucepan, combine the sugar/cornstarch mixture and the salt. Whisk in the water, lemon juice, and lemon zest. In a separate bowl, whisk together the egg yolks and add to the lemon/sugar mixture. Heat over medium heat to a simmer, stirring constantly with a wooden spoon. Add the butter and continue cooking until the mixture thickens, about 1 to 3 minutes. Remove from the heat and pour into the cooked pie crust. Cover with a piece of plastic wrap pressed to the lemon curd surface to prevent a film from forming. Set aside and begin the meringue immediately.

In a small saucepan, sift together the cornstarch and flour. Whisk in the water and place over medium heat, stirring constantly, until the mixture becomes transparent. Remove from the heat and cover.

In a grease-free bowl, beat the egg whites on medium speed until soft peaks form. Add the vanilla and the cream of tartar. Add the superfine sugar very slowly. Beat on high until peaks are stiff and glossy. Slowly beat in the cornstarch paste until all has been added. With a spatula, gently fold the mixture to ensure that none of the cornstarch paste has settled to the bottom. Beat for another 30 seconds.

Remove the plastic wrap from the lemon curd, which should still be very hot, and spread the meringue. Begin by spreading part of the meringue around the edges, ensuring that it touches the crust. This has a twofold effect. First, the meringue is prevented from shrinking while cooking, as it adheres with certainty to the crust. Second, covering the edges prevents the curd from spilling out due to any extra weight in the center!

Bake in the preheated oven for about 20 minutes, or until an instant-read thermometer reads 160° F. This temperature ensures that all potential pathogens have been killed. Do not overcook, however, as this can cause the meringue to weep.

Remove from the oven and let cool to room temperature. Serve each slice with a garnish of summer-ripe blackberries and a sprig of fresh mint.

Delicious for up to three days in the refrigerator (if it lasts that long).

# Fresh Blackberry Crisp

Serves 8–12

A simple and perfect summer dessert. Serve with a little fresh cream or Homemade Vanilla Ice Cream, page 164. If you absolutely must, you can use frozen berries, but the outcome is not quite as perfect.

5 cups fresh blackberries
1 cup brown sugar, lightly packed

½ cup flour
4 tablespoons unsalted butter

TOPPING:

½ cup flour
½ cup brown sugar

4 tablespoons butter
1 cup old-fashioned oats

Preheat the oven to 325° F. Rinse the berries and drain. Mix together the cup of brown sugar and the ½ cup of flour. Spread just enough of the mixture over the bottom of a 9 x 13-inch baking dish to cover. Dot the 4 tablespoons of butter atop the sugar/flour mixture. Toss the remaining mixture with the berries, and spread over the bottom crust mixture.

For the topping, mix together the flour and brown sugar. Cut in the butter with a pastry blender. Toss in the oatmeal to evenly incorporate. Sprinkle this topping over the berries.

Bake in the preheated oven for 30 to 35 minutes, or until the top is browned and the berry mixture is bubbling. Remove from the oven and let sit for about 15 minutes before serving. Serve hot with Homemade Vanilla Ice Cream, page 164, or Cinnamon-spiked Whipped Cream (recipe follows).

### Cinnamon-Spiked Whipped Cream
Makes 4 cups whipped cream

2 cups heavy whipping cream
1 tablespoon sugar

1 teaspoon ground cinnamon
1 teaspoon vanilla

In a medium mixing bowl, beat the whipping cream until soft peaks form. Slowly add the sugar, cinnamon and vanilla, and continue beating until the cream has reached firm peaks stage. Be watchful, as overbeating will produce a curdled, butter-like mess.

# Nectarine and Blueberry Crisp

Serves 8–12

Another perfect summer fruit dessert, best using sweet and tart summer-ripe nectarines and blueberries. Serve to finish a menu of grilled meats and vegetables. Top with whipped cream or Homemade Vanilla Ice Cream, page 164.

2 cups flour
1 cup granulated sugar
1 cup brown sugar
¼ teaspoon nutmeg
½ teaspoon salt

1 cup unsalted butter, cold
2 cups oatmeal
6 ripe nectarines
1 pint blueberries

Preheat the oven to 350° F. In a medium mixing bowl, stir together the flour, sugars, nutmeg, and salt. Cut in the butter with a pastry blender until it is pea-sized. Stir in the oatmeal to blend.

Cut the nectarines into thin slices. Rinse the blueberries and toss with the nectarines. Put about 1 cup of the crumb mixture in the bottom of a 9 x 13-inch baking dish. Layer the fruit on top of this bottom crumb mixture and top with the remaining crumb mixture. Cover with aluminum foil and bake in the preheated oven for 45 minutes. Remove the foil and continue baking until the crisp has browned and the fruit mixture is bubbling, about 15 to 20 minutes.

Remove from the oven and let sit for about 15 minutes. Serve hot with whipped cream or ice cream of your choice.

# Russian Cream
Serves 8–12

This dessert inspires childlike pleasure in adult women of distinction. Have you ever wanted to lick your plate clean? It sounds quite unusual, but I know of several Waldemar "girls" who have thought twice about it. Once you've tried this dessert, you'll understand why. Smooth and creamy, its sweet and mildly tangy flavor is complemented by the contrasting tart brilliance of the Raspberry Sauce.

1 cup light cream
¾ cup heavy cream
1 cup sugar
2 tablespoons (3 packages) unflavored
    gelatin

½ cup cold water
1½ cups sour cream, whipped
1 teaspoon vanilla

In a medium saucepan, combine the light and heavy creams and the sugar, and heat until the sugar has dissolved and the cream forms small bubbles on the side. Meanwhile, stir the gelatin into the cold water to blend. Let stand until it begins to congeal. Whip the sour cream in a separate bowl until light and fluffy.

Add the gelatin mixture to the cream and stir to blend. Slowly add the sour cream and vanilla. Stir until smooth. Pour into a ring mold and refrigerate until the mixture has set, at least 4 hours. Serve cold and top with the Raspberry Sauce (recipe follows). Garnish with fresh raspberries and edible flowers or sprigs of fresh mint.

## Raspberry Sauce
Sweet and tart, perfect for this dessert or as a topping for vanilla or chocolate ice cream.

1 cup sugar
1 cup water
1 teaspoon vanilla

1 one-pound bag frozen raspberries,
    defrosted and juice reserved
1 tablespoon orange liqueur

Combine water and sugar in a medium saucepan. Simmer over medium heat until the sugar has dissolved and it comes to a rolling boil. Let boil until it reaches 220° F. Add the raspberries and their juice, the vanilla, and orange liqueur. Let cook for several minutes more. Remove from the heat and let cool. Store in the refrigerator for up to three days.

# Lemon Baked Alaska

This is Teak Elmore's favorite dessert. And with good reason. A wonderful nutty crust is toasted, then frozen. A layer of creamy vanilla ice cream follows, topped by a layer of perfectly tart lemon curd. This layering is repeated, and it is all topped with a wonderful layer of meringue. At service this masterpiece is flambéed.

This recipe requires substantial time in the freezer. Start it at least two days in advance of serving. It qualifies as a special-occasion treat, but you can define "special occasion" for yourself! Always use fresh lemon juice and the best quality vanilla ice cream.

CRUST:

| | |
|---|---|
| 1 cup ground pecans | 1 tablespoon sugar |
| 2 tablespoons unsalted butter, melted | ⅛ teaspoon vanilla |
| ⅛ teaspoon salt | |

Preheat the oven to 350° F. Pulse together all the ingredients in a food processor for about a minute, or until the mixture binds together loosely. To prepare the crust, spread evenly in a 10-inch springform pan and bake in the preheated oven for 15 minutes, or until it begins to brown. Set aside to cool. Cover and freeze until ready to use.

LEMON CURD:
(Makes about 1⅔ cups)

| | |
|---|---|
| 4 whole lemons, zested and juiced | 1 teaspoon vanilla |
| 5 egg yolks (save 4 egg whites for the meringue) | ⅛ teaspoon salt |
| | 1 cup sugar |
| 3 whole eggs | ½ cup unsalted butter |

Whisk together the lemon juice, lemon zest, 5 egg yolks, 3 whole eggs, vanilla, salt, and sugar. In a double boiler over simmering water, melt the butter with the lemon/egg mixture. Stirring constantly, cook until the curd has thickened. Remove from the heat and cool to room temperature. Refrigerate until cold, about 2 hours. This can be stored in the refrigerator for at least three days. Cover with a piece of plastic wrap pressed gently to adhere to the surface of the curd. This prevents moisture buildup on the plastic.

½ gallon Homemade Vanilla Ice Cream,
    page 164, or your favorite
    store-bought brand, softened
    just enough to spread

MERINGUE:
Do not make the meringue until you are ready to serve. It will not sit at room temperature for long.

| | |
|---|---|
| 1 tablespoon cornstarch | ½ teaspoon vanilla |
| 1 tablespoon sugar | ¼ teaspoon cream of tartar |
| ⅓ cup water | ½ cup superfine sugar (pulse granu- |
| 4 large egg whites, room temperature | lated in a food processor) |

Mix together the cornstarch, sugar, and water until smooth. Heat over a medium flame in a small saucepan, stirring constantly, until the mixture has thickened and is transparent. Remove from the heat and set aside.

In a stand mixer or with a wire whisk, beat the egg whites until foamy. Gradually add the vanilla and the cream of tartar, and beat until soft peaks form. Add the superfine sugar, 1 tablespoon at a time, and continue beating until glossy peaks are formed. Reduce the speed to low and slowly add the reserved cornstarch paste, a little at a time, beating until thoroughly incorporated. Scrape the bottom with a spatula to be certain that none of the paste has settled at the bottom.

ASSEMBLY:

½ cup superfine sugar                          1 cup rum or cognac

To assemble the dessert, spread a layer of ⅓ of the vanilla ice cream evenly over the crust, about 1 inch thick. Spread a layer of ½ of the lemon curd atop the ice cream, about ½ inch thick. Cover and place in the freezer for 6 to 8 hours, or until the curd is frozen. Repeat with another ⅓ of the ice cream and the remaining lemon curd, and freeze another 6 to 8 hours. Top with the remaining ice cream and freeze until solid, about 4 hours.

Preheat the oven to 450° F. Remove the dessert from the springform pan and cover with the meringue. Sprinkle with about ½ cup superfine sugar. Cook in the hot oven for about 4 minutes.

Meanwhile, heat 1 cup rum or cognac until simmering, but do not overcook, or all of the liquor will burn off. Working with ½ cup at a time, carefully light the liquor in the ladle and pour the burning liquor over the Baked Alaska. Let burn until it goes out. Serve immediately.


# Brownie Fudge Pie                                                   Serves 8

Another wonderful chocolate dessert contributed by the Elmores. Serve with Homemade Vanilla Ice Cream, page 164.

4 ounces unsweetened chocolate          ½ cup flour
1 cup sugar                              ¼ teaspoon salt
½ cup melted butter                      1 teaspoon vanilla
2 eggs

Preheat the oven to 325° F. Melt the chocolate in a double boiler, or in the microwave on high for about 2 minutes. Meanwhile, mix the sugar and melted butter until combined. Add the eggs and continue to mix thoroughly. Add the flour and salt, and stir to combine. Add the vanilla and the melted chocolate and mix well. Scrape the bottom to incorporate all of the batter.

Pour into a well-greased and floured 9-inch pie pan. Bake in the preheated oven for 30 to 35 minutes. The pie will be done when the edges have begun to pull away from the sides and a toothpick inserted into the center comes out with still-moist, but not runny, crumbles.

# Homemade Vanilla Ice Cream

Makes 2 quarts

It is far better to serve creamy homemade vanilla ice cream than any other dessert in the world. Lucille used to make it for the camp, although nowadays we serve Blue Bell Homemade Vanilla, which is as close to homemade as we have found. This recipe requires an ice cream maker. It is worth the investment to purchase one, as they will last many summers. Serve this atop hot Apple Pie, page 155, or Brownie Fudge Pie, page 163. Also use it in Lemon Baked Alaska, page 162.

| | |
|---|---|
| 1 cup sugar | 2 cups heavy cream |
| 1 tablespoon flour | 1 tablespoon vanilla |
| ½ teaspoon salt | 3 eggs, beaten |
| 2 cups milk | 1 10-ounce can of evaporated milk |

Sift together the sugar, flour, and salt. Set aside. In a saucepan, scald the milk and cream. Whisk in the sugar/flour mixture until smooth. Heat until the mixture thickens and coats the back of a spoon. Add the vanilla and remove from the heat.

In a large bowl, whisk the eggs. Slowly add the cream mixture to the eggs, about ½ cup at a time, whisking continuously. Repeat this 2 more times, then add the egg mixture to the remaining milk mixture. Return to the heat and continue stirring until the mixture thickens like a pudding. Remove from the heat and cool. Add the evaporated milk and chill for at least 4 hours. Make in an ice cream maker according to manufacturer's directions.

# Brownies

Makes 1½ dozen

Very rich and moist, with a slightly chewy texture, these are some of the best brownies ever. George Anne loves chocolate, and she thought that these were the best she had ever eaten. Teak agreed. Well, with an endorsement like that, you're bound to concur! Easy and quick, these will satisfy all of your bake sale and school-related dessert requirements. Serve warm with a glass of cold milk.

| | |
|---|---|
| 1 cup unsalted butter | ¼ teaspoon salt |
| 4 ounces unsalted, unsweetened chocolate | 1 cup plus 2 tablespoons flour |
| | 2 teaspoons baking powder |
| 4 eggs | 1 cup pecans or walnuts, toasted |
| 2 cups sugar | (optional) |

Preheat the oven to 350° F. Melt the butter and chocolate in the top of a double boiler, stirring to blend. Set aside to cool.

In a large mixing bowl, whisk together the eggs, sugar, and salt. Add the chocolate mixture to the eggs and blend well. Sift together the flour and baking powder and stir into the chocolate/egg mixture ½ cup at a time. Stir until smooth. Add the optional nuts and stir to mix.

Pour the batter into a greased and floured 9 x 13-inch baking pan. Bake in the preheated oven for 30 minutes. Let cool in pan. The brownies will continue to firm up while cooling. Cut into squares and serve warm. Will keep in an airtight container for at least four days.

# Chocolate Chip Cookies

Makes 2½ dozen

A childhood classic. This is our favorite version, a buttery, caramel cookie with lots of chocolate and pecans. Serve with a tall, cold glass of milk.

2⅛ cups flour
1 teaspoon salt
1 teaspoon baking soda
1 cup unsalted butter, softened
1 cup brown sugar, firmly packed
½ cup granulated sugar

2 eggs
1 teaspoon vanilla
1½ cups semi-sweet chocolate chips
½ cup chopped toasted pecans or
    walnuts (optional)

Preheat the oven to 375° F. Sift together the flour, salt, and baking soda. In a mixing bowl, cream together the softened butter and sugars. Add the eggs one at a time, beating well after each one. Add the vanilla and mix to blend.

Beat in the flour mixture, ½ cup at a time, mixing until fully blended. Stir in the chocolate chips and the optional nuts.

Drop by teaspoons onto a parchment-lined cookie sheet. Bake for 9 to 11 minutes. Remove from the oven and cool on a cooling rack. Store the cookies in an airtight container for up to a week.

# Oatmeal Raisin Cookies

Makes 2½ dozen

Oatmeal raisin cookies have a perfect blend of sweetness and spice. They are also chewy and wonderful and, as far as cookies go, pretty good for you, too. Substitute golden raisins, dried cherries, dried cranberries, or dried blueberries for a delicious variation.

1½ cups flour
1 teaspoon baking soda
1 teaspoon cinnamon
½ teaspoon salt
1 cup unsalted butter, softened
1 cup brown sugar, firmly packed

½ cup granulated sugar
2 eggs
1 teaspoon vanilla
3 cups old-fashioned oats
1 cup raisins

Preheat the oven to 350° F. Sift together the flour, baking soda, cinnamon, and salt. Set aside.

Cream together the butter and sugars until light and creamy. Add the eggs one at a time, beating well after each one. Add the vanilla and mix to blend. Slowly add the flour to the butter/egg mixture. Mix well to incorporate. Stir in the old-fashioned oats and the raisins.

Drop by teaspoons onto a parchment-lined cookie sheet and bake for about 10 minutes, or until the cookies begin to brown. Cool on a cooling rack and serve warm.

# Mexican Wedding Cookies

Makes 2 dozen

Light and refreshing, this cookie is a wonderful finish to a spicy Tex-Mex meal. Serve with your favorite sorbet.

¼ cup powdered sugar
1 cup all-purpose flour
¼ teaspoon salt
½ cup unsalted butter, softened
1 teaspoon vanilla

¼ cup pecans, coarsely chopped and toasted
1 cup powdered sugar, sifted, for the finish

Preheat the oven to 350° F. Sift together the flour, powdered sugar, and salt. Cream the softened butter, and add the flour/sugar mixture until well blended. Stir in the vanilla and the pecans.

To shape the cookies, roll about 1 teaspoon of dough between your palms to make a round about the size of a marble. Flatten with your hand into a disc the size of a quarter on a parchment-lined cookie sheet. Bake in the preheated oven for about 15 minutes, or until golden brown. Remove from the oven and roll in the sifted powdered sugar until well coated. Allow to cool and roll again.

# Gingerbread

Makes about 2 dozen

A warm and spicy cake, best served with lightly whipped cream. Serve with a hot cup of Louisiana coffee and chicory. This is great for a cold, rainy day.

3 cups flour
2 teaspoon baking powder
2 teaspoons ginger
1 teaspoon cinnamon
1 teaspoon cloves
1 teaspoon nutmeg
½ teaspoon baking soda

1 cup milk
½ cup unsalted butter, softened
½ teaspoon salt
1 cup brown sugar
1 cup molasses
2 eggs

Preheat the oven to 375° F. Sift together the flour, baking powder, and spices (ginger, cinnamon, cloves, and nutmeg). Set aside. Stir the baking soda into the milk. Set aside.

Cream together the butter and salt. Add the sugar and molasses and mix well. Beat in the eggs one at a time and mix well to blend. Alternate adding the flour and milk to the butter mixture, mixing lightly between each addition. Be careful not to overmix, or the cake will dry out.

Pour into a 9 x 13-inch well-greased and floured baking pan. Bake in the preheated oven for about 25 minutes. Serve warm with lightly sweetened whipped cream.

# Chocolate Roll

Serves 6–8

Several of you may remember the Fourth of July celebrations held when Lucille was still in the kitchen. Elegant chocolate rolls were carried out of the kitchen into the dining room, each balanced in the skillful hands of the kitchen wait-staff, alight with sparklers to celebrate the birth of our nation.

This dessert is notoriously difficult to perfect. If the cake is not handled just right, it will split when you try to roll it. Don't despair. The whipped cream in the center will generally hold it together. Chill the cake well before cutting, and use a heated knife with a very sharp edge. To heat the blade, dip it into a pitcher of very hot water. Dry on a clean cloth.

THE CAKE:
3 tablespoons cake flour
5 tablespoons powdered cocoa
6 eggs, at room temperature, separated

1 cup sugar, divided
1 teaspoon vanilla
¼ teaspoon salt

FOR ROLLING:
1 tablespoon cocoa powder

1 tablespoon powdered sugar

THE FILLING:
1 pint heavy whipping cream
2 tablespoons sugar

1 teaspoon vanilla

Preheat the oven to 350° F. Sift together the flour and cocoa. Set aside.

In a large bowl, beat the egg yolks until lemon colored and thick. Whisk in ½ cup of the sugar until the mixture is smooth. Fold in the sifted flour mixture. Stir in the vanilla.

In a separate bowl, beat the egg whites with salt until soft peaks form. Add the remaining ½ cup sugar and beat until firm, but not dry.

Gently fold the egg whites into the egg yolk mixture. To prepare the jelly-roll pan, line with parchment paper and lightly spray with cooking spray. Pour the batter onto the prepared jellyroll pan and spread evenly, using a spatula. Bake for about 15 minutes, or until done (the cake will begin pulling away from the sides of the pan, and the center will spring back from a light touch).

Remove from the oven and invert onto a clean, dry, lint-free cloth to cool. Remove the parchment paper from the cake.

Whip the cream with 2 tablespoons sugar until firm. Do not overwhip, as it will begin to break down.

Sift together the tablespoon cocoa and powdered sugar.

To roll the cake, remove the cake from the jellyroll pan and lay onto a lint-free dishtowel dusted evenly with the cocoa and powdered sugar mix. Let cool for about 3 minutes. Begin rolling the cake, starting with the short end. Use the towel to assist you in lifting the cake. Set the rolled cake seam side down on a cake rack.

While the cake is cooling, whip the cream with the sugar and vanilla until firm. Do not overwhip, as it will begin to break down. Set aside.

Unroll the cooled cake and spread the whipped cream evenly over the surface. Roll the cake and place seam-side down on a platter. Chill for several hours.

Slice and serve with a garnish of fresh strawberries or raspberries.


# Lemon Soufflé

Serves 8

This wonderful dish is like lemon-flavored air. Many of you have requested this recipe. Enjoy!

| | |
|---|---|
| 4 tablespoons butter | 4 eggs, separated and at room temperature |
| 3 tablespoons flour | |
| 1 cup milk | ½ teaspoon cream of tartar |
| ¾ cup sugar | ¼ teaspoon salt |
| 3 lemons, juiced, zests grated | |

Preheat the oven to 375° F. In a small saucepan, melt the butter and stir in the flour to make a roux. Slowly add the milk, 1 tablespoon at a time, stirring to blend. Add the sugar and the lemon zest, and continue cooking until the mixture is thick and coats the back of a spoon, about 10 minutes. Remove from the heat.

In a large bowl, beat the egg yolks until light and thick. Stir in the lemon juice to blend. Very slowly whisk the milk sauce into the egg yolks.

Beat the egg whites until foamy. Add the cream of tartar and the salt, and beat on high speed until stiff peaks form. Fold ¼ of the egg whites gently with a spatula into the egg yolk/milk mixture. Then carefully fold in the rest.

Position a rack in the lower third of the oven. Prepare the 2-quart soufflé dish by buttering the sides and sprinkling evenly with sugar. Place the soufflé in a hot water bath and fill the soufflé dish with the batter.

Cook in the oven for 45 minutes to an hour and 15 minutes. Test for doneness after 45 minutes by sliding a long toothpick into the center from the side. If it comes out slightly moist, it is ready. If it is very moist, return the soufflé to the oven.

Serve warm with freshly whipped cream.

# Mrs. English's Cheesecake

Serves 16

This is the cheesecake that Marsha Elmore's mother used to make. It is a wonderfully creamy cake with a thick graham cracker crust, a fully rich body of silken cream cheese, and a topping of sour cream. Topped with a sauce of fresh berries, sugar, and a splash of vanilla or your favorite spirit, this is a sublime perfection. It is easy to make; however, this is a partially baked cake that requires a twenty-four-hour chilling period. Do not skimp on the time, or your dessert will not be fully set. The wait is worth it, though, so plan ahead and enjoy this old-fashioned wonder.

THE CRUST:
| 18 graham crackers, finely ground (about 2½ cups) | ½ cup sugar |
| | 4 ounces unsalted butter, melted |

THE CAKE:
| 36 ounces cream cheese, softened | 3 tablespoons fresh lemon juice |
| 5 whole eggs, lightly beaten | 1 tablespoon vanilla |
| 1⅓ cups sugar | |

THE TOPPING:
| 16 ounces sour cream | 1 teaspoon vanilla |
| 2 tablespoons sugar | |

Preheat the oven to 400° F. Process the graham crackers in a food processor until they are finely ground. Stir together with the sugar and the melted butter. Pour into the bottom of an 11-inch springform pan and press evenly to cover the bottom and halfway up the sides. Set aside.

In an electric stand mixer using a flat paddle, beat the cream cheese until smooth. Slowly add the beaten eggs. Continue to beat until the eggs are fully incorporated. Add the sugar and beat until blended. Stir in the lemon juice and vanilla. Pour atop the crust in the springform pan and bake in the preheated oven for 30 minutes. The cake will still be very loose in the center. It will continue to firm up in the final chilling. Remove from the oven and let cool for 15 minutes.

Stir together the sour cream, sugar, and vanilla until smooth. Spread evenly over the cheesecake and return to the oven for 10 minutes. Remove from the oven and let cool completely. Cover with plastic wrap and refrigerate for twenty-four hours.

Serve with fresh berries, Raspberry Sauce (page 161), or the Fruit Sauce (recipe follows).

## Fruit Sauce

2 cups frozen mixed berries
    (raspberries, blueberries,
    blackberries), defrosted

½ cup sugar
1 ounce vanilla or brandy

In a glass bowl, stir together the mixed berries, sugar, and vanilla or brandy. Let sit for 30 minutes. Serve a spoonful atop each serving of cheesecake.

# Chocolate on Chocolate on Chocolate Cake   Serves 6

This cake is a specialty of Roy Spears, the creative genius and chef behind Waldemar for eighteen of the last twenty-one years. It is a decadent pleasure for all chocolate lovers, light and wonderful génoise sponge cake with a chocolate buttercream icing and shavings of dark chocolate for a garnish. Perfect for any occasion. This recipe makes enough for six proportionally small but very satisfying servings.

THE CAKE:

4½ ounces bittersweet chocolate
1½ ounces unsweetened chocolate
3 tablespoons strong coffee
¾ cup sifted cake flour
½ teaspoon salt
6 ounces unsalted butter,
    softened

1 cup plus 2 tablespoons sugar,
    divided
5 eggs, separated
½ cup finely ground blanched
    almonds
½ teaspoon vanilla
⅛ teaspoon almond extract

Preheat the oven to 350° F. Butter and flour a 9-inch square cake pan.

Melt the bitttersweet and unsweetened chocolates together with the coffee in the top of a double boiler. Remove from the heat and set aside to cool. In a small bowl, sift together the cake flour and the salt. Set aside.

Cream together the butter and ¾ cup of the sugar in a stand mixer. Add the egg yolks and continue to beat until smooth.

In a food processor, combine the almonds and 2 tablespoons of the sugar. Pulse to combine. Stir this into the butter/sugar/egg mixture. Add the melted chocolate/coffee, the vanilla, and the almond extract to this mixture and stir to combine. Set aside.

Whip the egg whites with 2 tablespoons of the sugar until firm peaks form. Fold ⅕ of the egg whites into the reserved chocolate mixture gently with a spatula to lighten the mixture. Fold in the remaining egg whites. Working with ¼ cup of the flour mixture at a time, sift over the chocolate/egg mixture. Gently fold into the chocolate/egg mixture. Repeat with the remaining flour. Pour the cake into the prepared pan and bake in the preheated oven for about 20 to 25 minutes, or until the cake pulls away from the sides and a toothpick inserted in the center comes out clean. Remove from the cake pan and let cool on a cake rack.

THE ICING:

| | |
|---|---|
| 3 egg yolks | 1 cup softened butter |
| 6 tablespoons sugar | 3 ounces bittersweet chocolate, |
| ¼ cup corn syrup | melted and cooled |

In a stand mixer, beat the egg yolks until a very pale yellow.

In a saucepan, combine the sugar and corn syrup and cook over medium heat, stirring constantly, until the mixture reaches a full boil. Immediately transfer the mixture to a heat-proof glass measurer to stop the cooking of the syrup.

Working quickly, add a small amount of the hot syrup to the egg yolks and immediately beat in to incorporate. Stop the beaters and add another small amount of the syrup. Repeat the process until all of the syrup has been added. Clean the sides periodically with a rubber spatula. It will look like a very fluffy, very pale yellow mixture. Beat until the bowl is cool to the touch, about 15 minutes.

Slowly add the softened butter to the egg/sugar mixture. It is very important that the butter be soft and at room temperature. This recipe will not work if the butter is too cold. Beat in the butter on a medium speed, working in small quantities until it is all incorporated. Add the melted chocolate and stir to blend.

To ice the cake, cut off the top "bulge" of the cake to level it, using a bread knife. Trim off the sides with the knife to give a clean, square edge. Using a clean piece of fishing wire, hold each end of the wire firmly in each hand and carefully cut the cake horizontally into halves, making two layers. With the bread knife, cut the cake down the center. This will give you four evenly sized pieces of cake Set aside three of the four layers. Spread the buttercream icing evenly across the top of the bottom layer to about ¼ inch thick. Lay the second quarter layer atop the iced bottom, and evenly spread the icing. Repeat with the remaining layers. Ice the top and sides. Place in the refrigerator until ready to serve.

THE DECORATION:

4 ounces bittersweet baker's chocolate

Melt the chocolate and spread onto a greased pan. Let harden at room temperature. It is best to work in a cool kitchen—otherwise, the chocolate may not harden. In this case, place the pan in the refrigerator until the chocolate hardens, about 30 minutes to an hour.

Break the hardened chocolate into large pieces and decorate the top of the cake. Serve with a garnish of fresh berries or edible flowes.

# Angel Food Cake

Serves 8–12

An egg-white cake, almost devoid of fat! Bake in a smooth-sided tube pan. Be certain that all of your utensils, as well as the pan, are free of any oil, as oil will affect the rise of the cake. Serve with fresh fruit, fruit sorbet, or fruit sauce such as the Raspberry Sauce, page 161.

Use cold egg whites, as this will produce sturdier air bubbles—that is the secret to the leavening of this cake. Also, once the cake is done, remove it from the oven and immediately invert the cake pan and let cool for at least 1½ hours. This will help prevent the cake from falling.

| | |
|---|---|
| 1 cup sifted cake flour | 1 tablespoon water |
| 1½ cups sugar, divided | 1 tablespoon fresh lemon juice |
| ½ teaspoon salt | 1 teaspoon cream of tartar |
| 1½ cups cold egg whites | 1 teaspoon vanilla |

Preheat the oven to 350° F. Sift together the cake flour, ¾ cup of the sugar, and salt—three times. Set aside.

In a large bowl, whisk together the cold egg whites, water, lemon juice, cream of tartar, and vanilla until fluffy. The mixture will have small, sturdy air holes. Beat in the remaining ¾ cup sugar, 1 tablespoon at a time, until the mixture has soft peaks. Do not overbeat to the stiff peaks stage.

Work with only about ¼ cup of the flour mixture at a time, sifting it over the top of the egg whites. Very gently fold in until the flour is just incorporated. Repeat this step until all of the flour is incorporated. Do not mix or stir the batter, as this will cause the egg whites to fall.

Pour the batter into the clean, grease-free tube pan. Bake in the preheated oven for 35 to 40 minutes, or until a toothpick inserted in the center comes out clean.

Immediately invert the pan and set the edges atop 4 glasses. Let sit for at least 1½ hours to cool. To remove from the pan, gently slide a dinner knife along the smooth edges and tap the bottom of the pan with the dinner knife until the cake is loosened and comes clean from the pan.

# Blarney Stones Cake

Serves 8–12

The quintessential Waldemar cake, a sponge cake with buttercream frosting, loaded with chopped peanuts. It is served with coffee ice cream (we prefer Blue Bell). This has been served every year here since the 1940s.

| | |
|---|---|
| 4 eggs, separated | ¼ teaspoon salt |
| 1 cup sugar | ½ cup boiling water |
| 1 cup flour | 1 teaspoon vanilla |
| 1½ teaspoons baking powder | |

Preheat the oven to 350° F. Separate the eggs, reserving one of the yolks for the icing. Beat the remaining yolks until light and thick. Gradually add the sugar.

Sift together the flour, baking powder, and salt. Alternate the dry mixture with the boiling water, blending well between each addition. Stir in the vanilla.

Beat the egg whites until stiff peaks form. Fold ¼ of the egg whites into the egg yolk/flour mixture. Carefully fold in the remaining egg whites.

Pour into a 9 x 13-inch pan and bake for 30 minutes, or until a toothpick inserted in the center comes out clean.

Ice the cake with the Blarney Stones Icing and serve with coffee ice cream.

## Blarney Stones Icing

1½ cups butter, softened
1 egg yolk
2½ cups powdered sugar

1 teaspoon vanilla
1½ cups salted peanuts, crushed

Cream together the butter and the egg yolk. Gradually sift the powdered sugar over the butter mixture, and mix and smooth. Stir in the vanilla. Fold in the ½ cup of peanuts. Frost the cake with the icing and sprinkle the top of the cake with the rest of the peanuts. Cut into squares and serve with coffee ice cream.

# Waldemar Birthday Cake
# with Buttercream Icing
Serves 12

Every year, all of the summer birthdays are celebrated with a beautiful and tasty cake served at the birthday girl's lunch table. The cake is decorated in purple, orange, or green to honor the girl's tribe: Tejas, Comanche, or Aztec. It is a white cake with several layers separated by raspberry jam and topped with buttercream icing.

The cake is fairly forgiving as far as shaping goes. My brother, Stan Pipkin, was the cake baker in 1996. I doubt that there have ever been or possibly ever will be as imaginative and wonderfully decorated cakes at Waldemar. He made so many that he wanted to keep them interesting, and, in his inimitable style, he created three-dimensional shapes like Winnie the Pooh, a basketball entering a hoop, and Alameda 3 (one of the kampongs), just to name a few.

1 cup unsalted butter, softened
2 cups sugar, divided
3½ cups cake flour, pre-sifted
3 teaspoons baking powder
¼ teaspoon salt
1 cup milk

1 teaspoon vanilla
¼ teaspoon orange extract
6 egg whites
1 cup seedless raspberry, apricot, or
    blueberry jam

Preheat the oven to 400° F. Cream together the butter and 1½ cups of the sugar until light and fluffy. Set aside. Measure and sift together the cake flour, baking powder, and salt. Add the flour mixture to the butter, alternating with the milk until just incorporated. Add the vanilla and orange extract and stir to blend.

Whip the egg whites until soft peaks form. Slowly add the remaining ½ cup of sugar, and continue beating until the peaks are glossy. With a rubber spatula, gently fold ¼ of the egg whites into the flour/butter mixture. Fold in the remaining egg whites until well incorporated.

Pour the batter into 3 greased and floured 8-inch cake pans. Bake for 18 to 20 minutes in the preheated oven. Cake is done when the edges begin to pull away from the sides and a toothpick inserted in the center comes out clean. Let the cake cool in the pan for about 15 minutes. To remove the cake from the pan, slip a knife around the edges and invert onto a cooling rack. Tap the bottom of the pan with the handle of the knife until the cake is loosened. Let cool completely.

To build the cake, even out the tops of the individual cakes by gently slicing away any domes that may be present. Slice each cake in half. Spread the jam in the middle of each cake and cover with the tops. Spread about ½ cup of the buttercream icing between each layer. Stack the cake into the 3 full layers. Cover the entire cake with the buttercream, and decorate to preference. Chill for several hours before serving to allow the icing to set.

## Buttercream Icing

1 cup sugar
½ cup water
6 egg yolks

2 cups unsalted butter, softened
2–4 tablespoons vanilla or liqueur of
    your choice

In a saucepan, melt the sugar and the water over medium heat, stirring constantly. Once dissolved, stop stirring and continue cooking until it reaches the soft ball stage, 238° F on a candy thermometer. Quickly remove from the heat and transfer to a heatproof measuring bowl.

Meanwhile, beat the egg yolks in a stand mixer until light-colored and thick. Turn the mixer off to pour a small amount of the sugar mixture into the eggs, and quickly beat on high speed for 5 minutes to incorporate. Repeat this step until all of the sugar syrup has been added. Use a rubber spatula to clean the measuring bowl. Continue to beat until completely cool.

Gradually beat in the softened butter and the vanilla or liqueur. The final product will be a light and silky icing. It is best not to make this on a steamy, hot day, as the butter will melt if left too long at a warm room temperature.

# About the Author

LAURA PIPKIN KRAMER, a Waldemar camper from 1981 to 1984, has been in the kitchen as long as she can remember. She was the innkeeper for the Waldemar Bed & Breakfast for three years. It was during this time that she had the distinct pleasure of testing many of these tried-and-true recipes for her guests, as well as developing a few new favorites along the way. She feels very fortunate to have had the opportunity to work on this project and hopes that you will enjoy it as much as she!

Laura currently lives in Houston with her nine-year-old son, John, her cat, and her memories of Waldemar: cool morning air, mist rising over the Guadalupe River, and smells of freshly baked bread and good, hot coffee mingling with the sweet aroma of cypress trees. And she is dreaming of her next return.

# Index

# Notes